MW00467388

STOCK MARKET INVESTING FOR BEGINNERS AND OPTIONS TRADING CRASH COURSE

Master Like an Intelligent Investor the Stocks, ETFs, Bonds, Futures, Forex and Commodities Markets. Leverage Your Capital with Options Trading

DAVE ROBERT WARREN GRAHAM

©Copyright 2020 by Dave Robert Warren Graham

- All rights reserved –

Paperback Format ISBN: 978-1-80111-793-7
Hardback Format ISBN: 978-1-80111-789-0

The content contained within this book may not be reproduced, duplicated or transmitted without direct written permission from the author or the publisher.

Under no circumstances will any blame or legal responsibility be held against the publisher, or author, for any damages, reparation, or monetary loss due to the information contained within this book. Either directly or indirectly.

Legal Notice:
This book is copyright protected. This book is only for personal use. You cannot amend, distribute, sell, use, quote or paraphrase any part, or the content within this book, without the consent of the author or publisher.

Disclaimer Notice:
Please note the information contained within this document is for educational and entertainment purposes only. All effort has been executed to present accurate, up to date, and reliable, complete information. No warranties of any kind are declared or implied. Readers acknowledge that the author is not engaging in the rendering of legal, financial, medical or professional advice. The content within this book has been derived from various sources. Please consult a licensed professional before attempting any techniques outlined in this book.
By reading this document, the reader agrees that under no circumstances is the author responsible for any losses, direct or indirect, which are incurred as a result of the use of the information contained within this document, including, but not limited to, — errors, omissions, or inaccuracies

This book, as well as all the others dealing with this topic, was written to share every single ounce of knowledge and experience that has allowed me to achieve the life I want through stock market investments and trading. No courses will be sold after this book because it is already complete and useful for people who want to become a smart investor and successful trader.

I dedicate this book to all of you who, just like I was a few years ago, are trying to learn how to invest and earn in the financial markets using the many books available on the topic. Finally, a book for you. This is will be your guide. Congrats!

Good luck with your reading and studies!

Dave R. W. Graham

Table of Content

PART 1:
STOCK MARKET
INVESTING FOR
BEGINNERS

Introduction Part 1

The stock market is the place investors associate with buy and sell investments, usually stocks, which are shares of proprietorship in an open organization. Stocks, otherwise called values, speak to fragmentary proprietorship in an organization, and the stock market is where investors can buy and sell responsibility for investible resources. A stock market considered monetary advancement as it enables companies to get to capital from the general population rapidly. It is where shares of pubic recorded companies are exchanged. The essential market is the place companies glide shares to the overall population in the first sale of stock to raise capital.

Different elements go into the choices of traders and investors about where to buy and sell singular stocks. The most significant is the profitability of the organization, as well as its possibilities for profits. Traders are continually looking for advances. They use past value activity as charts to illuminate their choices to sell or buy; however, what chooses whether they settle on the correct choice or not is the thing that will occur.

Most beginners—investors and traders—have quite confused ideas when approaching the stock market, investing in stocks (or options, ETFs, commodities, etc.) or trading in general. One of the pivotal points that creates confusion in those interested in making their money work through investments is the lack of understanding of the crucial difference between trading and investing. The confusion derives from the fact that in the eyes of the investor or the uneducated and non-conscious trader, doing trading or investing seems to be the same thing.

Although they are united by the desire to make a profit, the two operations arise from different logic and follow different rules. Those who invest measure the value of what they buy (an action, a house, a business, an object of art, etc.), try to buy it at a discounted or otherwise balanced price. The entire operation is based on the prediction or hope that, over time, the good purchased will increase in value and that this increase in value will automatically be reflected in a corresponding rise in its market price, allowing it to be sold for a profit.

An easily understandable example of investment is that of those who buy agricultural land in the expectation that it will then be buildable. The greatest investors of history, such as the legendary Warren Buffett, are, in fact, masters in buying "depreciated quality." Of course, their time horizon is never very short, and the value of what they have purchased can remain or even go down for a specified period without this causing them to worry excessively.

Trades, however, do not bet on a change in the value of things. The hard and pure trader does not care highly about the objective quality or the nature of what he buys and only interested in acquiring it at a price in a short time frame he plans to grow, even though the value of what he purchased remains perfectly identical. What makes trading possible is that the prices of things and, therefore also investment objects such as shares, bonds, real estate, etc. may vary regardless of their value due to the law of the application and the offer.

The stock market fills two significant needs. The first is to give money to companies that they can use to fund and grow their organizations. If an organization issues one million shares of stock that at the first sell for $10 an offer, at that point that furnishes the organization with $10 million of capital that it can use to develop its business less whatever expenses the organization pays for an investment bank to deal with the stock contribution. By offering stock shares as opposed to getting the capital required for an extension, the organization abstains from bringing about obligation and paying interest charges on that obligation. The optional reason the stock market serves is to give investors the individuals who buy stocks a chance to partake in the profits of traded on an open market company.

The stock market empowers buyers and sellers to arrange costs and make exchanges. Investors would then be able to buy and sell these stocks among themselves, and the exchange tracks the organic market of each recorded stock. It helps decide the cost for every security or the levels at which stock market members, investors, and traders are happy to buy or sell.

Chapter 1.

How to Get Started?

S tock may seem incredibly intimidating for those starting in the investment world. It looks like a completely different world, and the hardest step for most is the beginning. However, it is quite simple to get started in stock investments. First, one must set goals for themselves and determine how they would like to invest in a stock. By writing down goals and ensuring that the investor's money is used in the best possible way, the investor is helping them yield the highest return on their investment. Once the individual's goals are made clear, they must plan on how to meet those goals. After this, they may choose the best investment method for achieving these goals. Then, it must be decided on where exactly the investor will go to invest their money. It is crucial, as this will be the platform by which the investor will trade their stocks. After this, the investor must open an account with whomever they choose. Before they start trading, the investor must make an initial investment using this account. While doing so, they may have to link their bank account to their stock trading account. The investor must then begin the process of buying and selling stocks using this account. Although this seems like a lengthy process, it is quite simple.

Planning and Meeting Goals

The investor must familiarize themselves with their goals. It is quite helpful to write down one's goals in each area and put it somewhere that is easily accessible. It is useful to have measurable goals to reach. This way, there may be a specific period and amount that may be assigned to the targets. It may help to come up with monthly goals. For instance, the investor may start with the purchase of 100 shares of stock in February. They may wish to increase that to 150 shares by March, 200 shares by April, and so on. This way, the investor may have a period to achieve their goals. It will allow them to measure their progress easily.

To set proper goals, one must reflect upon their past. How much will the investor be able to set aside for stock realistically? If one's goals are not realistic, it may become discouraging and set the investor back from their full potential. The investor must consider any past investments they have made. They must consider what worked and what did not. It is crucial to consider income and expenses when investing, and one must also consider any savings goals that they have. This will make it more apparent what may be invested in stocks.

Without a clear guide on how to invest, the investor will lack direction. It may lead to spur-of-the-moment decisions, and the investor may regret these choices. There may be some periods where one will not trade, as it won't be as profitable. Perhaps the market is down, and the trader does not wish to sell any stock. Perhaps the market is up, and the trader does not want to buy any stock. There will be events such as vacations, holidays, stressful events, or emergencies.

One must also consider how much money they have. Although it is possible to double one's money in a year, it is not likely for a beginner to do so. One may also choose to invest one time and hold it, or they may choose to invest more into their account often. This time and amount will depend on the investor and their financial situation.

The investor must also choose a strategy. They may wish to buy and sell stocks or to buy and hold stocks. They may even consider options trading. Whichever method that the investor chooses, there will be different goals to fit those strategies.

Long-term goals may be set to help the investor. Although planning for the following year may help the investor, longer periods may prove even more beneficial. Perhaps the investor wishes to acquire a million dollars' worth of stock in the succeeding ten years. Perhaps the investor wishes to save a certain amount for retirement, which they wish to have by the next 25 years. Whatever the end goal is, the investor must make that clear so that they can begin working towards it immediately. Once a proper plan is created for meeting the investor's goals, they may move to the next step.

Choosing an Investment Method

After the investor has set goals and created a plan to meet them, it is time to decide on which investment method they wish to pursue. For those that wish to trade on their own completely, the DIY (do-it-yourself) method is the best fit. The investor may conduct all their trades online, making transfers from the bank manually or automatically. It will allow full control of one's investments. There will also be complete independence over what the investor wishes to buy and sell, how much they wish to trade, and how often they wish to trade.

They will, however, need to dedicate time to researching, making any transfers, trading, and other procedures. There is also a higher risk for this choice, as a beginning investor will not have the education that a financial advisor will. They also won't be under the control of a Robo-advisor. However, all the profit that is made by the investor will be theirs to keep. They won't have to pay commission and fees outside of any required by the broker that they use.

The least independent approach to investing in stock is by hiring a financial advisor. It is for those who do not wish to touch their stock at all and to have it fully regulated for them. Hesitant beginners may benefit from this method. It is important to remember, however, that this method tends to be the costliest. It is most beneficial for those with higher assets and larger portfolios. It is also important to choose an investor that will work to meet the investor's goals, not just the goals of themselves. Therefore, the investor must set specific goals for themselves and how they wish to invest their money. They may more easily communicate with the advisor their desires, which may be carried out for them.

Choosing a Stockbroker

When investing for oneself, a proper stockbroker must be chosen. This will depend on the individual's needs and wants. For some, their bank that they already operate with offers stock investments through their bank. This is a quick and simple option, as their money will already be linked through the bank, and they may already be familiar with their style. There may also be options for financial advisors in the bank that are free-of-charge. Otherwise, the investor must research their options before settling on a broker.

When choosing a stockbroker, the investor should research any fees (transaction fees, maintenance fees, etc.), minimum funds required to open an account, any commission collected by the stockbroker, and accessibility. The investor may prefer a specific type of formatting for their broker to have. There may also be free education, customer service, and other ways to make investing easier for the investor.

The investor must choose the option that will allow them to make the highest return on their investments. The investor should keep in mind which services they are likely to use most frequently, and they should choose the broker that charges the least to use those services. There may be transactional fees, which are the costs of buying and selling stocks. Many beginning investors tend to forget this, so it is essential to take this into account.

Opening an Account

When opening an account, there are often a few steps that are required. This is typically not a lengthy process, but the investor should be aware of the potential actions associated with opening an account. The first step when opening an online account is typically to create an account. This will consist of a username and password, as well as some personal information. This may include setting goals, determining which types of features the investor wishes to use, and the investor's experience level. This information will help to create the optimal experience for the investor. There may also be an application for the account to ensure that the investor is qualified to hold the account. There may also be an agreement stating that the investor assumes all the risks of investing and understands that the money is not insured or guaranteed. Initial Investment and Linking Accounts. During the application process, the investor will most likely be prompted to fund the account. This can be done in several ways. The investor may transfer the funds electronically via an EFT (Electronic funds transfer). This is transferring the money from a linked bank account and will most likely only take one business day to transfer. The investor may also choose to make a wire transfer, which is a transfer directly from the bank. It is important to consider how much to invest in the account initially carefully. For those just starting, there may not be much money to invest at first. The minimum investment amounts for the broker should be looked over beforehand.

Buying and Selling Stocks

After the investor funds their account, it is time to start trading the stocks. It must be decided what stock, how much of the stock, and how the investor wishes to buy. Once these factors are decided, the investor must buy the stock. It is usually as simple as searching the stock symbol and selecting "buy." It is best to wait until the stock is at a low, but the investor must also begin investing as early as possible in experiencing the benefits of investing. When the stock is bought, it will typically take a bit to process and for the broker to receive these funds. After that, it will show up in the online portfolio of the investor. When it is time to sell this stock, the investor may typically visit their portfolio and click "sell" on the desired stock.

Chapter 2.

Do's and Don'ts

Y ou need to understand and realize a couple of things regarding stock investing. First, there is no sure-shot formula for profitable stock investing. Even the most successful and celebrated investors lose money in some cases.

However, some rules are followed by many successful stock investors. These rules prove to be useful over a long period and enough stock trades. If you follow them prudently and consider the specifics of a stock or market condition, you may increase the chances of a good return on your investments.

Do's

- You should have a long-term approach to stock investing with a broad picture of your investment goals in your mind.
- It would be best if you had a thoroughly grounded and realistic perspective. Making money in stocks is not an easy task, and it takes time and effort to become successful at it. Persistence is vital when learning to invest. Don't get discouraged.

- As a new investor, be prepared to take some small losses. Experience is a great teacher.

- You'll need to do much research and develop a sound understanding of the stock market before getting to start.

- You should follow a well-disciplined investment approach. If you put in money systematically in the right stocks and hold on to your investments for enough period, you would increase your chances of generating good returns.

- It would help if you always made an informed decision. Do a proper analysis of the fundamentals of a stock before investing in that stock.

- It would help if you created a well-diversified portfolio by investing in several good stocks of well-known companies with leadership positions in their industries. Diversification will reduce your risks and heavy losses.

- You should invest in the right stocks or companies. Strong sales and earnings growth characterize these as well as increasing or good profit margins, consistent and high return on equity of 15% or more, industry leader or with large market share, etc.

- You should have realistic expectations. In times of bull runs, some stocks generated returns of 25% plus. However, you cannot take such a performance as your annual benchmark return for your stock investment. It may lead you to take unnecessary risks. You should aim for a return of 10%.

- You should monitor your stock investments or portfolio regularly and rigorously. This will help you in making desired changes in your portfolio with the evolving market conditions. Concentrate your eggs in a few solid baskets, know each of them well, and keep on watching them vigilantly.

- You should learn from great investors. It is advised to never invest in the stock, but to invest in the business. You should invest in a business or market that you understand. This will help you in judging the proper value of a company and its stock and consequently increase your chances of identifying good stocks for profitable investing.

- It is also important to pick the right broker with a good track record, online facilities, tools and apps, high-grade customer support, etc.

Don'ts

- In the beginning, do not invest in companies or sectors that are characterized by much volatility or fluctuations in stock prices.

- As a beginner, do not set up a margin account; but set up a cash account.

- You should avoid more volatile types of investments, at least in the initial phase, like futures, options, and foreign stocks.

- You should not buy a stock just because it is cheap. You generally get what you pay for.

- You should avoid the herd mentality and invest in a stock because your friends, relatives, or acquaintances are buying the stock. Always invest in a stock after you do your own research and once understand the fundamentals of that stock.

- You should not try to time the stock market. Catching the top or the bottom of the stock market is not a good idea. You may lose money in trying to time the market.

- Do not allow your emotions and sentiments to cloud your judgment regarding stock investments. Many investors have lost money, mainly due to their failure to control their emotions. These emotions are usually fear and greed.

- You should never speculate by building heavy positions in some stocks, buying stocks of unknown companies, etc. The fabulous dream to become a millionaire overnight may even wipe out your hard-earned money.

Chapter 3.

Technical Analysis Vs Fundamental Analysis

T echnical analysis is a method of looking at stock charts and data to spot price trends. It is a method primarily used by traders who are interested in short term profits, but it can be helpful for long-term investors as well. Long-term investors can use technical analysis to determine (estimate) the best entry points into their positions. Note that technical analysis certainly isn't required, and most long-term investors ignore short-term trends and use dollar-cost averaging. Nonetheless, it's a good idea to become familiar with technical analysis in case you decide you want to use it in the future.

Fundamental analysis focuses on the underlying fundamentals of the company. These can include earnings, price to earnings ratio for the stock, and profit margins. The technical analysis ignored all these things and focused on the trades of the moment. It seeks to discover upcoming trends in buying behavior. So, whether a company was profitable in the previous quarter—It doesn't necessarily matter. Of course, profitability can drive more stock purchases, and so drive up the price. But many things can drive the price up or down over the short term. Simple emotion can do it, and so traders that use technical analysis study the charts themselves and pay far less attention to external factors or fundamentals.

Trend Seeking

The first thing that technical analysis seeks to discover is the trend. Simply put, a trend is a prevailing price movement in one direction or the other. The period isn't specific and will depend on the trader's needs and goals. For example, day traders are looking for a trend that might only last two hours. Swing traders may hope to ride a trend that lasts weeks or months. Position traders are looking for longer-term changes and want to enter a position at a low price and exit that position month or between 1-2 years later at a higher price to make a profit.

Trends are easy to estimate, but your estimations have no guarantee of being correct. For an uptrend, traders typically draw straight lines through the low points of the gyrations of the stock on the graph. This will help you estimate where the trend will end up at some future point in time. You can use this to set a selling point when you exit your position.

Support and Resistance

Over relatively short periods, stocks will stay confined between a range of prices. The low pricing point of this range is called support. The upper price point of the range is called resistance. The trader seeks to enter their position at a point of support. They can also place a stop-loss order slightly below support so that they will exit the position if they bet wrong and share prices drop substantially. Then they can sell their stocks when the share price gets close to resistance levels, on the theory that it's more likely than not to drop back down after reaching resistance.

Moving Averages

The number of periods defines a moving average. So, if we were using a chart that is framed in terms of days, a 9-period moving average would be a 9-day moving average. This helps eliminate noise from the stock charts and can be useful in spotting trends.

The real benefit comes from comparing moving averages with different periods. A short period crosses above a long period moving average indicates that an upward trend in pricing can be expected. That's because it indicates that buyers are moving into the market more recently. Conversely, when a short period crosses below a long period moving average, that indicates a coming downward trend in the market.

A simple moving average, one that simply calculates the average of the past given number of days, is going to give equal weight to prices days ago and prices more recently. This is an undesirable feature, and so traders prefer to use exponential moving averages to get more accurate data. Exponential moving averages weight the data, giving more weight to recent prices and less weight to more distant prices.

Chart Patterns

Traders also look for specific chart patterns that can indicate coming trend reversals. For example, you might be looking for signs that a stick is unable to move any higher in price after having undergone a large and long-lasting uptrend. What happens in these cases is that the stock price will touch or reach a certain price level that is slightly higher than where it is at present and do so two or more times. But each time it reaches the peak value, it will drop back down in price.

Traders also look for signals in the chart that a breakout is going to occur. A breakout can happen to the upside, that is, stock prices can increase a great deal, or it can happen to the downside, in which case a strong downward trend in share price will follow.

Bollinger Bands

Bollinger bands attempt to combine the idea of a moving average with moving zones of support and resistance. The levels of support and resistance for a stock are calculated at any given time using the standard deviation. Bollinger bands will include a simple moving average curve in the center to represent the mean stock price.

Value Investing and Growth Investing

Investing can further be divided into two main categories. These are value investing and growth investing. These two categories have been around for decades and have been used successfully by investors over the decades.

Value investing refers to the purchase of stocks of undervalued firms. The main purpose here is to identify the top companies with undervalued stock rather than investing in largely unknown firms whose potential is yet to be determined.

Most value investors prefer investing in stable and strong firms that appear not to reflect a company's real value. As such, they hope to benefit when the firm's real value is realized, and others show an interest in it. You need to know what some of the pointers are. What are some of the factors that indicate a company's shares are undervalued? There are a couple of tips, including high dividend yield, but more important is a minimal price to book ratio. This is a ratio most preferred by value investors.

As it is, the marketplace is hardly accurate all the time. Sometimes there are errors and mistakes on how companies are valued. Some stocks are overvalued, while others are undervalued. When these stocks are eventually valued correctly, they gain in value, and this gain will pass on to the investor. It can sometimes be a pretty significant gain, so this is the main reason why some investors go for value investing.

Sometimes this strategy can be a short-term affair but a long-term approach for other investors. While the strategy is rather straightforward and uncomplicated, it can be a little complicated, especially in the long term. Some investors hope to make a quick kill out of this strategy by making it short-term. This can be a mistake because it may take a while before the real value of the firm is known. Therefore, if you wish to become a value investor, you should think about investing in the long term rather than short-term so that you receive real benefits. Also, most investors are into investing in the long term. As such, it is advisable to always think about long-term investing as well as long-term benefits which are much greater than quick, short, gains.

Fundamentals of Growth Investment Strategies

Growth investment is crucial when it comes to stock investing. It is one of the two pillars of stock investing, the other being value investing. There is a distinct difference between these two groups of investors. One significant difference between these two investment models is that value investors approach is more focused on young companies with potential for above-average and significant growth in the coming years. On the other hand, growth investors focus on firms that have regularly displayed significant growth as well as a substantial increase in opportunities and profits.

There is an accepted theory behind the growth investment strategy. Investors think that an increase in revenue or earnings should result in increased share prices. Therefore, they prefer buying stocks that are priced either equal to or just above a company's latest intrinsic value. This is often based on the belief that the inherent value of the firm will increase based on the continuous fast growth rate. There are specific metrics used by growth investors, and they include profit margin, EPS or earnings per share and ROE or return on equity.

Combination of Value and Growth Strategies

The best approach, according to finance experts, is to combine these two strategies, especially for investors seeking fast, long term growth. A combination of growth and value investing is known to be a successful one and is the approach adopted so successfully by the billionaire investor Warren Buffet. It is advisable to consider this approach because it promises an even more successful outcome, especially in the long term.

There are several reasons why this is a worthwhile pursuit. For starters, value stocks are mostly stocks of firms operating in cyclical industries. Consumers spend their discretionary incomes in these industries only when they believe it is necessary. Take, for instance, the airline industry. Consumers mostly choose to fly a lot when the economy is on an upward trajectory and then keep airlines when times are tough. As such, the airline industry is cyclical, and its stocks can be deemed to be value stocks.

As a result of seasonal gains and stagnation, value stocks tend to do well during times of prosperity and economic recovery, then perform rather dismally when a trending market is sustained for lengthy periods. Such stocks thrive during low-interest rate situations and grow even in the final stages of a long-running bull market. However, the minute that the economy experiences a downturn, these industries are the first to suffer loss.

If you choose, as an investor, both value and growth investing, you are likely to enjoy bigger returns even as you also reduce your risks substantially. In theory, you will easily generate optimum profitability if you purchase stocks using both value and growth strategies. And even though the economy fluctuates with each economic cycle, you will emerge the winner after things even out eventually.

Chapter 4.

How to Build Your Investment Portfolio

As an investor, you should not invest all your money in a single stock. This is very similar to putting all your eggs in one basket. Identify several stocks from different industries such as the financial services sector, industrial, automotive, oil and gas, transport, and so on. If you can identify some good shares in some of these sectors, then you will improve your chances of success at the stock markets. Statistics indicate that diversified portfolios are much more successful and earn more money that single stock portfolios.

Diversification also saves you from imminent loss should anything negative happen. People have been known to lose their investments for a lack of diversification. For instance, let us assume you purchase Boeing stocks, and shortly after that, major incidents involving airplane crashes happen. The stock would plummet in value, and you would lose most of your investments.

When you invest in stocks, you need to be on the lookout for price changes regularly. Prices rise and fall based on a variety of factors. For instance, when interest rates fall, the economy will have a positive outlook, and stock prices will very likely rise. On the other hand, when an industry-specific incident happens, or the economy falls into recession, then prices are bound to fall. In general, the stock market is a static entity, and prices are always falling and rising. You should know when you want to benefit from this regular rise and all-in price, also known as volatility. You can benefit greatly by buying stocks when the price is low, then selling when prices go up.

The main goal of any trader or investor is to take advantage of short-term price movements. We have learned that stocks are never static, and there is almost always some volatility in the markets. This volatility translated to price movements. A seasoned trader can monitor these movements and take advantage of them to profit in a big way. Most traders at the markets do this regularly. They spend their time monitoring the markets and observing price movement.

Take, for example, a person who has $10,000 they wish to invest in the stock market. You will first open an account with a broker then fund it with your trading capital. Once your account is up and running, you should scan the markets for the most suitable stocks. This will teach you how to identify such stocks. However, past performance at the markets and the company's fundamentals are examples of things to watch out.

Now, once you identify the desired stocks to buy, you should then purchase them in enough quantities. Remember to spread out your purchases and not to purchase just one stock. This way, you will spread out the risk and minimize exposure. As an investor, you will not engage in active trading even though you are free to do so.

Also, as an investor, you may not necessarily need a lump sum amount to invest in stocks. All that you will need is an amount as little as $100 plus fees and costs charged by your broker. However, it is advisable to grow your investments with time. This means investing small amounts like $100 each week, or every fortnight or even monthly. This is how a lot of people in America grow their money. They invest in the stock market and then grow their investments over time. The income generated is then used for other purposes such as capital to start a business or a down payment for a home.

Building an Investment Portfolio

As an investor, the best approach is diversification. Diversification means investing your funds in different securities. This is highly advisable because of the inherent and underlying risks posed by the markets. It is a fact that the price or value of stocks keeps changing almost all the time. Diversification means no matter what happens, you can still be profitable.

Therefore, to invest wisely, you will need to develop or come up with a suitable investment portfolio. It is easy to imagine an investment portfolio where all your investments are held. A portfolio is in other ways like a safe that stores crucial personal or business documents. However, unlike a safe, it is more of a concept rather than a tangible product.

When you diversify your investments into a portfolio, it means that you will own a myriad of assets. These assets could be exchange-traded funds or ETFs, mutual funds, bonds, stocks, and many others. However, it is best to approach the diversification of a portfolio with a well-thought-out plan and not haphazardly.

We can define portfolio management as an approach to balancing rewards and risks. To meet your investment goals, you will need to invest in a wide variety of products, including SMAs, REITs, closed-end funds, ETFs and others. It is an excellent idea and highly recommended to have an investment plan and determine what your end goal is, especially when there are numerous options available.

Portfolio management often means different things to different investors. Think about a young person fresh from college and on his first job. Such a person views portfolio management as a way of growing investments and providing a pretty decent amount over time for future use.

Such a person will view portfolio management as an excellent chance of holding on to their wealth, possibly accumulated over the years. There are different ways of organizing and planning portfolio management. A portfolio manager should be able to handle the various needs that different investors have when coming up with a diversified portfolio. Therefore, the individualized approach is a highly advised option. Here are some basic principles for developing a portfolio.

It is advisable to note the availability of numerous options. A client or investor needs to determine whether they wish to create wealth over time, put away funds for future use, generate a regular income, and so on. This way, it will be possible to come up with a suitable investment plan. Such a plan should incorporate appetite for risk, period, and similar aspects.

By spreading your wealth into different types of investment vehicles, you prevent one type of risk from wiping out the entire value of your portfolio. Here are some strategies that you can use to diversify your asset distribution:

- **Investing in Other Sectors**

If your portfolio value is still small, you may consider diversifying by investing in the other sectors. Make sure that you learn about the new sector first, and the companies in it before you pull the trigger.

Investing in a second sector widens your circle of competence. It increases the number of companies that you can invest in safely. It also allows you to spread your funds to another industry so that you will be able to avoid exposing your money to one type of sector-related risk.

One way to do this is by dividing your portfolio fund into two. You could leave one of the funds you first invested in. You could then distribute the other half in the new sector you've selected.

You could also go about it by leaving your old positions alone and investing only new funds into the new sector. This strategy is better if you are in no position to sell your older positions. With this strategy, you will be building up your fund in the new sector from scratch.

- **Index Investing**

Index investing is another strategy that you can use to diversify your fund's distribution. With this method of investing, you no longer need to spend too much time doing fundamental analysis. Instead, you only spread your wealth among the companies in the index you have chosen. This method of investing is used by people who believe that it is impossible to beat the market consistently. This belief has some statistical backing.

In the year 2010, more than 90% of fund managers failed to beat the performance of the S&P 500. Most of the managers who did beat the market were significant in hedge funds, mutual funds and banks that were only accessible to the rich. Because you are a beginner, we could assume that you will not be able to beat the performance of the market in your first year of trading. If you believe this too, you may be better of using the index investing method.

To invest in an index fund, you will need to pick a company to do it. You could then ask them if they are offering index funds. The best time to start investing in an index fund is when the market is doing well. Index funds tend to be of higher risk compared to other types of mutual funds. They are riskier than other types of managed funds like balanced funds and equity funds because of the tendency of its price to fluctuate. However, this higher risk is directly proportional to the potential rewards that you may get.

- **Investing in Other Types of Securities**

If your goal is to maximize your diversification, you could also consider investing outside of the stock market. If your funds are totally invested in the stock market, you are exposing 100% of it to stock market-related risks. As your funds grow bigger, you may want to put some of it in other types of securities. One option that you may consider bonds. While company stocks are regarded as equity investments, bonds are considered debt investments. The companies and government agencies who issue these bonds are basically borrowing money from you. The bond is the proof of the transaction, and it states the amount of money borrowed, the schedule of repayment and the interest rate of the loan.

Aside from bonds, you may also choose to invest in commodities. Commodities trading applies a similar trading strategy as stocks, in that it requires you to buy low and sell high.

- **Investing in Real Properties**

If your fund grows in value, you may also invest in properties. Investing in another type of asset, one that is tangible, can increase the diversity of your asset distribution.

Investing in real estate, though, just like any type of investment, requires you to study what you are buying. You also need to time your entry into the market.

If the price of real estate in your area is low compared to its potential value, you may choose to use it as your method of diversifying your income. There are multiple ways that you can earn through real estate investing. Just like with securities, you can also buy and sell properties. You also have the option of renting your properties out.

Chapter 5.

Master the Stocks Market

T here are numerous ways of investing in stocks. All these ways have some advantages and disadvantages, but every individual's situation is different. What's right for you may lead to a problematic situation for another. Considering the period and market value, while looking for stocks to invest in, is highly recommended.

Sometimes, the market may be going through a smooth and steady path, and your emotional aspects may get in the way to make the right decision. You may invest in expensive stocks due to the success of the market. On the other hand, in a poorly performing market during situations like inflation, you may start to sell off your stocks.

So how can you decide where to invest? First off, you need to analyze how much a specific investment method would be affected by the risk and potential losses. If the risk is too high, but the gains from it would be more fruitful, you would know what step to take. Such decision making requires proper research of all the methods, and a proper understanding of how much would be at stake, in different situations.

We know that all methods would have specific effects, but in the end, the success relies on how much risk you are ready to take, as well as how much knowledge you have in stock marketing. If you're into a more modern and technological way of business, then you should know, online buying of stocks is a thing.

However, it is only recommended if you know how the stock market operates and can give useful advice to yourself, as this one doesn't involve any advice to be given, so you're on your own. Also, it is far riskier, as you are charged only a flat fee for each transaction. Also, to mention, it's time-consuming, as you would have to train yourself until you're confident enough to take the next step.

Investment Club

The next method which you can consider is through the investment clubs. You meet a lot of people who may be going through the same situation you are, and people who can give professional and financial advice. Other people's experiences can make you learn a lot too. It is affordable and can help you to understand and differentiate between different market situations. Increased involvement and investing in stocks through this can help you gain a new perspective and a sense of direction.

If you purchase some clothes and neglect the fact that trying them on would help you decide whether to buy them or not and come home to only find out that the clothes don't fit, you'll be pretty disappointed unless there is an exchange or return policy at the outlet. If not, you're at a loss. Trust me, investing in a market is nothing close to purchasing clothes. Hence, neglecting important facts can lead to the loss of a fortune. Louder for the people at the back, investing in stock markets is nothing close to managing your day to day spending. So, you got to be smart about it.

Investing in stocks for the first time has a much higher risk. However, these risks are to be taken, but as mentioned before, there is always supposed to be a margin. The potential risk still needs to be managed.

Research gets you a long way. You don't want to trust the company blindly. It is important to analyze and study how the company is doing in the market. Their marketing tactics, financial weaknesses, and productivity need to be kept in mind.

If the business doesn't have a good marketing department, it's likely to go crashing down as soon as the competition gets tough. The finance department needs to be checked and observed at every point, as they handle a major part of the business. Any fishy business being done, the greater is the effect on you. Whatever the company is selling, it needs to have a good production plan, method, and a skilled and efficient workforce.

Two Kinds of Markets and How to Trade Them

Several markets facilitate trade in exchange for assets. Each market runs under different trading mechanisms, which seem to affect liquidity and control of the company. A positive effect on the liquidity of the market would mean the ball being in your court.

The Dealers Market

The dealer's market is the type of market in which the dealer acts as a counterparty between the seller and the buyer. He sets the bid and asks the prices for the security in question. Any investor, who accepts the price, would be involved in the trade.

The term 'over the counter' dealers emerged from this when dealers sell securities. This leads to increased liquidity in the market, which means a lesser risk of bankruptcy and loss. The market would be able to get out of its debt without selling the assets. This would happen at the cost of a small premium. In this, you would expect an additional return, for holding a risky market portfolio, instead of risk-free assets.

In this market, the dealer holds counterparty risk. He often sets the bid prices lower than the market price and asks for higher prices instead. In this way, the spread between the prices will be the profit the dealer would make. Such markets are more common in bonds and currencies, instead of stocks. There are more future opportunities for many dealers in this market. It holds more long-term future success and options, as well as useful for derivatives. One important aspect of this is that foreign exchange markets are usually dealt with within the dealer's market. The banks and currency exchange acts as the dealer intermediary. The dealer market is known as the most liquid market. Hence, it is good for you, as a beginner, as paying the debts would be easier.

The Exchange Market

The exchange market is one is known to be the most automated, but the irony is that, without the presence of a buyer and the seller, there is no execution of the trade.

In this market, no brokers are used for stock trading, as the order matches the buyers and the sellers. This is a quicker and less time-consuming method, which also avoids any delay in the trade to take place. However, the buyers and sellers are expected to find a counterparty, as there is no involvement of a broker or a dealer intermediary.

Exchanges are most appropriate for standardized securities, including stocks, bonds, futures, contracts, and options. Exchanges will typically specify characteristics for the securities traded on the exchange.

Fundamental Analysis

Those who trade based only upon the return offered and who do not evaluate the fundamentals are not in the game very long. Fundamental analysis is more detailed than the elements presented here. The goal is to assure we of the stock's worthiness and to look for danger signs.

If a stock does not cut, you should find it quickly to waste as little time as possible. For this reason, the most important fundamental elements are viewed first.

The Price to Earnings (P/E) Indicator

The P/E ratio is not perfect and reveals to us nothing about the nature of profit, or whether income is growing or taking a downturn. Be that as it may, it regardless fills in as a valuable measurement to look at stocks in a similar industry. A P/E ratio is fundamentally higher than the business average outcomes because the market prefers the stock, yet that preference can change abruptly. If market opinion changes negatively towards that stock, you, as a holder of that stock can sell it. Sell off would be more worthwhile if the stock sold for an overvalued price.

Earnings Growth and Quality

On numerous occasions, earnings, including one-time, unprecedented events, are unimportant to earnings quality. By quality, we allude to operational profit (and income), not phenomenal occasions like the offer of a division or a one-time discount. What's more, companies that focus more on earnings, usually report their financial outputs to show more earning quality. Now and then, these incomes exhibited here are sometimes misdirecting. Tragically, profit quality is hard to evaluate without a point by point assessment of companies' financial statements. Hence, you may wish to concentrate on earnings development over time and its dependability, since robust earnings growth is a more applicable metric than earning quality.

Earnings per share (EPS) is emphasized in this respect since it relies upon the number of offers exceptional. A stock buyback would blow up EPS without a relating income increment. What's more, giving new offers such as public offerings, mergers, etc. would diminish EPS, yet the money inflow may be very positive.

Average Day by Day Volume

Although this is more a technical analysis tool, it is also very relevant in this discussion. Volume is, by and large, a proportion of the stock's liquidity and dependability, however not really of its necessary sufficiency. Low-volume stocks can give high returns; however, they are dependent upon control and cannot move much of a stretch. There are an excessive number of incredible assets with substantial volume to allow for the trading of the low-volume stocks. Regardless of whether you are searching for progressively unstable stocks for exchanging openings, pick high volume. The average day by day volume is what makes a difference.

Stock Volatility

Volatility reveals to us how unpredictable the stock is, take the most recent incident; for example, Tesla, how has been it rose and dropped sharply in the market. Instability might be level when contrasted with records, and it can also be expanding or diminishing. Then there is implied volatility that demonstrates whether alternative prices are inferring a potential future unpredictability that is lower than or higher than the records of volatility.

Remember that the markets frequently show general volatility of under 15%. 20-40% is a medium degree of instability, and over 40% could be viewed as high. Over 80% is high as can be. Choose what instability level you are eager to go up against, however staying with more prominent companies with reliable records in the twenty to fifty percent volatility range can yield enormous profits for your investment.

Inferred or implied volatility ought to be estimated against the 10-day volatility. If implied volatility is following the lower 30-day unpredictability rather than, the higher 10-day instability, at that point, the later volatility primarily isn't being estimated into the choice; the market isn't worried about it because there is no cause for alarm.

A final group you should consider are the Insiders (officials, chiefs, and significant investors). They are bound to record reports when they purchase or sell protections of their companies. These reports are broadly held to demonstrate whether the insiders think about their organization's stock a purchase or a short. This view is commenced on chronicled perceptions that insiders will, in general, purchase their organization's stock when the viewpoint is splendid and sell in front of terrible occasions for the organization. This means well since they have a definitive instructive favorable position.

Many analyses and forces affect when to choose stocks, how to choose them, when to sell, and hold on to your stock. A strong understanding of these factors and their respective fluctuations would help make you an investment guru.

Chapter 6.

Dividend Stocks Creating Passive Income

For hundreds of years, long-term investors invested in dividend stocks. At the beginning of the 20th century, most of the money made in the stock market in the US came in the form of dividends that companies paid to their shareholders. It is one of the opportunities that an average investor can enjoy now, too. This age is dominated by speculation in various securities. People tend to believe that they can make a killing in the stock market by selecting the right stock that would rise by a thousand percent and win a jackpot. Unfortunately, most speculators end up losing it all.

They ignore long-term profits and tend to choose short-term strategies to invest in stocks. Very few investors now think about a company in terms of whether it pays dividends or not. Most are searching for growth stocks that start their existence in the market from $5 or something and, in a matter of a few years, skyrocket to $100 or even more. They search for future stocks of CISCO, Wal-Mart, Apple, or Google that are going to fly like rockets to the moon and make them wealthy beyond their wildest dreams. Very few finds these stocks. Some pick up some penny stocks and lose a substantial amount of their money investing in them.

However, the facts speak for themselves. Some say that for the past 100 years or so, more than forty percent of the famous S&P500 returns came from dividends. The statistics should make one think whether it is better to leave short-term strategies and concentrate on the long-term ones. One of the best strategies is, of course, investing in dividend stocks. When you start delving into the subject, you will see how many advantages this kind of investing has over other most popular trading strategies. Let us look through some of the benefits of buying and holding dividend-paying stocks.

Benefits of Dividend Investing

You earn from dividends and rising share prices. So, this shows that there is a possibility to make money in two ways. Firstly, you get dividends, and most are paid quarterly. Secondly, you can also make substantial amounts of money from a rise in your shares. As you know, stocks rise and fall, and since you are in these dividend stocks for the long haul, you will surely benefit in these two ways: from steady dividends and rising prices of your stocks.

- **Steady income year after year**

Those who only expect to make money as shares rise will often have to sit out through bear markets when all stocks are falling, and they do not get the privilege of getting a steady income from the market in those times. However, those who own dividend stocks can enjoy never-ending streams of cash in good times and bad. Even if your shares' price is falling, your dividends are still paid, and your steady stream of income never stops.

- **The power of compounding when reinvesting your dividends**

Some investors talk about the power of compounding that they get when they reinvest the dividends. In a nutshell, compounding is getting current/future earning from previous earnings. So, if you get dividends and use them to buy more shares of a company that pays them, next time, you will get more dividends (and consequently more cash). If you invest those, you will again get more shares and more dividends. These earning will keep growing if you continue doing this, year after year until you retire and have probably created yourself a nest egg.

This type of investment protects your wealth from losing its value during inflation. We do know that during inflation, money starts losing its value. As prices grow, your money gets less and less power to buy things due to rising prices. For centuries, investors have tried to protect their hard-earned cash gold and in dividend stocks. Inflation often follows an overheated economy when everything is booming, and various new businesses spring up. That's when companies make bigger profits and, consequently, pay more significant dividends. Your price of shares rises, and so do the dividends from depreciation by investing in

- **Dividend stocks outperform those that do not pay dividends**

Growth stocks may do very well during booms. However, as fast as they rise, they plummet when financial bubbles burst. Those who have held to those stocks lose all their profits and even more. Dividend stocks may not take you for such an extraordinary ride upward, but they will also not take you down hard when the economy heads south. So, those who follow long-term investment strategies and do not jump in and out of the market try to get a quick buck and will earn cash in good times and bad.

Value stocks that they hold make them money even during very bad times because dividends do not stop coming. On the other hand, those who have been following short-term strategies have no streams of income from the market in bad times, and they need to wait for another boom to make money from rising prices in stocks. These stocks provide you with financial safety and stability. As people grow older, they want less risk and more stability and security. That is what investing in dividend stocks is all about.

You protect yourself from falling markets by keeping a steady stream of income. Prices of these stocks are often cheaper, but as dividends rise with prices of shares, you earn more. In the same fashion as gold, dividend stocks have proven to be one of the safest ways to invest in the stock market. It relieves you from the pressure of where to enter and exit the market.

Short-term investors are very concerned as to where they must enter and exit the market. They intend to capitalize on fast stock price moves, and it is crucial to be right when the move starts. Long-term dividend investors do not have to worry about that. They select the best-paying dividend stocks and accumulate their wealth slowly but surely. They do not have psychological pressure regarding daily market fluctuations, as they know they are there for the long haul.

How to Pick Dividends

There is no magic key to tell you exactly how to pick the winning dividend. That magic key would be almost as good as a lottery tracker that would tell you the exact number to choose. Make sure you are picking everything in the right way so that when the time comes, you can truly cash in on the dividends. Choosing the right ones will allow you to do so more quickly and give you the chance to make even more money.

Profits in the Company

The company profits are the number one thing that you should look at when you decide whether to choose them for your dividend investment. A company needs to have high profits for you to choose them, and they need to show that they are going to have these profits for a long time in the future. Ensure that the profits are going in the right direction and to make sure that you are going to be able to make money from the investment that you make. A company that has good profits is good.

Size of Payouts

You can always check the size of the payouts that the company has made to find out possible payments you can expect from the company. By simply looking at the company's trading profile, you will be able to see how much they payout, how often, and what it takes out of the profits that they have made. When you look at this amount, you need to consider all the aspects of the payouts, and this also includes the initial investment amount. Compare that amount to what you are planning on investing in the company and see if the payouts will be worth what you are going to invest in the company.

It is vital to ensure that you are looking at all this information in a way as if you were going to invest in the company.

Just because a company has great profits and appears to be healthy does not mean that it will continue to be healthy. One of the most popular cases to look at is the case of Whole Foods Market. They are a huge company that has a lot of help from the people who shop and the profits they make. They did well when the crunchy organic movement was happening, but their health has failed drastically since the recession hit. They are no longer profiting in the way that they would have been. When you are considering an investment, consider the future health of the company.

If you are hoping to make money from these companies, you can always invest more money into it so that you can get higher payments.

Be sure that you choose a company that works with you because that is what you want. Do not decide to invest your money in a company because a book told you to or someone else told you. Do your own research, learn about the companies, and figure out exactly what you want to get out of the investment opportunity.

Chapter 7.

Make Money with Growth Stocks

A growth stock is simply the stock of any company that is expected to grow its revenues or earnings rapidly. Here's the first rule for trading growth stocks:

Ignore the High P/E

Great companies that are rapidly growing will always trade at high P/E's. They might not even have any earnings. They might be losing a lot of money as they grow their market share, like Uber. They might also grow their market share for many years before they turn on the profit spigot. That's what Facebook did. It raised the social network for many years, before finally turning on advertising.

Value investors will always tell you to stay away from companies with high P/E's or companies that are losing money. But if you do that, you will miss some of the greatest stock runs of all time. Microsoft, Starbucks, Home Depot, and Amazon all traded at very high P/Es for many years. Amazon still does. But these stocks have gone on to make their holders very rich.

Companies with high P/E's are pricing in high growth in future earnings. If the growth is slowing or that those earnings may never appear, the market will trash the stock. That's why we always trade growth stocks with a clear stop loss.

If you are Warren Buffett investing in a mature company, the P/E does matter. If you are holding a growth stock for a few weeks or even months, nothing could matter less than the P/E.

Let me explain how to trade growth stocks:

I like to buy growth stocks that are hitting new 52-week highs, or even all-time new highs. This may seem counter-intuitive to some. Isn't it risky to purchase a stock that is at all-time new highs? Doesn't that mean that it has further to fall?

If you study the highest growth stocks of the past, you will notice that they spend a lot of time trading at all-time new highs. This makes sense simply because any stock that goes up a lot must spend a lot of time trading at new highs.

There is, in fact, something wonderful and magical about a stock at an all-time high: Every single holder of the stock has a profit.

By contrast, when a stock has crashed or is continuously hitting new 52-week lows, many investors and traders have been left holding the bag. If the stock then tries to rally, these investors will be happy to get out by selling their shares at their break-even price. This provides constant downward pressure, and thus makes it more difficult for the stock to bounce back.

At a new all-time high, everyone who owns the stock has a profit. All the losers are gone and have already exited at a loss or their break-even price. At new highs, there are only happy traders and investors left. Well, except for one group of traders that no one feels sympathy very much for the short-sellers. These are traders who have shorted the stock (probably because "it has such a high P/E") and are betting that it will go down. At a new all-time high, everyone who has shorted the stock previously now has a losing trade on their hands. They are sweating bullets.

And there's only one thing that they can do to stem their losses: They must "cover" their shorts by buying back the stock. This buying only adds more fuel to the fire, driving the stock higher, and forcing out more short sellers.

Meanwhile, a stock that has recently moved up a lot begins to be featured on CNBC and explained by online commentators. This publicity brings in a new wave of buyers, who continue to drive the stock higher and make it hit even more new all-time highs.

The next step is to look at a daily chart of each stock. I want to make sure that the stock is trading above its 50-day moving average; and that the 50-day moving average is above the 200-day moving average.

Never buy a growth stock if the stock is trading below its 200-day moving average, or if the 50-day moving average is trading below the 200-day moving average. If either of those two criteria is true, the stock is in a downtrend. There is nothing more dangerous than a growth stock in a downtrend. A growth stock might go up 300% over three years, and then fall 80-95% once it enters a downtrend. This can happen even with major companies.

If a growth stock is trading above its 50-day moving average, and the 50-day moving average is trading above the 200-day moving average, I am happy to belong. If the stock is trading at new 52-week highs or all-time highs, that's even better. If a stock gaps up to new highs after a strong earnings report, that can be a great buy signal. Due to an anomaly called "Post-Earnings-Announcement Drift" (PEAD), a stock that has gapped up like this will tend to continue moving in the same direction for many days or even weeks. As a small investor, you can ride the wave, as larger institutional investors add to their positions over time, causing the stock to drift higher.

Understanding IPO's

IPO (Initial Public Offering) is viewed as a privately-owned business that has developed with a moderately modest number of investors, including early speculators like the originators, family, and companions alongside expert financial specialists, such as financial speculators or holy messenger speculators.

IPO furnishes the organization in collecting a great deal of cash and gives a more prominent capacity to develop and grow. The expanded straightforwardness and offer posting validity can likewise be a factor in helping it acquire better terms when looking for obtained assets.

The first sale of Bear parts of an association is esteemed through due underwriting steadiness. When an association opens to the world, the as of late had private offer ownership changes over to open ownership, and the present private financial specialists' offers become worth the open exchanging cost. Generally, the private to open advancement is a key time for private examiners to exchange out and win the benefits they were envisioning. Private speculators may grasp their ideas in the open market or sell a piece or all of them for augmentations.

Meanwhile, the open market opens an enormous open entryway for some money related authorities to buy shares in the association and contribute subsidizing to an association's financial specialists' worth. The open involves any individual or institutional monetary master who is enthusiastic about placing assets into the association. As a rule, the number of offers the association sells and the expense for which offers sell are the making factors for the association's new financial specialists' worth regard. Financial specialists' worth still addresses controlled by examiners when it is both private and open, anyway with an IPO the speculators' worth augmentation on a very basic level with cash from the fundamental issuance.

Greatest IPOs

- Alibaba Group (BABA) in 2014 raising $25 billion
- American Insurance Group (AIG) in 2006 raising $20.5 billion
- VISA (V) in 2008 raising $19.7 billion
- General Motors (GM) in 2010 raising $18.15 billion
- Facebook (FB) in 2012 raising $16.01 billion

Lenders and the IPO Process

An IPO involves two areas. One, the pre-advancing time of the promotion. Two, the primary clearance of Bear itself. Exactly when an association is excited about an IPO, it will elevate to underwriters by mentioning private offers, or it can, in like manner, possess an open articulation to make interest. The underwriters lead the IPO technique and are picked by the association. An association may pick one or a couple of agents to supervise different bits of the IPO technique agreeably. The lenders are related to each piece of the IPO due to constancy, document course of action, recording, publicizing, and issuance.

Steps to an IPO going with:

1. Underwriters present suggestions and valuations discussing their organizations, the best sort of security to issue, offering esteem, the proportion of offers, and assessed time apportioning for the market promoting.

2. The association picks its underwriters, and authoritatively agrees to ensure terms through an embracing understanding.

3. IPO gatherings are confined, including agents, legitimate counsels, guaranteed open clerks, and Securities and Trade Commission masters.

4. Information as for the association is amassed for required IPO documentation.

- The S-1 Registration Statement is the basic IPO recording report. It has two areas: The arrangement and subtly held account information. The S-1 joins basic information about the ordinary date of the account. It will be adjusted as often as possible, all through the pre-IPO process. The included blueprint is in like manner refreshed interminably.

5. Marketing materials are made for pre-publicizing of the new Bear issuance.

- Underwriters and authorities promote the offer issuance to measure solicitation and set up a last offering expense. Underwriters can revise their money related examination all through the advancing technique. This can consolidate changing the IPO cost or issuance date as they see fit.

- Associations figure out how to meet unequivocal open offer offering essentials. Associations must hold quick to both exchanges posting essentials and SEC necessities for open associations.

A common hold is a kind of money related vehicle made up of a pool of funds assembled from various examiners to place assets into insurances, for instance, Bears, protections, cash market instruments, and multiple assets. Normal resources are worked by master money directors, who allocate the save's favorable circumstances and attempt to convey capital increments or pay for the store's theorists. A typical store's portfolio is sorted out and kept up to match the endeavor targets communicated in its framework.

Regular backings give close to nothing, or individual theorists access to expertly supervised courses of action of esteems, bonds and various securities. Each financial specialist, along these lines, takes an intrigue generally in the increments or hardships of the store. Normal resources put assets into many assurances, and execution is pursued as the modification in the outright market top of the save.

Chapter 8.

Investment Strategies

N ow that you have an idea of why you need to invest and some fundamental principles in investment as well as asset classes, you can invest in it. For you to start winning in a big way, you would have to put in the time. You would have to put in the effort. You would have to have the proper experience and groundwork to make that happen. And in many cases, even with the best-laid plans and with the best strategies laid out, things still don't pan out.

The better approach is to do the best with the situation you are facing. In other words, use specific strategies that would enable you to position yourself to come out ahead. They might not necessarily result in you making tons of money or experiencing truly stupendous returns, but they can position you for solid gains. The following strategies enable you to do just that.

Buy Depressed Assets

Now, this might seem straightforward. After all, this is just a reiteration of the classic investment and commercial maxim of "buy low, sell high." However, the big challenge here is in determining what constitutes a "depressed asset."

You might be thinking that a stock that was trading at $50 and pops to $150 might not be all that depressed if it fell to $100. You might be thinking, where's the depression? This is not a fire sale. It hasn't fallen enough.

If you look at the stock's trajectory and how much growth potential and market attention, it might very well turn out that the stock is headed to $300. Do you see how this works?

If that's the case, then scooping up the stock at the price of $100 after it fell from $150 is a steal. After all, buying something worth $300 for a third of its price is one heck of a bargain.

Now, the big issue here is how do you know the stock's full future value? This is where serious analysis comes in. You can't just buy stocks on hype. It would be best if you looked at facts that would inform the growth trajectory of that stock.

For example, is it a market leader? Does it have certain drugs in the approval pipeline that have little to no competition? Is it on the cusp of a breakthrough drug patent? Is it in the process of buying out its competition?

There are many factors that you should consider, which can impact the overall future value of a stock. You should pay attention to its current developments, and you should pay attention to the news cycle surrounding the company.

You should also pay attention to its industry. Is its industry fast-expanding, or is it a "sunset industry" on its last legs? If it's in a sunset industry, there might still be opportunities there because usually, such industries witness a tremendous amount of consolidation. Whatever the case may be, always be on the lookout for the future value of a stock based on what you know now, as well as its past performance.

Dollar-Cost Averaging

What happens if you buy a stock that subsequently crashes? This happens to the very best of us. If this happened to you, don't get depressed. Don't think that you suck at investing. Don't think that all is lost. If you get caught in a downturn, it might be an amazing opportunity.

Now, it's important to note that almost all stocks experience a pullback. I have yet to come across a stock that has appreciated positively with no dips in its trading history. I'm not aware of a stock that hasn't experienced a day-to-day dip in pricing. All stocks experience a pullback. Even stocks that are well on their way to becoming breakthrough or high-valued stocks will experience dips.

What happens if you bought a stock that drops in value tremendously? Well, you have two options at this point. You can wait for the stock to keep going up and then start buying some more. You're taking bets on its recovery.

The better approach would be to use this as an opportunity. For example, if you bought, for the sake of simplicity, one share of stock at $100 a share, and the price crashes 50% to $50 a share, you can buy one share at $50, and this would average out your holdings to $75 per share.

Ideally, you should wait for the stock to drop so much and then buy a whole lot. This enables you to set your break-even point at a much lower level. For example, using the same hypothetical facts mentioned above, instead of buying one share, you buy 9 shares at $50. So, what happens is, the average price per share gets reduced to $55.

Even if the depressed stock manages to limp along and possibly pop up here and there, it doesn't have to pop up all that much to get all your money back from your position because once it hits $55, you're at break-even territory. Compare this with breaking even at $75 or, worse yet, waiting for the stock to come back to $100 a share. It's anybody's guess whether it will back to that level.

This strategy is called dollar-cost averaging, and it is very useful. You must have free cash available, and you must use that free cash at the right time.

That's how you maximize its value. That's how you fully take advantage of opportunities that present themselves. Otherwise, you might be in a situation where the stock crashes so hard that you could have broken even very easily with little money spent, but unfortunately, you were locked out because you don't have the cash to do it.

Buy Self Liquidating Assets

Another investing strategy you can take is to buy assets that pay for themselves. For example, if you spent a million dollars buying a building, but the building generates rents totaling $100,000 per year, the building pays for itself in roughly 13 years or more, factoring taxes and other costs.

Self-liquidating assets may seem too good to be true, but they are very real. Most of this applies to certain types of real estate, like commercial properties. However, this strategy also applies to stocks and bonds.

For example, if you buy stocks that have no dividend and you buy bonds, you can use the bond interest to start paying off your stock's portfolio. Of course, this can take quite a bit of time if you factor in interest rates as well as taxes.

Smart Money Valuation

Another winning strategy is to buy into private corporations as a sophisticated investor at a much lower valuation. Now keep in mind that many mobile app companies are popping up all over the United States. You don't necessarily have to live in Silicon Valley of California to have access to these types of companies.

The great thing about these companies is that in the beginning, they require very little capital. Many require "Angel," "per-Angel," or even raw seed capital. The founder would have a rough idea of a software, an app, or a website. This is the most basic stage of a company's evolution.

Now, when you come in as a source of seed capital, you can lock into a large chunk of the company's stock for a very low valuation. For example, somebody comes up with a startup idea, and the initial cost is a maximum of $1 million. If you were to invest $250,000, you have a 25% stake in the company.

You may be thinking that 25% of a company that's not worth that much, which is very, very risky, doesn't seem like a winning proposition. Well, keep in mind that after the seed stage, the company's valuation usually goes up. So, once your money has been used to push the company further along its developmental path, the company's valuation starts to go up, especially if they now have something more concrete to show other investors.

You may be asking yourself, okay, the smart money valuation thing sounds awesome. This is great in theory, but is it real? How can the Average Joe investor get in on such deals?

There are websites like Angel List and others, as well as LinkedIn groups that publicize startup projects that are actively recruiting investors. Of course, you need to do your homework and pay attention to the track record of the founders.

Chapter 9.

Master the ETFs

E xchange-Traded Funds (ETFs) are unique investment funds that are comprised of different securities like stocks, bonds, commodities, international or U.S. only holdings. They combine the features of open-end and closed-end funds with the structure of an open-end investment company.

They can be traded like regular stocks throughout the day on stock exchange markets. ETFs operate using an arbitrage mechanism to keep the net asset value (NAV) close to the trading price. They can also track both bond index and stock index. With a lower cost of transaction and management fees, stock-like features, and tax advantages, they attract a lot of investors.

ETFs already covered almost all conceivable market niche, sector, and trading strategy when introduced in the United States in 1993. They became available in Europe around 1999. Some of them own thousands of stocks in different industries, while others prefer to concentrate on one sector. With the capacity to hold multiple underlying assets, ETFs provide diversification, versatility, and convenience.

Some of the most popular ETFs are the SPDR Down Jones Industrial Average (DIA), SPDR S&P 500 (SPY), iShares Russel 2000 (IWM), and Invesco QQQ.

There are different types of Exchange-Traded Funds (ETFs):

- Bond ETFs—Invest in corporate bonds, government bonds, and municipal bonds (state and local bonds)
- Stock ETFs—track stocks and indexes
- Index ETFs—attempt to copy the performance of an index
- Currency ETFs—Invest in foreign currencies like the Canadian dollar or Euro
- Industry ETFs—track specific industry like oil or gas sector, banking, or technology
- Commodity ETFs—Invest in gold, crude oil, and other forms of products
- Inverse ETFs—attempt to create profits out of stock declines through the shorting strategy, which sells it, expects a reduced value, and repurchases the stock at a much lower price
- Leveraged ETFs—attempt to gain returns which are 2x or 3x more aggressive than non-leveraged ETFs

Buying and Selling of ETFs

The supply of shares of the ETF is regulated under the creation and redemption mechanism. ETFs are available only through authorized participants (APs) who are large specialized investors or broker-dealers.

Distributors buy or sell them in creation units (large blocks, which are around 50,000 shares). Purchases or redemptions of the creation units are in kind, wherein the investor contributes or receives a basket of securities (assets).

The process by which the APS sells stocks to an ETF sponsor, in exchange for ETF shares, is referred to as creation. When the ETF requests for additional shares, the APs will purchase stocks from the index and sell them to the ETF or opt for new shares at an equal price. After the trading, the APS has the discretion to sell the new ETF shares for a profit.

Redemption is the process that is used by APs to reduce the number of their ETF shares. They buy ETF shares on the open market and sell them to the ETF sponsor. Payment is in the form of individual stock shares, which the APS sells on the open market.

ETFs operate much like mutual funds because they blend the resources of many financiers to acquire a basket of stocks, bonds, or both. ETFs vary from traditional shared funds in a couple of important ways:

Switch on Platforms

As the name suggests, these securities are traded on almost the same markets as stocks. ETF rates change from second to second, just like stock prices.

Mostly Index Funds

While a couple of ETF managers actively handle their funds to top standards, the bulk of them tracks indexes.

Greater Openness

Unlike traditional mutual funds—which the SEC requires to divulge their holdings quarterly—ETFs need to disclose daily. Considering that indexes don't change their holdings typically, a lot of ETFs don't either.

Pros

- **Convenient Trading**

Unlike the way shared funds reprice at the end of the day and trade only at that cost during the following day, ETF costs rise and fall intraday like stocks.

Hedging. Financiers can purchase and sell options on ETFs, just as they can on the majority of Inventory. Starting buyers will probably avoid stocks, but the flexibility to buy and make choices. ETFs permit has contributed to their popularity.

- **Trading Costs**

Numerous brokers charge more to trade mutual funds than stocks. When investors buy or offer exchange-traded shared funds, they pay the same commissions charged for stock trades.

Cons

- **Fund costs**

Bear in mind that every shared fund charges fees. Since ETFs trade like stocks, investors often treat them like stocks and forget about those charges. And ETFs rarely draw much attention to the fees they gather.

- **Selection**

Many ETFs track indexes, indicating they're passively managed. While some ETFs use active managers, financiers looking for active management will discover a couple of choices amongst ETFs.

- **Viewed Complexity**

While ETFs appear like mutual funds in most aspects, many investors avoid them. A 2010 survey by Mintel Compere Media, a consulting firm, found that almost 60 percent of financiers decided not to buy ETFs because they did not understand how they operated.

Mutual Funds

Shared funds pool the properties of several investors, supplying purchasing power that surpasses that of all but the wealthiest individuals. Suppose you have $10,000 to invest. If you try to spread out the cash around 50 stocks, commission costs alone may cripple you. Yet spend the same $10,000 in a mutual fund that holds 50 stocks, and you've got that. Buy a small piece of each of those companies without the cost or trouble of acquiring them separately.

Professional money managers decide when the fund sells and buys, and all the financiers either win or lose together. If shared, the investment pays 10%

in one year, and every person who holds the fund at the beginning of that year will see the fund—very same 10% return on his investment.

At the end of 2012, financiers worldwide had $26.8 trillion purchased mutual funds, with $13.0 trillion of these assets in the hands of the U.S. cash supervisors, according to the Investment Company Institute (ICI). Of that, $13 trillion bought the U.S. shared funds, 45% remained in stock funds, and 26% were in bond funds.

Stock and bond mutual funds can be found in two tastes:

Passively Handled Funds

Frequently called index funds, quietly managed funds try to match the performance of an index.

Actively Handled Funds

Unlike passively managed funds, proactively handled funds purchase and offer securities to exceed the return of their standard—generally index or index party. It's hard to overstate the value of mutual funds as a financial investment automobile. More than 92 million people own in the United States alone shared funds, frequently through retirement plans. Additionally, most 401 (k) retirement plans invest employees' possessions in pooled funds, so if you take part in a company-sponsored retirement plan, you probably currently own funds.

Pros

- **Professional Management**

Many individuals do not know much about evaluating financial investments because of a lack of interest, an absence of training, or both options. With almost 9,000 standard mutual funds on the market, practically any investor can find a fund to resolve her investment objectives.

- **Diversification**

Portfolios containing a range of stocks or bonds tend to be less unpredictable than an individual stock or bond. Mutual-fund supervisors utilize their purchasing power to acquire numerous securities, which, most of the time, supply diversity.

Cons

- **Every Shared Fund Charge Fee**

Remember that specialist you worked with when you purchased the mutual fund? Also, some funds charge costs called loads, gathering additional money to compensate for the salesperson or investment company.

- **Complacency**

Mutual-fund investors typically presume that considering that they have a professional handling a diversified basket of stocks, they can relax and relax. Don't make that error.

- **Poor returns**

Last year, only about a 3rd of actively handled shared funds surpassed their criteria. A lot of academic studies recommend this pattern isn't brand-new, which fund fees should have much of the blame. While the persistent underperformance shouldn't scare you away from shared funds, it needs to hammer home the significance of choosing your money wisely.

Chapter 10.

Master the Forex, CFD and Commodities

A t the core of Forex, you are dealing with currency trading and at the base of that currency trading, you have speculation about the values of currencies. Currency trading is speculation. It is as simple as that. You are using what knowledge and information you must make a profit by buying currencies. It is like buying stocks or any other financial security; you make a transaction and hope to make a profitable return. However, in the Forex market, the securities you are dealing with concern about the currencies of nations.

Typically, when you invest, you aim to minimize the risks and maximize the returns over a certain period (usually months or years). In Forex, you are maximizing returns over a short period (usually minutes, hours, or days). You will read the trends, understand the shifts, and even use the latest news to make calculated risks. The best way to understand your actions is by taking the example of a business. If you are the owner of a business, then you will be making calculated risks. Should you increase the available stock that you have? Do you want to hire more employees? Should you think about expanding your business or opening a branch in another location? Do you need to spend heavily on big marketing campaigns?

You may never be certain about the outcomes of any of those decisions. But you do make choices based on the information you have. For example, you notice that there is a demand for your products in another state. After conducting a market survey, you decide that it would be profitable for you to have a branch in that state. You immediately open another business. But what if you are not receiving profits that way you had expected? What are you going to do then? Are you going to pack up and call it quits? Or will you try some other tactics to attract customers to your business?

It is the same with Forex. When you speculate, you are making decisions about your investment based on the information you have with you.

Therefore, not many people realize before venturing into Forex that they need to be equipped with a specific frame of mind and skill set.

- You need to be dedicated. You can invest in the Forex market and ignore it for a few days, but then you must return to it to make a few changes.

- You need to have financial and technological resources. Even though you can start small, you will not last long if all you have is lunch money. When it comes to technical resources, you need to make sure that you have steady access to the internet and the trading platform.

- You need to have financial discipline. You do not need to have a finance degree. Instead, you should be capable of understanding trends and numbers.

- You need to be emotionally strong. Things do not always go your way. But some of the biggest successes in Forex happen because people do not get emotional over their trades. They figure out ways to bounce back.

- You need to have the perseverance always to seek out new information, new ways to manage your risk, and look for new opportunities.

- Finally, you should be a sponge, able to absorb knowledge about the politics, economics, and market situations of a country. That means it is time to renew your newspaper subscriptions.

Buying factors, you are acquiring the base currency while trading the quote currency. This connotes that you want a rise in the value of the base currency and peddle it back at a higher price. In Forex, we use terminology such as taking a "long position" or "going long." To make it easier, long is equivalent to buy. Selling in Forex means you sell the base currency while buying the quote currency. It is the exact opposite of buying the base currency. In other words, you want a fall in the value of the base currency and later buy the currency recedes at a diminished price. The terminology for this situation is taking a "short position" or "going short." Short is for selling.

Bid and Ask Price

Now you know the difference between buying and selling the base currency in Forex, it is essential to talk about the bid and ask price. Do not be confused when you see currency pairs quoted at two different prices. This indicates the bid and asking the price, and in a better situation, the bid price is always lower than the asking price.

The bid price is the price your intermediary decides to purchase the base currency against the quote currency. It is the best price convenient at that time at which the trader is inclined to sell. Alternatively, the asking price is that a broker is willing to sell the base currency in exchange for the quote currency. The asking price is also known as the offer price. The spread is the difference between the bidding and asking price.

Time to Make Money

I know you are fired up to know how to make money in the market. Well, in the examples below, I will teach you how you can use essential analysis to select to either buy or sell a currency pair.

- **EUR/USD Pair**

By now, I am convinced you now know the base and quote currency. The euro is our base currency in this example and the basis for which we buy/sell. This is how traders make a profit—when they anticipate that the U.S. economy will fall, which is terrible news for the dollars; they will trigger a buy option of the EUR/USD pair. By doing so, the trader has purchased the euros in anticipation that it will rise against the U.S. dollar.

Alternatively, if the trader believes the U.S. economy will be strong. In contrast, the euro will fall adjacent to the dollar and trigger the sell option, which allows him to sell the euros in anticipation that the price will fall.

- **USD/JPY**

Always remember, the base currency is on the left while the quote currency is on the right-hand side. In this example, our base currency is the U.S. dollar and is the basis for our buy/sell. You will execute a buy option if you think the Japanese government will weaken its currency to boost its export industry. By this option, you have purchased the U.S. dollar in anticipation that it will rise against the Yen.

However, if your hunch tells you that Japanese investors will pull their money from the U.S. financial market and exchange their dollars to yen, this will affect the U.S. dollar, and the best option is to execute the sell order. In this situation, you have sold the dollar while anticipating that it will depreciate when compared with the Japanese yen.

- **USD/CHF**

This will be the last example of this session. The base currency is the U.S. dollar. If, as a trader, you consider the CHF is overvalued, then you can trigger the buy order. In doing so, you have anticipated that the dollar will inflate over the Swiss Franc. However, if you consider the opposite, then you could execute the sell order. This means you anticipate a depreciation in the value of the U.S. dollar over the Swiss Franc.

Pips

A pip is the unit of measurement representing a change in terms of value that exists between two different currencies. Do not mind my English definition. Let us assume the following pair GBP/USD moves from 1.3250 to 1.3251. In this situation, the currency moves a pip. You will observe that the pip is the last decimal place of a pair. It is usually the fourth decimal place of any currency. However, if such a pair contains the Yen, then it is two decimal places.

Note that some brokers quote pairs beyond the standard "2" and "4" decimal places we know to "3" and "5" decimal places. In this situation, what they quote is the fractional part, which is called the pipettes. I know this may look confusing, and I always use examples to make my point clear.

For example, the pair GBP/USD moves from 1.35421 to 1.35422, moving a single pipette. Because every currency has its unique value, it is essential to evaluate the value of a pip for each currency.

Chapter 11.

Bonds and Futures

I nvesting in bonds should be part of an overall strategy to achieve financial independence. To accomplish that, you need to know how to build a solid financial structure to deliver the desired result. Financial independence means having a guaranteed regular income to support your lifestyle without having to work.

Whatever the figure that comes works for you, financial independence means if you lose your primary source of income (wages, pensions, proceeds from a business), your life goes on normally without you having to seek a bailout.

To build a solid or stable financial structure, you need to understand what it is and how to go about building one that works for you, and you need a proper foundation. That foundation is financial security. This security does not come from your job or your business. It comes from earning enough from other guaranteed (relatively risk-free) income sources to live your life normally if you lose your job or your business goes belly up. This means your life is independent from income you must work for.

You need to build the right financial structure to achieve financial stability through the ups and downs of any economic cycle. This financial structure is built on having your money work for you. Your job is to convert a part of your earned income (that you work for) to passive income (that you don't work for)—building a structure whereby money works for you so that you eventually don't have to work for money anymore, but for love.

Whatever you are doing will come to an end someday. Your job will not last forever. You will leave it one way or the other, including mandatory retirement at a certain age. The marketplace is continuously evolving. Your line of business will be overtaken by new market trends, technology, etc. someday. The economy goes up and down, and this has an impact on your business. You need to build a financial support structure, a financial portfolio that will give you financial stability.

This financial structure is made up of two plans:

- **Financial Security Plan**

This plan is to secure your family financially in terms of sustaining your current standard of living. It is not to make you rich. Investments under this plan are fixed-income investments whereby the returns are guaranteed, and risk is almost zero. Investments in this plan include money market investments like fixed deposits, treasury bills, etc., that also includes bonds.

- **Financial Growth Plan**

This plan is to enable you to grow financially, become richer, essentially increase your net worth and raise your standard of living if you so desire. Returns under this plan are potentially higher than under the financial security plan. The risks are also higher (higher risk, higher reward). You can make a lot of money and can also lose a lot of money. Investments under this plan include stocks, real estate, forex trading, etc., investments that appreciate.

For those who desire to be very rich, there is a third plan:

- **Financial Abundance Plan**

This plan is to make you very rich, a multi-millionaire, or even billionaire (in dollars), whereby you can virtually afford anything you want. Investments under this plan, as you may have rightly guessed, are high risk and high reward. You can become very rich if it goes well, and you may be wiped out financially if it goes wrong, and you accumulated huge debts while pursuing this dream. Such investments include investing in startups, think Apple, Facebook, Twitter, Google, LinkedIn, WhatsApp, YouTube, and Instagram. There is also another list—those that did not make it. This plan is often considered as part of the financial growth plan.

So how do you tie all this together to build a solid financial structure? The answer is asset allocation.

Asset Allocation

You are working hard, saving before spending, and using your savings to invest. Where do you put the money? If you have a regular income, you need to start building the plans or portfolios, starting from the foundation, which is the financial security plan where the risk is virtually zero.

When you are just starting, you don't know much and are probably afraid of losing your hard-earned money. Every building starts from the foundation. Building a financial security plan is the starting point, and bonds are a valuable addition to your financial security plan.

However, you need to understand that you need to build and keep both plans, rather than build your financial security today, demolish tomorrow, which is what most people do. Like liquidating bond investments to build the financial growth plan, or worse still lend to a friend with a business idea.

Futures

Futures represent financial derivatives, and their value is determined by the changes in the price of another asset. This suggests that its inherent value does not determine the price of futures; rather, it depends on the price of the asset being tracked by the futures contract.

A key benefit of the futures market is that it is centralized and that people from all parts of the globe can create futures contracts electronically. The price of the merchandise will be determined by these futures contracts and the delivery time. Important information is included in each futures contract regarding the quantity and quality of the goods sold, the specified price, and how the goods will be transferred to the buyers.

The overall worth of the contract is not paid by the individual who has bought or sold a futures contract. Rather, he pays a small percentage as a fee to take up an open position. For instance, if the futures contract has a value of $350,000 and the S&P 500 is 1,400, then the initial margin payment that he makes is just $21,875. This margin is established by the exchange and may be modified at any point in time.

When the S&P increases to 1,500, the value of the futures contract is going to be $375,000. Therefore, the individual will attain a profit of $25,000. However, if the index decreased to 1,390 from the initial level of 1,400, he will face a loss of $2,500 as the value of the futures contract will now be $347,500. This loss of $2,500 has not yet been realized. The individual will not have to add more cash to his trading account.

When the index decreases to 1,300, the value of the futures contract will be $325,000. The individual will experience a loss of $50,000. The broker will ask him to add more cash to his trading account because the initial margin of $21,875 is insufficient to cover the deficits.

All futures contracts have a few similarities. However, distinct assets may be tracked by each contract. Hence, it is vital to assess the different markets.

Categories of Futures Markets

Agriculture:
- Grains
- Livestock
- Dairy
- Forest

Energy:
- Crude Oil
- Heating oil
- Natural gas
- Coal

Stock Index:
- S&P 500
- Nasdaq 100
- Nikkei 225
- E-mini S&P 500

Foreign Currency:
- Euro/USD
- GBP/USD
- Yen/USD
- Euro/Yen

Interest Rates:
- Treasuries
- Money markets
- Interest Rate Swaps
- Barclays Aggregate Index

Metals:
- Gold
- Silver
- Platinum
- Base Metals

Futures contracts can be traded on various assets and categories. However, for a new trader, it is important to trade those assets that they are aware of. For instance, if you have been involved in stock trading for some time, you should use stock indexes at the start of your futures contract trading. This would make it easier for you to comprehend the underlying asset. You just need to comprehend the working of the futures market.

Once you have selected your category, you should determine which asset to trade. For instance, after choosing the energy category for trading futures contracts, you may focus on natural gas, coal, heating, or crude oil. Market trading takes place at different levels; hence, you should know different things, such as market requirements, liquidity, contract sizes, and volatility. Before trading in futures contracts, it is important to research the important aspects.

Investors making investments worth these tricks influence a large amount of money or those purchasing a significant number of products as price fluctuations can have a huge impact on the money spent on products. These "ticks" vary for different merchandise. The "ticks" of each commodity being traded in the futures and the minimum price fluctuation for each is distinct, depending on its kind.

Chapter 12.

Make Money with Futures

Exchanging fates is a type of contributing that can give broadening to a portfolio and assist you with overseeing hazards. Fates contracts apply to agrarian wares, rising and falling as the market interest of things, for example, corn, steel, cotton and oil change. You can make cash exchanging fates on the off chance that you pursue patterns, cut your misfortunes and watch your costs.

Follow Trends

Fates markets have patterns, much the same as different protections markets do. Items tend not to have a similar unpredictability as stocks, however, can likewise be less unsurprising. At the point when you distinguish a pattern through thorough research and testing, it speaks to your most obvious opportunity to benefit. Research includes investigating which components sway the organic market of the item that you're keen on. Testing includes making mimicked interests in prospects that you think you see slants in, to see whether a genuine venture would have worked out.

Cut Losses Short

Any individual who puts resources into fates long enough is going to buy gets that lose esteem. On the off chance that a specific agreement begins to move in opposition to your desires, firmly consider undercutting and assuming a little misfortune. The option might be trusting that the agreement will ascend in esteem, just to see it fall further. Since each agreement you purchase is with the desire that it will see gains inside your time skyline, stopping misfortunes by selling will expand the arrival that you return to contribute somewhere else, and counterbalance different additions when you ascertain salary venture for your charges.

Margins and Expiration Dates

Financial specialists exchange fates on edge, paying as meager as 10 percent of the estimation of an agreement to possess it and control the privilege to sell it until it lapses. Edges consider duplicated benefits, yet additionally profit you can't stand to lose. Keep in mind that exchanging on an edge conveys this unique hazard. Select gets that terminate aft   er when you anticipate that costs should arrive at their pinnacle. A March prospects contract is pointless on the off chance that you get it in January yet don't anticipate that the product should arrive at its pinnacle an incentive until April. Regardless of whether April contracts aren't accessible, a May contract is increasingly proper since you can sell it before it lapses yet hold up until after the ware cost gets an opportunity to rise.

Brokers and Expenses

Financial specialists exchange prospects contracts through conventional representatives just as online agent administrations. Online administrations offer less customized exhortation, but at the same time, are more affordable, offering exchanges for under $1 now and again. Utilize an online specialist and play out your own market investigation to minimize expenses and increment your net addition from exchanging fates. Track all costs, including intermediary charges and memberships on the web or print productions that help you contribute, to deduct them as speculation costs on your annual expenses.

Significant Method to Make Benefit in Futures

Have you at any point needed to figure out how to profit on the fates showcase? It is a high hazard, high reward condition, be that as it may on the off chance that you recognize what you are doing, you can profit, even procure a living from exchanging the fates showcase.

Before considering going all in, you should initially comprehend the concealed insider facts that are hiding underneath the dinky surface. Too often do you see beginners bounce directly into exchanging fates without first acknowledging what the shrouded gets are.

There are some concealed gets, however, once you realize how to utilize them furthering your potential benefit, then you will have the option to take steady benefits from the prospects showcase over and over.

- Try not to attempt the fates advertise on the off chance that you have no cash.

Many individuals get the possibility that creation cash on the prospects trade is simple, and they feel free to put enormous sums on that they can't stand to lose. That is a major NO.

- Try not to attempt some trick or mystery you read in a book.

The fastest method to lose cash on the fates showcase is to go out and attempt one of the mysteries you got notification from a companion or read in a book. These are simply gossipy tidbits and, for the most part, don't work. If you are going to test a specific methodology, guarantee you do it relaxed and with modest quantities of cash before going hard and fast. Little tests will assist you with seeing reliable results. You won't profit yet the dangers are little, and you won't lose your whole record on the off chance that things conflict with you.

- Think in the present moment and long haul.

Try not to attempt to make sense of what will occur in the fates showcase in the following 2 hours. Indeed, this can profit, however, there are a ton of effective merchants that are making cash long haul in fates moreover. They couldn't care less about the every day variances, or what happens each moment of consistently.

- Don't over investigate.

There is such an incredible concept as making a decent attempt on the fates trade. Regularly the great merchants will discover something that works, and afterward, continue attempting to make the framework and procedure work better. Simply acknowledge, there is no sacred goal to exchanging. There is no framework that is going to profit 100% of the time. Acknowledge you will take little misfortunes and discover a framework that works reliably and stick to it. Keep it near you and use it as your weapon against the market.

- Utilize an expert exchanging stage.

There are numerous great stages you can use to exchange prospects. In any case, there is a darker side to exchanging prospects, where numerous broking houses offer carriage stages that are more regrettable than inferior. Simply do your schoolwork first and discover what the top dealers are suggesting. These stages ordinarily play out the best and keep customers cheerful. At the point when your cash is in danger, you need to guarantee you have a wellbeing and dependability on your side. Generally, there can be radical outcomes.

- Know what's going on out there in the economy.

After the worldwide money related emergency, a few nations are doing ineffectively, and there is at present a few monetary standards issues. It may merit your opportunity to discover how the economy is getting along in your general vicinity of the world. If things are not looking great, it is smarter to set aside cash to purchase day by day things before you go gambling everything on the fates advertise.

- Utilize a demonstrated stop misfortune the board framework.

This is the main motivation behind why numerous merchants out there come up short. They toss cash into the fates advertise without pondering what their arrangement is if things conflict with them. Things won't work out as expected 100% of the time. Taking misfortunes are a part of the game, and increasingly like a cost of doing business for proficient brokers. Simply acknowledge it and consistently leave a position on the off chance that it conflicts with you. It is difficult to concede you aren't right, yet simply acknowledge it and get out the exchange. That will guarantee you have cash for the following exchange that presents itself.

For you to start
winning in a big way,
you would have
to put in
the time and the effort.
Use
these specific
strategies
that will enable you
to position yourself
to come out ahead

Chapter 13.

Common Mistakes to Avoid

Mistakes happen in every field, sector, and industry. Some are always anticipated, while others happened unexpectedly. When it comes to stock trading, there are several mistakes that you can make. Understanding these mistakes can help you avoid them, thus ending up successful in your stock investments. Here are some of the common mistakes made by most investors, beginners, and professional traders alike:

Failure to Understand the Trade

It is always wrong to invest in a trade or business you know nothing about. It is a great mistake to engage in stock trading when you do not understand the business and financial models involved. You can avoid this mistake by taking the time to research the stock market and stock trading before investing your money. Know the different markets, the driving forces, as well as trading procedures.

Most investors tend to buy stocks from the latest companies and industries they know very little about. Although such companies may look promising, it is difficult to determine whether they will continue to exist. Understanding a specific company gives you a better hand over other investors. You will be able to make accurate predictions about the company or industry, which may bring you more profit. You will quickly tell when the business is booming, stagnating, or closing way before other investors get this information. Individuals who do not take time to study companies miss out on future trends of these companies. Failing to establish such trends leads to several missed opportunities. For instance, a person who invests in a company that is higher than his capital may quickly lose all his investment. That is why it is always advisable that you invest in the industry you understand better. For instance, if you are a surgeon, you can invest in stocks that deal with medicine or related stocks. Lawyers can invest in companies that generate income through litigation, and so on.

Impatience

The stock market is for patient investors. It is a slow but steady form of investment. Although it bears various opportunities that can bring you money, you cannot make enough profit in one day. Most stock investors are always faced with the challenge of being patient. Some end up losing trade positions before they mature in the quest to make quick money. Exiting the market too early will always cost you some returns. As a new investor, you must never expect your investment portfolio to perform more than its capability, as this will always lead to a disaster. Remain realistic in terms of the time, duration, and resources needed to earn from the market.

Failure to Diversify

Another mistake that easily causes disaster is the failure to diversify. Professional investors do not have a problem with this since they can easily profit from a single type of stock. However, young investors must be able to diversify to secure their investment. Some of them do not stick to this principle. Most of these lose a great fortune as soon as they get onto the stock market. As you seek to invest, remember the rule of thumb governing stock diversity. This states that you should not invest more than 10% of your capital to one type of stock.

Getting Too Connected with a Certain Company

The essence of trading in stock is to make a profit. Sometimes, investors get too deep into a certain company that they forget that it is all about the shares and not the company itself. Being too attached to a company may cloud your judgment when it comes to stock trading since you may end up buying stocks from this company instead of getting the best deal on the market. As you learn more about companies, always remember that you are into the business to make money, besides creating relationships.

Investment Turnover

Investment turnover refers to the act of entering and exiting positions at will. This is one other mistake that destroys great investments. It is only beneficial to institutions that seek to benefit from low commission rates. Most stock trading positions charge transaction fees. The more frequent you buy and sell, the more you pay in terms of transaction fees. You, therefore, need to be careful when entering positions. Do not get in or exit too early.

Have a rough idea of when you want to close positions so that you do not miss some of the long-term benefits of these positions.

Timing the Market

Market timing results in high investment turnover. It is not easy to successfully time the market. On average, only 94% of stock trading returns are acquired without the use of market timing. Most traders time the market as a way of attempting to recover their losses. They want to get even by making some profit to counter a loss. This is always known as a cognitive error in behavioral finance. Trying to get even on the stock market will always result in double losses.

Trading with Emotions

Allowing your emotions to rule is one of the things that kill your stock investment returns. Most people get into the market for fear of losses or thirst to make returns too fast. As a young trader, you must ensure that greed and fear do not overwhelm your decision making. Stock prices may fluctuate a lot in the short-term; however, this may not be the case in the long term, especially for large-cap stocks. This means that you may get lower profits in the short-term, but these may increase in the long-term. Understanding this will help you avoid closing trades when it is not the right time yet.

Setting Unrealistic Expectations

This always occurs when dealing with small-cap stocks such as penny stocks. Most investors buy such stocks with the expectation that the prices will change drastically. Sometimes this works, but it is not a guarantee. To make great fortunes, people invest a lot of capital on these stocks, and then the prices do not change much. If these investors are not prepared for such an eventuality, they may feel frustrated and may quit the business completely. However, this is something that you must be able to manage if you want to grow your investment. Do not expect more than what a certain type of stock can deliver.

Using Borrowed Money

This is probably one of the greatest mistakes that investors make. Some investors get carried away with the returns they are making. As a way of getting more profits, they borrow money and use it to enter more stock positions. This is a very dangerous move and can result in a lot of stress. Stock trading is like gambling. You are not always sure how much you take home at the end of each trade. It is therefore not advisable for you to invest borrowed money in it.

As you try to avoid these mistakes, you must also avoid getting information from the wrong sources. Some traders have lost a fortune because they relied on the wrong sources for stock information. It is important to isolate a small number of people and places where you will seek guidance from. Do not be a person that follows the crowd. Take time before investing in new stock opportunities. Carry out proper due diligence, especially with small-cap stocks since these involve a lot of risks. Remember, you must trade carefully and implement expert advice if you want to succeed in stock trading.

Chapter 14.

Tips and Tricks for Successful Stocks Trading

There are some tips and tricks that you can keep up your sleeve to help you invest in stocks. Let us look at some of them.

Always be Informed

You need to be informed about what happens in the market. This is the only way you can trust your decisions. You should go through different resources and publications if you want to obtain more information about the various stocks in the market.

Buy Low, Sell High

This is a strategy that most investors will use. It is always good to buy low and sell high, and you must follow this to the tee. It is when you do this that you can expect to make large profits in the market. When you buy low and sell high, you will purchase a stock at its lowest value and sell it at its highest value. It will be easy for you to determine when the stock price will reach the highest rate based on some methods and data you collect. You need to ensure that you always act according to the data that you have collected. Experts recommend that it is a good idea to buy stocks the minute the market opens. Most stocks reach their highest price in the afternoon, and that is when you should sell them.

Scalping

This is a very popular technique in the stock market. When you use this technique, you can always buy and sell stocks within a matter of a few seconds. Your purchases and sales depend on how fast you are. This is a very strange method, but it is very effective, especially in volatile markets. Let us assume that you purchased a stock at 10:00 AM and sold it at 10:02 AM The price of that stock is $3, and the selling price is $5. So, in a matter of two minutes, you made a $2 profit per share, and this is a great profit for a scalper. This does not seem like a profit, but if you do this at least twenty or thirty times a day, you can make a huge profit. You should only use this form of trading once you have enough experience in the market. If you want to take up this technique, you should have at least a year's worth of experience to help you make the right decisions.

Short Selling

Many traders use the concept of short selling when they invest in the market. Short selling refers to when you need to borrow stock from the holder and sell it to another buyer. Then, you will wait for the stock price to fall before you give the stocks back to the lender. This is one of the easiest ways in which you can capitalize on the volatility of the prices. You must make the right decisions about the investments you make and don't invest or borrow useless stocks. You must always ensure that you maintain a wide margin that will make a few mistakes. You should ensure that you have enough capital to support any other investments if things never work out. It is always good to buy shares back at the earliest if you believe that the price of the stocks will continue to increase.

Identify the Pattern

It is important to remember that stocks and every other stock in the market will follow a pattern. Once you notice this pattern and understand it, you can invest in stocks successfully. This pattern has all the information you need about the high and low points of the stocks and gathers some information on how you can trade between those points. It is important to have the history of the stock with you since it will help you determine the previous trend and predict the future trend of the stock.

Look at the Results

Every company is result-oriented, which means that the report published by the company will tell you how well the company is doing. The report that the company shares will shed some light on how well it is doing in the market. You should go through this report to ensure that you are making the right choice. The data collection results should show you that you could make enough profits when you invest in it. A small company will always aim to sell a large volume of stocks, and if you are impressed with the company and its numbers, you can invest in the stocks of that company. Remember that a company only publishes the results quarterly. Therefore, you need to look at all the results before you invest in the company.

Look at the Company Name

When choosing to invest in the stock market, you should understand that its name does matter. You must see if the company is well known and is doing well in the market. You can invest in a company that does not have any significant changes. Some people steer clear of such companies. If you are not a fundamentalist and are willing to take on a few risks, you can use technical analysis to help you make the decision. It is always good to learn more about the company if you choose to invest in shares in that company.

Understand the Company Better

You need to look at how the stock performs in the market, but it is important to spend some time understanding the company you are investing in. You need to know if the company is working on the right products and services. Understand the industry of the company. See if they are developing new products, technology, or services. Remember that whatever the company does affect the price of the stock. The best way for you to do this is to learn more about the company through fundamental analysis. You should always read the news about the company too. It is only this way that you can assess how well the company is doing. If you have any knowledge about the company or the products, you should spend some time to see where the company is heading.

When you start looking at a company, you need to ensure that you obtain the information from the right sources. Read this information carefully to understand whether the company is doing well or not. Ensure that the sources you use to obtain this information are reliable. If you get a fax, tip, or email from a person stating that one company is better than the rest, you need to make sure that you do not rush into investing. Take some time out and read about the company. Never invest in any company simply because of some information you may have received. Always conduct thorough research before you invest in the company. This is the only way you will learn if the company is doing well or not. Never waste your time or money. So, always stick to reliable sources and use that information to invest in the correct stocks.

Don't Trust Mails

You mustn't trust any emails that come from companies that claim to have enough knowledge about the stocks of other companies. These emails will also suggest the stocks that you should invest in, but the information in those emails is untrue. Companies cannot go through their investors' portfolios and suggest which stocks they should invest in. Even if a company does choose to do this, they may give you a suggestion that will not work for you. So, it is good to avoid these stocks and only invest in those stocks that you have all the information about.

Understand the Corrections

Remember that the price of stocks will be corrected in the market, and it is important that you remain patient. The price of the stock will drop when the market is correcting the price of the stocks in the market. If you are impatient, you will make a mistake and lose a lot of money. Always look at the company and make the right decisions about your investments. If a stock is either overpriced or underpriced, it means that the corrections will be made soon. Never sell your stocks in a panic and wait for the corrections to be made. You need to follow the news regularly, so you understand how or why the correction is being made.

Hire A Broker Only If Necessary

You should never hire a broker to do the job for you unless you need one. The only reason is that a broker will charge you a fee for helping you with your investments. They will also ask you to pay a commission, which will eat into your profits. You also need to remember that you need to pay your broker a fee regardless of whether you make a profit. So, they do not have to work hard to ensure that you make a profit. There are theories that companies hire brokers to increase the price of the stock in the market. They request the brokers to motivate investors to trade in a specific stock even if they do not want to invest in that stock. You will purchase these stocks if you can be swayed easily, which will lead to huge losses. You should always look for discounts online and see if you can trade independently. Avoid depending on your broker to buy and sell your stock.

Diversify Your Risks

This has been mentioned repeatedly across the book, so you can imagine how important it is for you to do this. You must always diversify your risks depending on the type of investment you make. This holds for any instrument. When you choose to invest in stocks, try to invest in stocks from different industries and sectors. If you invest in stocks only in one sector, you will lose a lot of money if the industry were to crash. It is because of this that you need to ensure that you diversify your capital. You must invest in different instruments in the market. Yes, one industry may be doing well compared to other industries, but this does not mean that you put all your money on stocks in that industry.

Money Movement

If you notice a sudden change in the price movement and the flow of money in the company, you know that the stock value will increase. If there is a sudden increase in the capital through external sources or it pumped its profits into its business, then it means that the company wants to expand. This will mean that the stock prices will rise, and it will benefit you as an investor. You must always keep track of the news and make the right decisions.

Look at the Stock Volume

If you notice that the volume of the stock has suddenly changed in the market, it is always a good idea to invest in that stock. The sudden changes in the price and volume of the stock will happen when there is some information in the news about the stock that makes people buy or sell stocks. Ensure that you capitalize on these situations so that you can make a huge profit. According to Timothy Sykes, you should always purchase a stock if you experience a high price after one year. The price of the stock will change only when the company talks about its earnings and bonuses.

Chapter 15.

Factors Affecting the Stock Market

The stock market can be described by one unique element called change. It continues to change due to so many forces and influences. The volatility can be brought about by several issues. Take note that the following factors are not exhaustive. They are not the only factors that can affect the movement of stocks in the market, but have a role in the performance of stocks.

Economy

The economy is very much connected with the stock market. You can tell if the economy is doing well by looking at the stock market. States that have a good economy also tend to have a stable stock market.

Political events

As can be expected, the stock market cannot escape the influence of politics. For example, when JFK was assassinated, the U.S. stock market sank since investors were hesitant to invest. And, since stocks and bonds operate within a legal framework, the state's power to enact laws can also affect the stock market. After all, laws can directly affect many businesses.

Media

The media greatly affects the stock market. Due to the attention that the media can bring, it can either make or break companies, as well as their stocks. Media announcements can also cause lots of reactions, which can significantly affect the volatility of certain stocks.

Supply and Demand

As can be expected in any business, supply and demand affect the stock market. When the prices are low (high supply), many investors make a buy-in order, thereby creating demand. Then, the price will rise, and supply decreases. However, once the price gets too high, the demand drops, and the investors wait and look for other opportunities. Demand and supply will always fluctuate. Occasionally, they may appear balanced. Part of their nature is a continuous fluctuation, which also affects the stock market.

Natural Disasters

As ironic as this may be, natural disasters tend to be beneficial to the stock market. This is because right after a natural disaster, people tend to spend lots of money on their rebuilding efforts and projects. Also, while natural disasters may damage the market for some time, they mostly initiate growth.

Investors Themselves

Each moment an investor purchases stock or makes a sell that affects the stock market. Now, just imagine how many investors engage in the same activity. For example, certain investors have confidence in a stock, and they purchase the said stock, and its price naturally increases. Say, due to the increased value, it manages to draw attention, and other people also start buying the same stocks. Now, when it has reached its peak, and the confidence in the stock begins to wane, the market simply collapses and fails.

Marketing Hype

It is so easy to promote something these days. You can easily share something with the world with just a few clicks of a mouse. Hence, many people have taken advantage of this by marketing some stocks to raise their value. In the stock market, the more attention the stocks draw, the higher their prices tend to increase. These days, some people promote themselves to be an "expert."

World Events

World events, regardless of whether good or bad, affect the stock market. They simply draw so much attention, and issues like having a change of leadership, international relations, and others, can either cause a boost in the market or cause it to panic.

News

News, especially that relating to businesses and the economy, can dramatically affect the stock market. Depending on the news, it can cause the value of stocks to rise or fall. Company news and announcements can also affect how investors analyze the market. If there is a likelihood of a company being successful, there will be an improvement in the performance of its stock and thus experience growth.

Deflation

When prices decrease, companies also experience lower profits, which also creates less economic activity. The prices of stocks may then drop, which will compel investors to share their shares and simply move to a more secure investment like bonds.

These are some factors influencing a stock's volatility. It is suggested that you learn to understand just how these forces influence the performance of certain stocks, as well as market behavior.

When Should You Sell Your Stocks?

An important element in making money with stocks is to know when to sell them. Many investors lose their money not only because of choosing the wrong stocks to invest in. Sometimes, they lose their money by holding on for so long to what once was a good stock.

When the Company Shows Signs of Weakening

When a company experiences changes that are likely to weaken its performance, it is the right moment to sell the shares before it is too late. For example, when the sales of a company that has shown good performance through the years suddenly face a significant decline, it is time for you to reconsider whether it is still a good investment to keep your stocks in that company.

When the Company Removes Dividends

If there are no dividends at all or show signs of instability, it may indicate that the company is headed to no good. This is a serious red signal. When the situation occurs, you are advised to sell your stocks immediately.

When You Attain Your Objective

Many times, you can avoid losing your money by not being greedy. Some investors decide to sell their stocks once they are already satisfied with their profit. For example, say you buy certain stocks at $10 per share, and you aim to get a 50% profit. If the value of those stocks increases and reaches $15 (50% increase), you sell them right away. Avoid greediness and hope for it to reach $20 or even $16. By doing so, you get to minimize your risks, which also minimizes your losses.

Factors to Consider While Choosing A Stock

You must take the time to perform an analysis to select the right stocks to invest in. A wrong choice of stock can make you lose a lot of money and be a wastage of your precious time. Get more information about a given company you have an interest in and scrutinize their financial reports to know if you can invest with them. It is best to understand all the financial information you get about a company before making the final investment decision.

It is important to choose to invest in a business that is doing well. You will be able to enjoy the peace of mind that your investment will not waste and that you will enjoy the gains. To know if a company is performing well, be keen on some clues that include:

- The company's profit margin.

- A company's return on equity.

- Past performance and expected growth.

- Its historic rate of earnings growth compared to its peers.

- The debts that the company has.

- The debt-to-equity ratio, which means taking the company's debt and dividing it by shareholder equity. The lower the percentage is, the better and safer your investment will be.

Here are some factors that will help you make the right choice of stock to invest in:

Effective management of the business – It is a pertinent issue to study. However, not many investors can access how effective business management is; therefore, they do not consider this. Return on equity and the income shareholders earn per their investments is a great indication of how the business management uses the money investors have invested in the business. A business with a return on equity of 5% or more is a good one to consider investing in.

Stocks from a suitable business sector – It is important to choose the industry sectors where you want to invest it wisely. Some sectors do better than the others, which is why this is important. Do not concentrate on one sector of the economy; this can be risky for your investment. When you are diversifying, only go for stocks in the leading industry sectors to ensure that at least all stocks will perform well. If, after some time, you will want to invest more money, you will invest in the sector that is doing better than the others. If there is a sector that is not doing well and you have already invested in it, you can always withdraw your investment as soon as possible and reinvest the money in a better performing sector.

The growing profits – Consider investing with a firm showing the potential for profits. Go for a company whose earnings per share growth is steady and at least 5% or more. This is what will assure you that you will be getting some money at the end of every year for as long as you will be investing in that company.

Small companies are riskier to invest in the size of the company when compared to the big companies. Big companies that have established themselves already know how to survive in the market; therefore, it is hard for such companies to go down. That is why they are the best to invest in. If possible, avoid penny stocks unless if you are willing to deal with all the risks involved. To be guaranteed of regular returns, buy stocks of big businesses.

Manageable debt – A business can borrow money to build itself, but too much debt is not good for the business. Ensure you have information on this before investing your money so that you will know if the debt per capita ratio is healthy or not. A rate of 0.5 or less is a good one, but if it is more, then there will be a problem after that. A business that is in debt will not be able to compensate its investors, and you might end up losing all your investment in the repayment of those debts.

Dividend payments – Companies that return part of their profits to the investors in terms of dividends are good companies to invest in. A dividend payment of 2% or more is a good one to consider and an important factor too. Dividends are important to investors. This is where the return on your investment on an annual basis comes in.

Stocks with enough liquidity are stocks that can easily be sold out if you no longer want to continue owning them. Some stocks are hard to sell, and these will give you a lot of problems when you finally want to sell them off. It is good to consider investing in stocks that will allow you to sell your position as fast as you want when the need arises.

Chapter 16.

Major Stock Exchanges

The stock market has a few major stock exchanges that are worth talking about in more detail. These markets are where most of the volume and liquidity (money) will be, thus the markets that have the most movement and profit to offer.

The Four Major Exchanges

NYSE

The New York Stock Exchange sees about $13.4 trillion in movement a day. The NYSE is the largest stock exchange in the world in terms of trade volume. It is also located in a physical location like all stock exchanges. The NYSE regulates stocks, commodities, and other product exchanges. Companies from around the world list their IPOs on the NYSE to gain the attention of investors. Companies can be locally listed on their country's exchange and then launch on the NYSE when they become large enough to sustain the interest in their shares. Companies can only be listed on one exchange at a time to avoid regulatory issues, and some countries do not allow their companies to list on the NYSE. Any stock listed on the NYSE can be purchased by traders to make a profit and earn dividends.

In North America, there is more than one exchange, like the Philadelphia exchange and Toronto. However, it is the NYSE, Dow index, and NASDAQ that gets the most media.

Tokyo Stock Exchange

Japan's stock exchange is the TSE, and it sees $3.8 trillion in movement per day, although in 2014, it was listed as $4 trillion. The Tosho (TSE) is considered the third largest in terms of market cap, but the number of companies listed is only 2,292 making it the fourth largest for the number of companies listed on the exchange. In 2012, the TSE merged with Osaka Securities Exchange to become the JPX or Japan Exchange Group. The exchange runs from 9 am to 11:30 am and from 12:30 to 3 pm during the weekdays. These are hours based on the Asian time zone.

LSE

The London Stock Exchange dealt with approximately $3.6 trillion market movement for the day before 2014. The LSE was formed in 1801 and, as of 2014, had $6.06 trillion as a market cap. The London Stock Exchange is considered the second largest by market cap data; however, it is behind the NASDAQ in terms of overall size. The LSE has merged with certain exchanges like Borsa Italiana, MTS, Turquoise, NASDAQ Bids, and there is a proposed merger with TMX Group. The LSE has primary markets with premium listed main market companies, which are the biggest UK markets. There is the Alternative Investment Market for smaller companies, a professional securities market, and a specialist fund market. The LSE is open daily, on weekdays from 8 am to 4:30 pm, GMT.

Euronext

This is the European Stock Exchange. It was smaller, dealing with only $2.9 trillion in market movement per day before the split with the NYSE. In 2015, the exchange started seeing closer to $3.7 trillion as a market cap. This was after Euronext made a public offering to become a separate entity. The market offers equities, exchange-traded funds, bonds, derivatives, commodities, warrants and certificates, and indices. It was established as an exchange in Amsterdam, London, Brussels, Paris, and Lisbon, as well as part of the Intercontinental Exchange.

Other Popular and Major Exchanges

In this list, you will see three other major exchanges, which are popular in certain markets like Asian stock investments. They are listed because they have a higher market cap in comparison to other exchanges that exist around the world:

Shanghai Stock Exchange

Shanghai is another Asian market that sees a high volume of $2.7 trillion.

Hong Kong Stock Exchange

Hong Kong has the same amount of traffic as the Shanghai Market.

Toronto Stock Exchange

Toronto is home to Canada's stock exchange. The market cap for this exchange is $2.2 trillion.

Stock Market Performance and Indexes

The NASDAQ and Dow Jones are two important indexes to discuss and determine market performance. Each needs to be explained to help you understand how the stock market works.

NASDAQ

The NASDAQ is a stock exchange that also offers options trading. It is an exchange that was the first electronic stock market, which lowered the spread charged to investors. The spread is the difference between the buy and sell price and is where most brokerage firms make their money. The NASDAQ offers a premarket period to fit into the London Stock Exchange part of the trading system. These hours are 4 am to 9:30 am EST and then from 9:30 am to 4 pm for the normal trading session. There is a post-market session that fits in the Asian time zone trading period, and those hours are 4 pm to 8 pm.

The NASDAQ has market tiers: small, mid, and large-cap. They are referred to as the capital, global, and global select market, respectively.

The stock exchange sees $9.6 trillion in daily movement. Approximately 3,600 companies are listed on the exchange. Investors can do more on the NASDAQ with options trading than on other exchanges. Options are a complicated process that you will want advanced stock market investing information to understand. You need to know it is an exchange with a different list of companies than the NYSE that may offer you room to grow into options trading.

The Dow Jones

It is a stock market index that measures the price of a specific unit of the stock market. It is computed based on selected stocks based on an average of the price of these shares. Investors use it to figure out the market movement and market health based on the average prices of top companies. Mutual funds and exchange-traded funds tend to use this type of index to track what the funds will do or have done in reacting to news and economic data. The Dow Jones was the first stock market index to be started. It was devised by Charles Dow in 1896. Edward Jones was his partner and a statistician. They weight 30 components that have to do with traditional industries.

Stock market investors will use the Dow Jones to determine the performance of a specific industry sector for American companies and overall weighting of the USA's economic stability. The Dow Jones is not meant to be influenced by economic reports or corporate reports, but by price movement alone.

You can use the Dow Jones for ETF, leverage, short funds, futures contracts and options contracts.

When you hear media experts talking about the market going up or down by a certain number of "points," they are usually talking about the Dow Jones index computation.

Chapter 17.

Indexing

Indexing is a passive investment style that buys index-tracking funds in various markets. Rather than buying individual stocks, you buy an entire market. It's a convenient way to diversify without too much effort or concern about picking the right stocks. We'll go over the basics of how an indexing strategy works and how you choose index funds or ETFs to include in your portfolio.

The Basic Guidelines of an Indexing Strategy

An index is a collection of stocks that have all been grouped according to some common factors and criteria. Then, they invest in this collection of stocks, spreading the actual investments across each stock according to their price relative to the rest of the group.

The most well-known indices are the ones that track entire markets like the Dow or the S&P. These index funds invest in the entirety of those markets and are said to be "tracking the market." As a result, you don't have to worry about the individual performance of any one stock in the market. Instead, your returns will be whatever the Dow's or the S&P's overall returns are.

Market indices aren't the only ones out there, though. Index funds can be created around any idea or characteristic. There are index funds that track specific industries like healthcare or energy.

There are a few advantages to index funds. The main advantage is that it's an incredibly easy way to diversify your portfolio. Rather than meticulously researching thousands of stocks for the ones you want to invest in, you can pick an index fund (or a few index funds) that agrees with your investing style and then invest in those. Your money is automatically diversified across the entire group of stocks the index is tracking.

This makes them extremely convenient and easy to use. Even the most novice investor can use index investing as an easier way to diversify and minimize risk while still enjoying a healthy return.

It can also be a lot more affordable since it's a more passive form of investing. The less active management a fund requires, the less fees investors must pay. When you invest in index funds, you're generally using a buy-and-hold strategy that will require little active trading over time, so you won't be paying as much in transaction fees, taxes, or other expenses that go along with investing.

As your wealth grows, however, an index fund becomes a less attractive choice. Even the most passive index fund is still being managed by someone, meaning you're earning a little less per share than you would if you had privately invested in the same set of stocks, using the same proportions. This slight difference is not worth considering for the average investor because, in general, the average investor doesn't have the capital needed to perfectly recreate an index portfolio, complete with the same weighting of stocks. In other words, most investors can't afford to buy full shares of every stock in an index.

When you invest in an index fund, however, you don't need to worry about that. The fund managers will spread the money you do have evenly across all their stocks, even if that ends up spreading so that you aren't buying a full share in every stock.

When your money has grown, however, an index investor would benefit from shifting away from index funds and towards building their index portfolio. Then, you could keep your money diversified in the same way that it has been up to this point, but you'll be pocketing even more of the returns by paying less in fees.

How to Pick Stocks for an Index Portfolio

Not all index funds are created equal. Within the index's world, you can still choose between more active investing styles and more passive ones. Before investing in any index fund, you do want to do your research to investigate the important details like:

- The past performance of the index fund itself.
- Any news and information that would be relevant to the stocks included in the fund. For example, for an energy index fund, you want to do your research about the energy industry and what kinds of policies, global trade news, natural disasters, technological developments, and others could influence the performance of the stocks in that index.

Where Will You Buy?

You've already read about the differences between ETFs and mutual funds. It's the difference between directly investing your money into the index fund or trading shares of it on the open market. If you don't plan on doing much active trading, direct investment in the mutual fund may be your best bet. Once you've decided whether you're going to invest directly or buy ETFs, you need to choose your broker. When choosing a broker, consider the following factors:

Available funds

What kind of index funds does that broker offer? How do they perform against similar index funds from their competitors? If you're going the ETF route, you need to make sure the broker offers ETF trading.

Additional services

Ideally, you want to find a single broker who can meet all your needs. If you're planning to put your money in and then just let it grow, you don't need too many additional services. However, if you're buying ETFs, you may want stock research, screening tools, portfolio management tools, or investing educational resources.

Reasonable costs

More and more brokers are offering free transactions (either unlimited or a fixed amount). However, mutual funds still charge commissions, and those prices increase; the more active management is required to maintain the fund.

Pick Your Index

An index funds track a variety of indices. This step is likely where the bulk of your research is going to happen as an index investor. While you are not limited to just picking one index, you still want to have in-depth knowledge of any index you choose. Here's a quick breakdown of the broad types of index funds you'll find:

Capitalization and Size

These are index funds that track stocks based on size. You can find large-cap indices, small-cap indices, or mid-cap indices. The large-cap index would be made up of larger, more stable stocks while the smaller ones would be less stable but potentially offer higher growth. So, you'll be making some of the same decisions that a value or growth investor would make, except for larger collections of stocks rather than individual stocks.

Sector or Industry

Another way to group stocks into an index is by sector or industry. You can find tech index funds, good consumer funds, and so on, all the stocks within that sector. Then, whatever the average returns are for that sector, that will be the returns on your index fund. With these types, you must be careful about the sector you pick. The up-and-down cycle of a single sector can be more dramatic than that of the market. So, you usually want to choose a few different sector index funds rather than putting everything into one.

Geography

Index funds defined by geography generally trade foreign markets. Rather than a Dow or S&P index, you might invest in an even broader index that tracks the entire US market. Geographically defined indices are a great way to diversify your portfolio beyond your home market and to protect against recessions because a recession in the US doesn't necessarily mean every market in the world is in a recession. You can hedge yourself against bear markets by investing in an index that's tracking another market altogether, ideally one that's more bullish than your own.

Market Opportunities

Market opportunity indices track growing sectors or emerging markets in search of stronger growth opportunities. They require a lot more research on your part because, by nature, they are a little riskier than other funds.

Type of Asset

The least popular type of index is one that tracks a particular asset class. For example, you can invest in a bond index fund that tracks government bonds from different countries around the world or a domestic bond fund that tracks federal, state, and corporate bonds within a single market. Other assets that tend to get grouped into an index include cash and commodities like oil.

Chapter 18.

Price Action Strategies

You do not need to be hitting home runs to be successful in the stock market. You should focus on getting the base hits and try to grow your portfolio by taking the most gains in the range of 20%-25%. While it may sound counterintuitive, it is always best to sell a stock when it's on the rise, consistently advancing and looking appealing to all other investors.

As you may have already figured out, trading on the stock market is a risky business, though the rewards that can come from these risks make it all worth it. Even though you will never be able to eliminate the risks, there are some things you can do to mitigate risks by actively managing your portfolio and making clever investments.

However, if you are not careful or don't know what you're doing, you could end up paying a pretty hefty price. The buy low and sell high strategy might have resulted in the success of many investors, but it is not how the real professionals become successful. Instead, smart investors deploy their money strategically to allow it to work in more ways than one. In layman's terms, they multitask their money.

There are ways to maximize your profits and get the most out of your investments.If you were to think of investing like a game, the way you would win would be to purchase a stock at a low price and then sell in the future at a higher price. If you are a homeowner, then you likely understand this concept quite practically. It's best to use one of two strategies to make a profit on your investment.The first is value investing, Like the products you buy from stores every day, stocks go on sale now and then, and value investors wait for this sale to happen. This makes it easier for them to make a profit, since stocks that are undervalued, or on sale, have more room for growth.

Unfortunately, your favorite stock might not be suited to this strategy since it must pay a dividend. It would need to have a price low enough for you to buy 100 shares, and it needs to trade many shares every day - at least 1 million shares of the daily volume are preferable.

You also want to avoid highly volatile stocks, as their more unpredictable shifts in price are more difficult to manage. This is where your stock evaluation skills and research will be put to the test.

Once you have found your stock, and you have decided that you want to value invest, you want this name to be in the middle or near the bottom of the trading range for the last 52 weeks. If it is not currently there, then you should either find another company or wait for the stock to be at a price you are willing to pay for.

The second strategy is known as momentum trading. Some investors believe that the best time for a stock to be bought is when its price continues to rise, since, as we learned in school, objects in motion tend to remain in motion. Most people want to think of the long term, as the longer you have stock, the better its potential returns can be.

Make Use of Covered Calls

Covered calls are slightly more complex. Using the method of purchasing a stock and collecting its dividend as it increases will still provide you with some significant gains. There are two important questions before you sell a covered call:

- What is the strike price?
- How many months do you want your contract to last for?

Strike Price

Covered calls are a kind of options contract strategy that allows the contract holder to purchase your 100 shares if it is at the strike price or above it. You probably do not want someone to take your shares from you, so the strike price will need to be steep enough that the stock does not rise above it, but low enough that you can collect a decent premium for taking a risk. This is a pretty tough decision to make, especially for new investors such as yourself. If your stock is currently experiencing a downtrend, you will likely be able to sell an option with a strike price not much higher than the current actual price of the stock. However, if the stock is experiencing an uptrend, you may want to wait until you are happy that the move up has run its course and that the stock will soon shift in the opposite direction. Remember that whenever a stock appreciates, your option value depreciates.

Expiration Date

The further you take your option into the future, the bigger your premium payout will be upfront, to sell the call, but that also means more time that your stock needs to be below the strike price, to avoid it being 'called away' from you. Consider going three or four months ahead for your first contract. As soon as you sell it, your covered call will make money for you, since the premium paid by the buyer will be deposited into your account directly. It will keep making money for you even if your stock's price drops. The premium falls with the price. You can buy back the contract from the buyer at any time, so, if the premium does fall, you can buy it for less than what you sold it for.

That means you're making a profit. At the same time, if your stock were to rise above the strike price, you would be able to buy the contract for more than you sold it, causing a loss, but also saving you need to hand over 100 of your shares. One of the most effective ways to use the covered call is to collect the premium at the beginning.

Even though you can repurchase the option if its price shifts, you will want to only do so under dire circumstances. It would be best if you kept in mind that the money you collect from selling your covered call can also be deducted from the price you paid for the stock.

The easiest way to get the hang of a new investment strategy is to make use of a virtual platform, like the ones many brokerage firms offer in their apps or websites. You can still buy the stock and collect dividends, but wait to sell the covered call until you feel comfortable with the way it works.

Chapter 19.

Stock Exchange Terms

I f you are planning to start investing your money in the stock market, then there are some common stock exchange terms that you must know. These terms are essential in understanding the behavior of the stock market.

You should also have known the basics before diving onto the live trade. These terms will help you achieve your goals and build your career in the stock market to become a successful trader.

Stock exchange terms are slang specifically for industry security. Professionals and expert traders use these terms to talk about different game plans, patterns, charts, and many other related elements of the stock market industry.

Common stock exchange terms are listed below:

Annual Report

The company specifically makes the yearly report of its shareholders. This report is designed in such a way that it attracts the shareholders. The annual report carries all the information about the company's shares and their game plan for the present and future. When you are going through the annual report, you gather information about the company's financial situation.

Arbitrage

This is one of the most advanced terms in the stock market, which every trader should know. This refers to buying stocks at a low price from one market and selling at a higher rate on another market.

For example, sometimes a stock ABC trade on 50$ on one market and the same stock on the other market trade on 55$ so traders buy shares on low price points and sell them on higher rates to make the profit.

Averaging Down

When stock prices fall, and you plan to buy stocks on lower rates, your average buying prices decrease. This strategy is used most commonly in the stock market. After buying, you plan to sell those stocks shares when the stock market rebounds.

Bear Market

A bear market is opposite to Bull market. It means that the overall market is negative or falling. In this stage, the market falls up to 20% the quarter after quarter. This is one of the scariest situations for big investors because their investments are at great risk.

Bull Market

Bull Market is opposite to the bear market. Bull market meant the rising of the stock points. In this stage, people start investing money in the stock market because of their positive behavior.

Beta

This is the whole relationship between the stocks and the overall market. If stock ABC has a beta of 5.5 means that every one-point movement in the market, the stock ABC moves 5.5 points and vice versa.

Bourse

In short, Bourse is a modern and more advanced name of the stock market. It means where people gather for the purchasing and selling of stock shares. Most commonly, it refers to Paris stock exchanges or non-US stock exchanges.

Broker

Many people who are beginners and don't understand the behavior of the stock market contact different brokers. These brokers are experienced traders who have sound knowledge of trading of stocks. These beginners contact these brokers and ask them to buy and sell stocks for them. Brokers charge high commissions for these services.

Bid

Bidding is as common and simple as we do in freelancing and other daily projects. In stock market, the bidder—who is a buyer—bid for a specific share. Bid means the buyer willing to buy the share on his desired rates. The bid is made according to the asking price of the seller.

Close

Simply this refers to the time when trading will stop, and the stock market will close. Its timings vary from country to country. Each stock market has its own time of closing and opening. After closing the stock market, it is not available for live trade.

Day trading

This is one of the most advanced terms in the stock market. Day trading refers to buying and selling of stocks shares on the same day. Many experienced traders use this method.

After buying shares, people wait for the following day to sell them at much higher rates. But there are 50/50 chances that they may end up with profit or loss. So, Day trading is a smart strategy, but it requires a lot of experience to make profits.

Dividend

Many companies offer incentives to attract more traders to their company. Some companies pay their shareholders one of their earnings portions, which are called the dividend. Some companies pay dividends annually or quarterly. Not all companies offer a dividend.

Exchange

Exchange refers to a place where thousands of investments are traded daily. There are many popular exchanges in the world. New York Stock Exchange is one of the most popular exchanges, which is present in the United States of America.

Execution

We are familiar with this term in the sense of computer where it means the completion of a task. In the stock market, it also acts the same as in the said case. When a trader buys or sells stock shares, after completion, it is said that the transaction has been executed.

Haircut

The haircut is the most known term used in the stock market. There is a slight difference between the buyer's bid and the asking price of the seller.

High

High indicates the milestone reached by the stocks. It points out that the specific stock has never reached such a high price before. In the stock market, there is also one other high. This high is used to demonstrate the milestone reached by stocks in a specific period. It may be fortnightly or in 30 days.

Initial Public Offering

Initial Public Offering means that when a company decides to expand its business and offers its stocks available for the public. The Securities Exchange Commissions is responsible for issuing Initial Public offering and is very strict against its rules.

Leverage

Leverage is considered the riskiest and dangerous game tom plays in the stock market. After having your complete research, you decide to borrow shares from your broker and set up a plan to sell them on higher rates. If you successfully sell those shares on higher rates, you again return those borrowed shares to the broker and keep the difference.

Low

Low is opposite to high. It indicates that the specific stocks have never fallen to this price before. Low is also demonstrated for a specific period may be weekly or monthly.

Margin

Margin is almost the same as that of leverage. It is also considered one of the riskiest games. It is an account that allows you to borrow money from the broker to invest that money into the stocks. Now the difference between the loan which you borrowed from the broker and rates of the securities is called margin.

Margin is not for beginners; even the most experienced traders fail to apply this strategy.

Moving Average

It is the average price of the stock shares at a specific time. 50 and 200 are considered the best common time frames to study the behavior of the moving average.

Open

Simply refers to the time when the stock market is open for the live trade. Traders start buying and selling of stocks according to their plans. This varies from country to country. Every stock market has its own time to open and close.

Order

Order is the same as bid, but in the order, you decide to buy or sell stock shares according to your plan after deciding your order to sell or buy the stocks. For example, if you are willing to buy 200 shares, then you must make an order.

Pink Sheet Stocks

Many beginners take start with pink sheet stocks. If you are just planning to invest in this stock market, you probably have listened to pink sheet stocks. These are penny stocks and are traded on a small scale, and each share price is 5$ or even less than that. Because these are the shares of smaller companies, you will not find them on the big markets such as New York Stock Exchange.

Sector

Dozens of companies belong to the same industry. These companies are available publicly on the stock market to buy their shares. These stocks groups which belong to the same industry are called sectors. There are many advantages to investing in the same sector because it is much easy to predict the fluctuations.

Chapter 20.

Classifications of Stock Market Investors

There is no doubt that stock investing provides a great opportunity to earn money. However, an investor must know when the best time is to buy or sell stocks. Before you begin investing in stocks, you may want to know first what type of investor you are.

The Conservative Investor

A conservative investor is an individual who does not take capital growth as an utmost priority when investing. Instead, he seeks for stable investments that can flourish gradually and practically not susceptible to high volatility. A conservative investor usually obtains moderate capital growth and a steady income stream. They may not get much from their investments, but they make sure to get a steady flow of earnings regularly. The conservative investor is cautious in making investment decisions.

Fundamental Trader

A fundamental trader is someone who focuses on company-specific affairs to help determine the right stock to buy and the best time to buy it. To depict this in another way, suppose this type of trader has decided to visit a shopping mall. A fundamental trader is someone who makes decisions based on fundamental things. They will visit each store, study the products that each store offers, and then arrive at the final decision of either making a purchase or not. The same thing happens when it comes to buying stocks. They may study them first before he/she decides to make a purchase. Trading on fundamentals can be a short-term or a long-term endeavor. It is often associated more with the investing strategy known as buy and hold than short-term trading. Some trading strategies rely on split-second decisions, and others depend on factors or trends that play out within the day. The fundamentals may remain the same for months or years.

The quarterly release of the target company's financial statement can provide valuable information regarding the firm's financial health or position in the stock market. Changes or lack of it can give a trader a sort of signal whether to trade or not. A press release that brings bad news has the power to overturn everything in an instant. Many investors find fundamental trading appealing because it is based on facts and logic—It practically ensures no room for errors. However, finding and deciphering the facts may take time, and it is a research-intensive task.

Sentiment Trader

A sentiment trader does not try to outsmart the market by seeking securities that may bring huge earnings. Instead, he identifies the securities that move with the market's momentum.

Most sentiment traders combine technical and fundamental analysis features to help them identify and take part in the market movements. There are sentiment traders that aim to seize momentous movements in price and try to keep away from idle times. Some traders try to take advantage of indicators of excessive negative or positive sentiment that may provide a sign of a possible reversal in sentiment.

The key challenges that sentiment traders usually face:

- Market volatility
- Trading costs
- Difficulty in making accurate predictions regarding market sentiment

If you think you are a conservative investor, your success depends on your ability to decipher the stocks that can give a steady flow of income. You may not get large amounts of money, but you will always gain something with little to no risk involved.

The Intermediate Investor

The intermediate investor takes some risks but still makes certain that the initial capital he invests will remain secure. This type of investor usually owns a rather volatile portfolio. These investors expect good (or near exceptional) capital growth. They may face some market fluctuations, which is unlikely to happen under normal market conditions. They usually own a balanced portfolio with assets that include a combination of bonds and stocks from established companies with a good record. This trader may choose to make a small investment in riskier assets that can provide better capital growth.

Market Timer

A market timer is a trader who tries to guess whether security will move up or down and if such a move can generate profit. To guess the direction of the movement, this trader checks the economic data or technical indicators. Some investors strongly believe that the direction of market movement is impossible to predict.

Market timers with long-term track records won't deny that it is quite challenging to achieve success using this method. Most investors know that they need to dedicate more time to gain a reliable level of success. These investors believe that long-term strategies are lucrative and, therefore, more rewarding.

Arbitrage Trader

This trader usually purchases and sells assets simultaneously to gain a substantial profit from price differences of financial instruments that are related or identical.

Arbitrage traders buy particular security in one market and sell it simultaneously at a higher price in a different market, taking advantage of the price difference. It is considered a riskless trade that can provide pure profit to the investor.

Let us use foreign exchange in our example to illustrate. A trader buys stock from a foreign exchange that is yet to adjust the price for the fluctuating exchange rate. At that time, the price of the foreign exchange is undervalued when you compare it against the local exchange. The trader can take advantage of it and generate profit from the price disparity.

Arbitrage exists due to market inefficiencies. It provides a means to keep prices from deviating too much from fair value for a long time. Understand that all markets can't impose uniform prices at the same time. Security may be traded at a lower price in one exchange market and a higher price in another market.

An arbitrage trader may still gain a lot of profit now, but one should not underestimate the technology advancement. Soon, it may become difficult to gain profit from a price disparity.

The intermediate investors may look like conservative investors at times, but they are not afraid to take some risks from time to time. Be extra careful when trading with risky stocks. You may gain more advantage than a conservative investor when you do that.

The Risk Taker

The risk-takers are dynamic investors willing to trade with greater risk to maximize profits. The investment portfolio of such trader could include stocks of young or new companies and emerging market equities. It may also contain a higher percentage of stock than bonds.

Noise Trader

In noise trading, whenever a trader buys or sells something, he does not refer to the fundamental data specific to a company that issues the securities. Noise traders commonly engage in short-term trades to gain profit from different economic trends.

Noise traders overreact to any good or bad news surrounding the stock market, and they have poor timing. The technical analysis of statistics that the market activity has generated could turn into useless data. They can't properly investigate the volume and past prices of the market that can somehow help them gain some insights on market activity and direction in the future.

Let us go back to the example that we had about the shopping mall. As compared to a fundamental analyst, a technical analyst may only sit outside and collect data regarding the number of people that each store has. He does not care about the products sold in each store. It is enough that he could see the number of people that each store can attract to help him arrive at a certain decision.

Most people can be considered as noise traders. Only some individuals use fundamental analysis when deciding on the investment.

If you are willing to trade stocks without knowing or weighing possible consequences that such trade may yield, you are a risk-taker. You may be able to earn much profit at once and then lose some at other times if you are too reckless.

So, what type of investor are you? You may need to improve something to make sure that you will gain more profits. Knowing the characteristics or psyche of a good investor can help you a lot.

Chapter 21.

Active and Passive Stock Investing

W hen it comes to making money from stocks, there are two ways to do it: actively and passively. And it's by understanding the difference between the two that you'll have a better idea of what investing and trading mean.

Active Investing

As you could infer from the term itself, active investing means a relatively high degree of activity. In other words, you'll need to be more active or involved in managing your stock investments. This means that on top of doing your homework in terms of choosing your stocks wisely, you'll need to monitor its performance regularly, depending on your investment time frame, i.e., short or long term. These are the things you'll need to do if you choose the active investing route: **Research and Evaluate:** What makes investing in the stock market much different from gambling in a casino, which some "geniuses" think is a very apt comparison, is that you don't just pick random stocks to trade or invest in and expect success. No, you'll need to research and evaluate stocks based on the information you're able to gather to come up with a candidates' shortlist. And from such a shortlist, you'll pick the stocks in which to trade or invest.

Take Positions: All the research and evaluation in the world will be for naught if that's where you'll end your journey. You'll need to act based on the information you've gathered and evaluated by taking a position on any or all the stocks in your shortlist, i.e., buy stocks. Unless you take actual positions, you will not earn anything from stocks. When you buy stocks, you're taking a LONG position. When you're selling stocks that you own, you're taking a SQUARE position. And when you sell shares of stocks that you do not own, you're taking a SHORT position.

Monitoring: When you're after a very quick buck with every stock purchase you make, the more important it is for you to keep track of the price of your stocks frequently. It's because there's a very good chance that you might miss the quick profits boat if you don't check market prices every few hours. And even if you're in it for the long haul, you will still need to monitor stock prices to make sure your investments are performing as desired, albeit less frequently say every week or every month.

At this point, I'd like to bring to your attention the words "trading" and "investment," in case you're wondering why I'm using them both or interchangeably. Here's the reason: Trading is the term often used to refer to very short investment periods. When stock market veterans say they're "trading" stocks, what they're saying is that their investment horizons are very, very short. How short? The longest would probably be a couple of days to a week, while many trades are daily. After they buy, they wait for the price to go up several points within the day of the week, and they quickly sell their shares to cash in on the profits. People who "trade" stocks this way must do it frequently so that over a month or a year, their small profits accumulate into a much bigger total. On the other hand, "investing" is often taken to mean as holding on to shares of stocks or any financial asset for a relatively long period. In many instances, investing is taken to mean as a minimum investment holding period of about three months and is often referred to as a "buy-and-hold" approach. Just buy stocks and leave it be.

However, there's no official barometer for considering whether a specific investment holding period's considered as trading or investing. It's because when you look at the grand scheme of things, trading and investing are practically the same and the only difference, albeit an arbitrary one, is the time frame. The goal of trading is buying-and-holding, which is to earn a profit. And either way, that's what investing is! And when you talk about the primary way you will successfully earn money via stock market investing, which is capital appreciation, it involves buying stocks at a low price and selling them at a higher one. And that's the real definition of trading, i.e., buying and selling.

Passive Investing

Passive investments are very popular these days, sometimes for the right reasons, but mostly for the wrong ones. For one, many personal finances "gurus" have painted passive investing to be the financial savior of every individual on earth who's living in poverty today. For others, many such gurus also make it appear—albeit not purposefully—as if building passive income streams that generate enough passive income is easy. And lastly, the same so-called gurus make it appear that passive investing is passive, i.e., a perfectly inactive form of investing where you do nothing, and riches will continue flowing to you. But is passive investing all that? Let's find out, shall we? Passive investing is taken from the word "passive," which means, among other things, inactive. Therefore, many people have the impression that passive investing means practically waiting for money just to come in. Now, this is where I'll have to shed a bit lighter on passive investing.

Passive investing means very little work or effort is needed to generate money. By inactive, what we're trying to say here is much less work. There's no such thing as a free—or inactive—lunch. You will always have to do something, even if it's very little.

The general passive investing approach taken by many is the buy-and-hold approach to make money in the stock market.

Compared to the active trading approach where you must monitor the market prices of your stocks very frequently and transact much more frequently, passively investing in stocks allows you to do other things during the day like work on a day job or enjoy life. It's also way less stressful. But still, it's not a completely inactive activity. And you can earn much more via trading. So, there's your tradeoff: less work, fewer earnings vs. more work, more earnings. Another reality about passive investing, you'll need to be aware of is that earning a significant enough amount of income to live on and become rich from is neither easy nor cheap! What do I mean by this? Let's say your goal is to live off passive income from stocks and that your average annual living expenses amount to $36,000. If the average annual rate of return on stock investments is 10%, you'll need to have at least $360,000 passively invested in stocks to make $36,000 annually. If you're in dire financial straits, it means you really can't rely on passive income to get you out of poverty or your current state of need. The only passive source of income that can do that for you is winning the lottery.

Active versus Passive Investments

Now that you're aware of what active and passive stock market investing looks like, which do you think will be more advantageous to you? Right off the bat, there's no outright winner because each approach has its advantages and disadvantages. What will determine the best approach for you will be your goals and current personal circumstances.

For example, if you don't have much time to spare to monitor your stock market investments on an hourly or bi-hour basis because of your day job, then passive stock market investing's the appropriate one for you. It's also the more appropriate type of stock market investing for you if you want to keep things simple and uncomplicated, and if your risk tolerance is relatively low. But if you're the type who has all the time to do practically nothing else but watch the stock market throughout the day, and have a high tolerance, then active stock trading may be the better approach for you. But what about in terms of profitability? Which of the two are generally more profitable? I'll give this round to active trading. Why? It's because it's highly unlikely to make money in stocks when the markets are down. Not impossible but highly unlikely. But with active trading, you can still make money even when the markets are crashing down.Keep in mind that I'm not saying passive investing isn't profitable, only that per my experience, an active trading approach to stock market investing's normally the more lucrative or profitable one.

Chapter 22.

Stock Orders

T here are types of stock orders that you can make. All of these can be accomplished by calling your broker with the instructions to execute the trade.

Market Orders

This is the utmost common kind of trading stocks. When you place a market order, you take the price presented to you when the order is executed. For instance, if you are interested in buying stocks from Microsoft and the price per stock is $90.23, you may end up getting it for $89.48 or $92.46. Therefore, the commission you pay your broker varies as well.

Limit Orders

You set a predetermined amount (the limit) that you are willing to buy or sell the stocks. First, your limit order may never be executed. Why? It is because the chance that share prices will rise or fall to your intended amount is next to none.

Second, brokers execute limit orders based on the order they are received.

This means that you might be looking at an excellent chance of your limit order being executed at the time you sent it. when your broker comes across it on the "queue," price for the stock you are eyeing may have already increased or decreased beyond your limit

All or None Orders

In normal circumstances, a bulk order for common stocks requires that the order be filled by your broker when the opportunity arises. This means that a single bulk order may be completed within weeks. This mechanism is in place to prevent sudden shifts in the market brought about by bulk stock purchases or sales.

There are moments you may need to purchase stocks in bulk. It may be that the current share price for that company is within your budget. It may also be that you wanted to become a shareholder for that company. Regardless of your plans, it is possible to accomplish bulk orders of stocks in a single transaction through all-or-none trading. This order tells your broker that unless he or she can execute the order in one transaction, your order will remain outstanding.

Stop Order and Stop Limit Orders

These trading types are what people have been talking about if you have heard of' stop-loss. 'The purpose of this is obvious: To avoid losses and lock in profits resulting from a profitable trade. Let's discuss each of them. Stop orders are executed once a stop price is reached. A stop price is a predetermined amount that triggers the execution of the order. In other words, once the stop price materializes, stop orders automatically become market orders. Stop orders are guaranteed to be executed. You will not know the actual share price until it is executed.

Stop limit orders, on the other hand, converts to a limit order when the stop price is reached. Still, in conjunction with share price, the order may or may not be executed.

Buy to Cover and Sell Short Orders

Both trading types are highly speculative and can lead to unlimited losses. However, if your speculations turn out to be correct, you can stand to make a profit.

Note that to sell short and buy to cover orders, you must hold the belief that the current share price is overvalued and that the price will decrease to its actual value in the future. So, what you can do here is to place a short sell order for 100 shares. Multiply it by the current share price of $100, and you get $1,000. Now, you approach your broker to borrow $1,000 worth of Twitter shares to cover for your short sell. You go to the open market and sell the shares. As you make a sale, you pocket the cash.

If in the future, your speculated share price for Twitter will become $50, you will repurchase the 100 shares you have sold for $50 through a buy-to-cover order. The amount of the buy to cover the order will now be $500. So, you can now return the shares you borrowed from your broker and keep the $500 profit. To successfully carry out short sell and buy to cover orders, you need two things:

- That your brokerage account is a margin account. Meaning that the account allows you to borrow money from your broker.

- That your money in the account is enough to pay your broker back if the shares you are keeping an eye on actual increase in the price instead of decreasing as you expected.

Trailing Stop Orders

Trailing stop orders are utilized to protect your capital gains and minimize your losses. This involves setting a stop price, which is a percentage of a stock's current market price or a spread in points.

To illustrate, let us say that you have chosen to buy 500 shares from PepsiCo for $50 per share. The price per share now is $57. Your goal is to lock in at least $5 from the per-share profit, but still intent on holding the stock, believing that its share price will still increase in the future. To meet your objective, you decide to place a trailing stop order at $2 per share.

At the time your trailing order was placed, your broker knew that, if the price fell below $55 ($57 - $2), he or she could sell your shares. However, if PepsiCo's share price ends up increasing to $62 per share, your trailing order is set to take effect. That is, it gets converted to a market order for a sale price of $60 ($62 - $2). From the market order, you stand to profit $10 per share ($60 - $50).

Bracketed Orders

Bracketed orders are like trailing stop orders, only this time, you add an upper limit to the trailing stop order. So, using the example above, you have placed a bracketed order with a trailing stop order of $2 and impose an upper limit of $65 per share. What happens then is that the order will follow the same tread as that of the trailing stop order. However, given the bracketed order, when PepsiCo's share price reaches $65 per share, then your order will automatically convert to a market order. As you can see, you stand to profit $5 more than what you would have made under the trailing stop order.

Day Orders, GTC Orders, and Extended Hours Orders

All stock orders you place must have an expiration date. When the trading day end, all orders are canceled. This especially applies to market orders. However, Good-till-Cancelled or GTC orders remain open until any of these three things occur:

- Orders are filled
- You canceled the order
- The order remained outstanding for 60 calendar days

Now, there are cons associated with GTC orders. For one, you might end up forgetting it. Take note that a lot of things can happen in 60 days. Two, you may end up paying multiple commissions to your broker as your order becomes partially filled. If you are lucky to have your order filled by numerous transactions, your broker will only need to charge you a single commission.

Still, some investors prefer to place an order after hours. A trading day takes place between 8:00 PM of the current day to 8:00 AM the following day. Placing orders after hours offer one advantage: It allows investors to take precautionary or profitable measures in response to corporate news

Chapter 23.

Risk Assessment Management

R isk management refers to the entire process of managing risks. Risks are inherent when trading and investing in the markets. It involves assessment, management, and loss prevention activities. Risk management is any action taken by an investor or even a trader to prevent losses. For instance, a trader may buy government-issued bonds that are considered extremely safe. This is a risk management approach to investing as the trader greatly reduces any potential for losses. If the trader had invested the fund in securities such as stock options or futures, the investment would have been highly risky. Risk management takes place almost always, like when an investor or fund manager or investor analyses risk and decides to adjust to minimize or prevent any inherent risks.

Risk management could be as simple as purchasing one security instead of another, or it could be a rather complex process. Think about traders who venture into complex securities such as futures and derivatives. Such instruments require serious risk management techniques as these complex securities are highly risky, even though they are also highly rewarding when successful.

A Closer Look at Risk Management

Every trader must consider risk management to avert possible losses in their trades. Without risk management, then traders and investors would just as well resort to gambling. Risk assessment and management ensure enough steps are taken to prevent losses.

There are great examples in the recent history of poor risk management approach that led to hundreds of billions in losses incurred by investors. Here we are discussing the collapse of the housing sector in 2007/2008 in the United States. Plenty of homeowners and mortgage holders across the country lost their investments due to the subprime mortgage collapse. This collapse led to the great recession that followed that. It took the US a couple of years to recover from this catastrophe, which also affected other sectors. The entire problem was a result of investments without proper risk management solutions.

Risk is Not Necessarily a Negative Thing

People tend to think of risk as a bad thing. They view it negatively and think of ways of shunning it. Risk does not have to be viewed in negative or derogatory terms. It is a good thing and can save investors and traders from losing their resources.

A lot of investors tend to define investment risk simply as a deviation or variation from an expected result. However, some of the most successful traders engage in very risky investments. The payoff is that they take the time to weigh the risks and even take measures to protect their investments. Good examples are options and futures traders. Options and futures are considered high risk yet high reward investments. If these investments and trading strategies were extremely risky, then nobody would touch them. However, some focus solely on these highly risky ventures, yet they are the most successful and profitable. As an advanced trader, you need to be able to implement appropriate risk management techniques so that your trades are safe and secure.

One crucial factor that traders need to keep in mind is their appetite for risk. How much risk is one able to take? An investor's appetite for risk will determine his or her strategy as well as the relevant risk-mitigating measures. This way, it will be possible to invest securely with little worry should things not work out as desired. Risk management is essential if you wish to make money in the markets for the long term. Even if you are a great trader and profitable most of the time, your profits can be wiped out in seconds without proper risk management.

Risk assessment can be defined as a general term that measures the chances of the likelihood of incurring losses when trading. Risk management also helps to realize the required rate of return so that a strategy becomes successful. As a trader, you need to incorporate risk management as part of your trading strategy. There are many different approaches to risk management, so it is advisable to consider the approach that best works for you.

Recommended Risk Management Approach

1. Plan your trades

The single most crucial aspect of your trade should be risk management. Without it, your whole trading life will be in jeopardy. Therefore, start all your trading ventures with a plan that you intend to stick by. Traders have a saying that you should plan your trades and then trade your plan. This means to come up with the best plan possible and then implement it and stick by it. Trade is very similar to war. When it is well planned, it can be won before it is executed.

Some of the best tools you will need as part of your risk management plan are take-profit and stop-loss. Using these two tools, you can plan your trades. You will need to use technical analysis to determine these two points.

2. The One Percent Rule

Traders often apply what is known as the one percent rule. This rule dictates that you should not risk amounts greater than one percent of your total trading capital on one single trade. For instance, if you have $15,000 as your trading capital, you should never risk more than $150 on a single trade. This is a great risk management approach that you can use as part of your trading strategy. Most traders who adopt this strategy have amounts of less than $100,000 in their trading accounts. Some are so more confident, so they choose to work with 2% instead.

3. Set Target and Stops

We can define a stop-loss as the total amount of loss that a trader is willing to incur in a single trade. Beyond the stop-loss point, the trader exits the trade. This is meant to prevent further losses by thinking the trade will eventually get some momentum. Collect any profits made and possibly exit a trade. At this point, stock or other security is often very close to the point of resistance. Beyond this point, a reversal in price is likely to take place. Rather than lose money, you should exit the trade. Traders sometimes take profit and let trade continue if it was still making money. Another take-profit point is then plotted. If you have a good run, you can lock in the profits and let the good run continue.

4. Use of Moving Averages

The best way to identify these two crucial points is to use moving averages. The reason why we prefer moving averages to determine the stop-loss and take-profit points—These are closely tracked by the markets and very simple to determine. Some of the popular moving averages include the 5-day, 20-day, 50-day, 100-day, and 200-day averages. Simply apply these to your security's chart, then decide about the best points.

You can also use support and resistance lines to determine the take-profit and stop-loss points. This is also a pretty simple process. Simply connect past lows and highs that happened in the recent past on key, high-than-normal volume levels. All you need to do is find levels where the price action will respond to the trend line on areas of high volume.

Assessing Risk versus Reward

Most traders lose a lot of money at the markets for a very simple reason. They do not know about risk management or how to go about it. This mostly happens to beginners or novice traders. Most of them simply learn how to trade, then rush to the markets in the hope of making a kill. Sadly, this is now how things work because account and risk management are not taken into consideration. Managing risk is just as important as learning how to trade profitably. It is a skill that every trader needs to learn, including beginners and novice traders. As it is, investing hard-earned funds at the markets can be a risky venture. Even with the very best techniques and latest software programs, you can still lose money. Experts also lose money at the markets occasionally. The crucial aspect is that they win a lot more than they lose, so the net equation is profitability.

Since trading is a risky affair, traders should be handsomely compensated for the risks they take. This is where the term risk vs. reward ratio comes in. If you are going to invest your money in a venture that carries some risk, then it is good to understand the nature of the risk. If it is too risky, you may want to keep away, but if not, then perhaps the risk is worth it.

Steps to Determine a Suitable Risk vs. Reward Ratio

- Identify the most appropriate stock or other security to trade. Make sure that you conduct exhaustive and thorough research to identify the most appropriate security.

- Determine the upside points as well as the downside points. The upside is where you take profit before a reversal while the downside is where you exit a trade to prevent further losses. Use the current price to make these determinations.

- Determine the risk versus reward ratio. Have a threshold for this, and do not take anything below your threshold. Most traders prefer ratios starting at 4:1, even though 2:1 is considered the minimum ratio for any trade. Should your ratio be insufficient, then raise your stop-loss levels to acceptable levels.

Always ensure to apply the risk versus reward ratio for all your trades. Keep in mind the indicated acceptable levels. If you are unable to find acceptable ratios after trying several times, find another security. Once you learn how to incorporate risk management into your trades, you will become safer as you trade without incurring any huge losses.

Chapter 24.

Chart Patterns to Know

Many new traders who are first getting started with technical analysis often have a hard time seeing the less obvious signs that are pointing them towards various positions regarding their desired underlying assets, which can lead to them missing out on key trades as the moment comes and goes without their notice. What these types of traders are often failing to take into account is that there is no single right way to trade, which means you will want to learn about many different types of chart patterns if you hope to use technical analysis to bring in the profits you have always dreamed of. While there are countless types of technical indicators that you could consider, the following are the ones you should get familiar with first, before expanding your horizons as desired from there. A chart pattern is any one of a variety of different metrics with a value that is directly tied to the current price of an underlying asset. The goal of all chart patterns, then, is to show the direction the price of an underlying asset is going to move as well as what the extent of that movement is likely going to be. This is done through a mixture of analyzing past patterns and determining how and when they are going to repeat themselves in the future.

Flags and Pennants

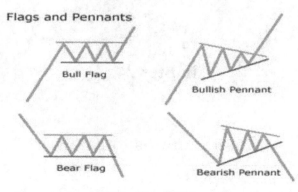

FIG1. Flag and Pennants

Both pennants and flags are signs of retracements or deviations from the existing trend that eventually become visible in the short term if viewed in comparison to the existing trend. Retracements rarely lead to breakouts occurring in either direction, but the underlying asset likely won't be following the dominant trend in the first place, so this shouldn't be much of an issue. However, the absence of a breakout will still result in a shorter trend overall. The resistance and support lines of the pennant occur within a much larger overall trend before coming together to a point. A flag is quite similar, with the exception that its support and resistance lines come together in a parallel fashion instead. Pennants and flags are both more likely to be visible within the middle portion of the primary trend. They also tend to last around two weeks on average before merging once again with the primary trend line. They are frequently associated with falling volume, which means that if you see a flag or pennant with volume that isn't dropping, then what you are likely really seeing is a reversal.

Head and shoulders

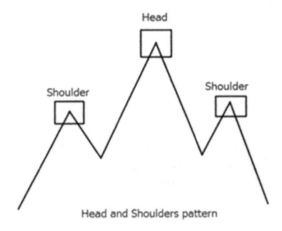

FIG2. Head and Shoulder pattern

If you are looking for indicators of the length of a trend, then the head and shoulders formation of three peaks within the price chart tends to indicate an overall bearish pattern moving forward. The peaks to either side of the main peak should generally be a little small than the main peak, which makes up the head. The price is the neckline in this scenario, and when it reaches the right shoulder, you can generally expect the price to drop off steeply. This formation most frequently occurs when a large group of traders ends up holding out for a final price increase after a long run of gains has already dropped most traders out of the running. If this occurs and the trend changes, then the price will fall, and the head and shoulders will become visible. It is also possible for the opposite to appear in the form of a reverse head and shoulders. If you see this pattern, then you can expect the price to soon be on the rise.

Cup with Handle Formation

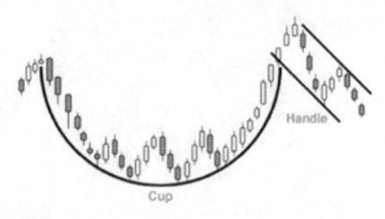

FIG3. Cup pattern

This formation typically appears if a specific security reaches its peak price prior to dropping hard and fast for a prolonged period. Eventually, it is bound to rebound, however, which is when you want to go ahead and buy. This is an indicator of a rapidly rising trend, which means you are going to want to try to take advantage of it as soon as possible if you want to avoid missing out. The handle forms on the cup after those who initially purchased the security when it was at its previous high decide they can't wait any longer and begin to sell off their holdings. This, in turn, causes new investors to become interested and then start to buy in.

The best-case scenario here would be to take advantage of the details as soon as the handle starts to form to ensure that you have the greatest length of time possible to benefit from the change. If you see the cup and handle forming, you will still want to consider any other day to day patterns that may end up derailing the trend as they will go a long way towards determining its true effectiveness when it comes to buying at a given point.

Ascending Triangle

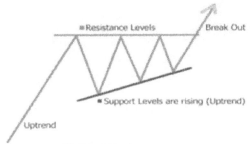

FIG4. Tringle pattern

This pattern typically forms during an upward trend and indicates that the current pattern is going to continue. It is a bullish pattern that says greater growth and volume are on the way. It can also be formed during a reversal, signaling the end to a downward trend.

Triple Bottom

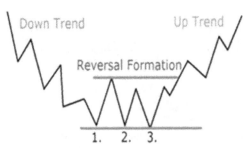

FIG5. Triple bottom pattern

The triple bottom, named for the 3 bottoming out points of a given stock, tends to indicate that a reversal is on the way. You can tell a triple bottom by the fact that the price rebounds to the same point after each period of bottoming out. After the third period, it is likely to reverse the trend by breaking out.

Descending Triangle

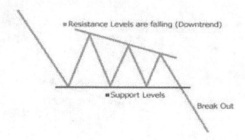

FIG6. Tringle Pattern (descending)

This is like the ascending triangle but is bearish rather than bullish. It indicates that the current downward trend is likely to continue. It can occasionally be seen during a reversal but is much more likely to be a continuation.

Bullish Triangle

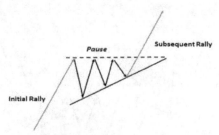

FIG7. Tringle Pattern (Bullish)

This is a symmetrical triangle pattern that can be easily determined by a pair of trendlines that converge at a point. The lower trendline tracks support while the upper tracks resistance. Once the price breaks through the upper line, then you know that a breakout has occurred that will rapidly pick up both steam and volume.

Rounded Bottom

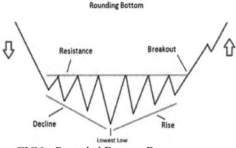

FIG8. Rounded Bottom Pattern

This pattern tracks a prolonged drop in price that will eventually rebound back to the point where it started. After the rebound occurs a reversal and breakout are likely to occur though it is best avoided as the new trend is likely not going to be strong enough to suit your day trading purposes.

Flag Continuation

FIG9. Flag Continuation

This pattern forms a rectangle with the support and resistance lines remaining parallel to one another. The slope of the parallel is likely to move counter to the original price movement. The point where the price breaks through can signal a strong indicator to buy or sell based on the direction of the breakout.

Chapter 25.

Right Tools to Trade Profitably

To make sound decisions, you need to base them on solid fundamentals. Some financial models can help you evaluate the performance of a company. Upon proper evaluation, you can determine if the stock is right or take a pass on it until its fundamentals improve. These models are based on quantitative analysis. Much like technical analysis, quantitative analysis refers to basing decisions on the number and measurable data. While your instincts are important, it is data-driven analytics that will give you the peace of mind that you need when making an investment decision. You can be confident that you made the right call based on the analytics you have used to base your investment decisions.

Tool #1: The Three-Statement Model

This model lives up to its name. It is based on the company's financial statements. Hence, the name "three statement model" refers exactly to this type of model. To conduct the right analysis, you will need to have the following financial statements: balance sheet, profit and loss, and cash flow statement. In this model, what you are doing is essentially linking all three statements to make sense of the company's financial situation. You can use this model to get an accurate idea of a company's overall financial position. If the numbers show health financials, you can feel that the company is in good shape and will produce good results down the road.

Now, the way this model works is to find a way to link all three statements into one model. What you can do is take the trend of each statement and look at how they all move together. If all three statements show a trend for growth, you can be sure that the company is in good shape.

However, if one of the balance sheets is growing, but the profit and loss and the cash flow show signs of trending in the opposite direction, you need to figure out why this is happening. There could be some unexpected situations, but the company is still solid.

If the company is posting profits, but their balance sheet is taking a hit, you can assume that their financials are out of whack. In this case, you would have to evaluate if this investment is worth it. Perhaps it might, but a very short-term deal. The use of this model is perfect for value investing and identifying the potential for a turnaround in a company that's been underwater in recent history.

Tool #2: Initial Public Offering Model

An initial public offering (IPO) is the even in which a company switches from being a private company to be a publicly traded company. In this event, the company is valued at a certain price per share by its financial team. Then the IPO is underwritten by the bank or investment firm, which is essentially sponsoring the IPO.

The issue here is determining the right IPO. This is based on the company's book value, and then a comparative analysis is conducted on the IPOs of similar companies to see where your valuation can fit in.

When you conduct your comparative analysis, you need to consider a set of variables that can be compared among companies. For example, you can compare revenue, gross sales, number of employees, annual turnover, growth rate, and so on.

The actual variables which will be considered can all be compared in a large spreadsheet. Then, each variable can be contrasted with the comparably sized companies so that you can visualize if the results obtained correspond to the comparable.

If you find that your company is above the variables seen in most comparable, then you might be able to value your company at a higher per-share price. If you see that it is below, you might want to reconsider going public. You might want to hold off going public at that time and wait until the company's financials improve.

Now, as an investor, the IPO valuation model is very useful since it allows you to see how individual companies stack against each other. This allows you to determine if your choice to invest in an IPO will make sense for you, or if you're better off waiting for the stock to prove it in the market first. Investors who get into the early stages of an IPO can make good gains. This can happen when you understand the comparison of that company's IPO. You can see if the valuation makes sense, or if it's being valued too high. In which, you might want to wait to see what happens in the market first. If you see that the valuation is below comparable, you might be looking at a potential bargain.

Tool #3: The Revenue Model

This model consists of charting a company's revenue over a given period to see the trends in that company's revenue.

You can build a model for each company you are interested in trading based on its revenue.

The best way to build this model is to take its historical revenue reports, chart them, and then calculate its trend line. You can do this on commercially available software such as Microsoft Excel, although your brokerage firm may offer you this type of analytics, so you won't have to calculate it yourself.

So, how can you interpret this model?

Once you have charted the historical data for a company's revenue, you can then look at its trend and determine if it is growing or declining. Look at 10 years' worth of data since it will give you an accurate picture of where the company is going. This would be 10 years of quarterly reports. That means that you could have 40 different data points where you can contrast the company's trend. With this model, you can see if the company is expanding, leveling off, or declining. When you see that a company's revenue is growing, you might consider it to be in an expansion phase. Depending on the age of the company, it could still be developing as part of its growth phase. If the company has been in the market for a longer period, say at least 50 years, you may want to take a look at older data, for example, 25 years, and see if the company is having a renaissance due to factors such as management turnover, the introduction of new products, or a shift in market conditions. This model is simple since it only looks at the behavioral patterns of one variable over time, but it is the most powerful variable in stock trading. You can then overlay a company's revenue trend line with that of other economic variables such as Gross Domestic Product (GDP), inflation, consumer confidence, and major stock indices to see if the company is responding to the factors around it, or it is producing results despite the trends observed in the overall economy.

The best part of this model is that you can overlay as many variables as you like to get a sense of where that company's revenue is going as compared to any number of variables in its surroundings.

Tool #4: The Forecasting Model

Industry experts will produce forecasts for companies' revenue.

These forecasts respond to the available data that analysts are looking at when determining where a company's earnings report should fall. These forecasts will produce an actual Dollar figure, which estimates where that company's earnings report should fall.

Usually, forecasting is done on an earnings per share basis. This means that the per earnings per share price are calculated based on that company's track record and other variables that can be taken into accounts, such as economic conditions affecting it and any other variables which may come into play. From that, analysts will produce a forecast where they expect that company's earnings per share to fall in line. This is where analysts' expectations are bred. If the company beats analysts' expectations,

Tool #5: Resistance Level Model

This model takes the trend in moving averages to determine where "resistance" levels can be found. A found resistance level is a psychological barrier that investors and traders must pass to continue with the stock trend.

Resistance levels are seen both at the top and the bottom, that is, both the floor and the ceiling of a stock. If a stock is trending upward, you may often see that it won't pass a certain point. This would be a resistance level. It is often hard for a stock to break through a resistance level because investors may not feel comfortable paying a certain price above a previous high. To determine resistance levels, you need to look at the candlesticks of a stock and compare it to its overall trend at the different points for moving averages. It could be that the 10-day moving average is trading in each range, but it is not surpassing the high point of the 200-day moving average. You can choose to approach the stock in many ways when you are in the presence of a resistance level.

First, you can choose today to trade the stock within that range. You can set up a buy order when the price falls to the lowest point you have observed in its 10-day or 50-day trend. Then, you can set up your sell order when it hits the resistance level ceiling.

This strategy can help you make some decent if underwhelming profits. But if the stock doesn't break the resistance level, you can feel confident about trading within that range.

Tool #6: The Gap up Model

When stocks close on high at the end of a trading day, investors may be looking to continue pushing the stock upward at the opening of the following trading day. This is common when a company's report data in the afternoon of a trading day.

As such, investors may choose to wait until the following trading day to pursue this stock. As a savvy day trader, you can purchase the stock right at the beginning of the trading day and wait for the gap to fill. When you hear that a "gap is filling," it means that the stock will go back to its previous highs after the euphoria has passed.

Chapter 26.

Benefits of Forex Trading

Liquidity

The first and most important benefit of forex trading is its liquidity. As you know, the forex market is extremely liquid, meaning you can sell your currency. There will be a lot of takers for it, as they will be looking to buy the currency. The highly liquid market can help you avoid any loss as you don't have to wait on your currency to be sold. And all of it is automatic. You only must give the sell order, and within no time, your entire order will be sold.

Timing

You can keep trading during the day and during the night if you are dealing with a country's currency whose day timings coincide with your night timings. Come up with a schedule to conveniently trade with all the different countries that lie in different time zones. You can also quickly sell off a bad currency without having to wait the whole night or day.

Returns

The rate of returns in a foreign currency trade is quite high. You will see that it is possible for you to invest just $10 and control as much as $1000 with it just look for the best currency pairs and start buying and selling them. The leverage that these investments provide is always on the higher side, making them an ideal investment avenue for both beginners and old hands.

Costs

The transaction costs of this type of trade are very low. You don't have to worry about big fees when you buy and sell foreign currencies. That is the one big concern that most stock traders have, as they will worry about having to spend a lot of money on transaction costs. But that worry is eliminated in currency exchanges, and you can save on quite a lot of money just by choosing to invest in currency.

Non-directional trade

The forex market follows a non-directional trade. It does not matter if the difference in the currencies is going upwards or downwards; you will always have the chance to remain profitable. This is because there is scope for you to short a deal or go long on it depending on the situation and rate of difference. You will understand how this works as and when you partake in it. The goal of investing in forex is to remain with a steady profit, which is only possible if you know when to hold on to investment and when to sell it off. This very aspect is seen as being a buffer by traders and is the main reason for them choosing to invest in forex.

Middlemen eliminated

With forex trade, it is possible for you to eliminate any middlemen. These middlemen will unnecessarily charge you a fee and your costs with keeping piling up. So, you can easily avoid these unnecessary costs and increase your profit margin. These middlemen need not always be brokers, and they can also be other people who will get in the way of your trade to make a quick buck out of it. You must be careful and stave such people off to avoid any unnecessary costs that they will bring about. Education is key here, and the more you know, the better your chances of avoiding fraud.

No unfair trade

There is no possibility of anyone rich investors controlling the market. This is quite common in the stock market where a single big investor will invest a lot of money in a stock and then withdraw from it quickly and negatively affect the market. This is not a possibility in the foreign currency market as there is no scope for a single large trader to dominate the market. These traders will all belong to different countries, and it will not be possible for them to control the entire market. There will be free trade, and you can make the most use of it.

No entry barrier

There is no entry barrier, and you can enter and exit the market at any time you like. There is also no limit on the investment amount that you can enter with. As was mentioned earlier, you can invest something as big as $10,000 or as small as $10 and control the market. You must try and diversify your currency investments in a way that you minimize your risk potential and increase your profit potential. You can start with little and then gradually increase it as you go.

Certainty

There is a certain certainty attached to foreign currencies. You will have the chance to avail guaranteed profits if you invest in currency pairs that are doing well. These can be surmised by going through all the different currency pairs that are doing well in the market. With experience, you will be able to cut down on your losses with ease and increase your profits. You must learn from your experience and ensure that you know what you are doing.

Easy information

Information on the topic of foreign currencies is easily available on the internet and from other sources. This information can be utilized to invest in the best currency pairs. You must do a quick search of which two pairs are doing well and invest in them without wasting too much time. If you need any other information on the topic, this will guide you through it. You can directly go to the topic that you seek and look at the details to provide there.

There are certain other benefits like minimal commission charged by the OTC agent and instant execution of your market orders. No agency will be able to control the foreign exchange market.

These form the different benefits of trading in the forex market but are not limited to just these. You will be acquainted with the others as and when you start investing in it.

Chapter 27.

Trading Full-Time or Part-Time

T rading to get long term profits is called longer-term position trading. This is different from the shorter-term scalping that is day trading. If you want to head into this direction, then it is imperative you get familiar with some strategies in order to achieve success. You need to know that the amount of money you inject into this venture is not going to come back in a short time, and you must, therefore, be very ready to make that investment. Below are some benefits of trading:

Source of Income

Financial independence is the dream of every individual. Day trading can easily get you this freedom. A trader can trade as many times as they can in a single day. Depending on how good they can trade, they can earn huge profits from the trades that they engage in. The main trick to becoming a good investor depends on how well an investor can utilize the various option strategies to earn a source of income. For you to become an expert trader, you need to have some tactics that you can utilize. Those tactics set you apart from the novice traders. You might be wondering how you can get to this point while you are just getting started.

Flexibility

We can describe flexibility in two ways. The first way is the fact that you can trade anywhere at any preferred time, and you can engage in any trade you would like. Most people do not get this, and that's why they make conclusions that options trading is a scam. Well, it is not as easy as it may seem. One must use their mind and spend some time learning more about how it works. It is an investment that you can easily engage in and earn your profits at the end of the day if you know how to do it right. The other way is the fact that once a trader purchases an option, they can trade as many times as they can to earn a profit.

Insurance

Options contracts can be utilized for insurance purposes. For a trader to use an option contract as insurance, they must build a good portfolio. Your portfolio indicates the profits an individual has made, together with the losses. A good portfolio needs to have more profits and fewer losses. As you trade, you need to ensure that you master the art of trading options.

This involves using the right trading plan and strategies to maximize your profits. Building a good portfolio is not a hard task. It is something that you can easily accomplish if you are committed to what you do. You keep getting better at it with every day that passes. In the beginning, you may encounter some challenges, but do not allow them to prevent you from getting where you would like to get. It is also important for you as a beginner to trust the process and believe that you will make it at the end of it all. Once you establish a good portfolio, you can use it as your insurance. It ensures that you do not acquire a complete loss in case a trade goes contrary to what you expected.

Cost-Effective

Different options contracts are priced differently. We have some that are more expensive than others. There are several factors that we must consider when it comes to pricing options. Some of these factors include; the strike price, stock price, dividends, underlying asset, and the expiry date. When it comes to the expiry date, the options contracts that have a short period before they expire tend to have low prices. On the other hand, the options contracts, whose expiry date is quite far, tend to be highly-priced.

Limited Losses

You think that you can make money within a short period of time, without having a strategy. You cannot invest blindly and still expect an income at the end of the day. A lot of effort, commitment, and dedication will be needed. Most people miss this fact, and that is why they end up making losses. Once they have incurred the losses, they conclude that day trading is a scam. We have had most of the traders engage in overtrading only to end up losing every penny that they have invested. To avoid this, one must be aware of the various option strategies. The different strategies are all aimed at increasing profits and reducing the losses. This is easily achievable if one is committed to learning how each strategy works and when to utilize each best.

Limited Risks

If you know much about investments, then you understand that most businesses, deals, or trades people engage in having risks. There is no single investment that an individual can engage in and fail to encounter risks. Day trading is no different from other investments. At times you will have to be open to the possibility of encountering some risks. If not controlled, it can result in fewer profits or no profit at all. Before engaging in a trade, evaluate all the possible risks. Get to know which you can afford to minimize as you live aside those that you have no control over. You need the right option strategy to do so. Depending on the type of trade you chose to undertake, you can easily get a suitable strategy to utilize. The strategy needs to be effective in minimizing the risks so you can earn more profits. As a trader, ensure you are aware of all the option strategies that you can utilize in a trade. This knowledge allows you to make the right decisions while trading, and you easily earn profits as you reduce the potential risks.

Make Huge Profits

Every investor aspires to earn profits from the investments that they make. With day trading, you can make your dreams come true. One of the good things about day trading is that you can trade multiple times. As you engage in different trades, it is good to keenly observe what you do to ensure that you avoid making wrong decisions. Ensure that you evaluate all the trades that you engage in. This allows you to evaluate the possibility of incurring a loss or a profit. You get to know the trades that you can engage in and those that you need to avoid. As a beginner, avoid the trades with a high possibility of earning a loss and, at the same time, have a high possibility of earning huge profits. Such trade may seem to be good, especially if you lean on the possibility of earning huge profits. However, do not forget that both possibilities are applicable, and you can also make a huge loss. In such cases, you will be required to make the right decisions that can result in you earning profits. You can also deal with multiple trades that earn small profits and get a huge profit at the end of the day.

Less Commission

Less commission means that you earn more profits. While selecting the best brokerage account to use while trading, this is one of the factors you will have to consider. Ensure that the brokerage account has fewer commissions so you can increase your income. Different accounts have different rates for their services. As you do your research, you will come across some accounts with high commissions and those with low commissions. If you go with the accounts with high commissions, it will affect your profit. You will find that a percentage of your profits will be slashed and go into catering for the high commissions. Avoid such accounts and work with those that have low commission. As a beginner, you need to properly analyze all your choices to come up with the best solution. It's a good thing that with a single click, you can get all the information you would like from the internet. The analysis given in various brokerage accounts can also help you identify the various services that they provide and their rates.

Liquidity

At the end of a trade, some traders like seeing the impact of their efforts on investing. Liquidity refers to the process in which an asset can be converted into cash. Upon investing in options trading, you can earn your money. As the holder of an option, you can exercise your contract and get paid depending on the payment method in the brokerage account. While opening a brokerage account, some accounts will require that you fill in your bank details.

This information will be useful while buying and selling options. In some accounts, you can fill in your E-wallet details. In case you have a PayPal account, your payment can be credited or debited from your account. We have some accounts that utilize cryptocurrencies. You find that a trader can use bitcoins to sell or buy a 55 options contract.

Profits Even with Low Investment

You may find it difficult to invest a lot in an investment that you are new to. The good thing about options trading is that you can invest in any amount you would like. Earlier on, I stated that options are priced differently. I also explained the factors that influence the pricing of options. You find that you can easily find cheap and affordable options contracts that you can engage in.

Chapter 28.

The Emotions of Trading

Many traders believe that the results (positive or negative) that are obtained by operating in the financial markets depend mainly on the psychological aspect. Discretionary traders are unlikely to be able to make steady gains without being able to control their emotional states. Knowing and analyzing them can, therefore, help avoid incurring errors that could be particularly heavy losses.

The mistakes that are made are essential for two types: cognitive errors and emotional errors. The first relates to a certain predisposition to make mistakes due to some prejudices that are formed in the head of the trader. The most common are hyper-optimism, over-confidence, and confirmation. All three-commit ex-ante, that is before entering the position.

Over-confidence leads us to believe that we know more than we know, thinking that we can control complex phenomena such as financial markets. Instead, you make a confirmation error when you only consider information that supports your point of view, discarding the information that contradicts it. Then there are cognitive errors that you make ex-post, that is after a position is closed. The first is the attribution error, which blames mistakes on others and never on themselves; the second is the error of hindsight and consists of judging the price movement as easily predictable in retrospect. Both mistakes do not allow you to have the necessary experience and avoid committing them again in the future.

Fear

It is the most frequent emotion and is linked to the risk of suffering losses and, in some cases, the fear of losing possible opportunities for earning. Fear can arise:

a. Before entering the position. The fear of losing money (particularly if you come from a series of negative results) can lead the trader to be hesitant to get into position despite the analysis indicating an interesting situation. In these cases, further confirmations are often sought from other indicators, and the danger is to waste valuable time and then be forced to chase the market (thus entering a higher level than the budgeted one, with the real danger of taking higher risk than that established in the construction of the strategy).

b. When the position is already in place. For example, a simple pause is enough to make us nervous and induce us to close a position in advance, without the market and indicators coming warning signals. An early exit, if the market then continues in the assumed direction, leads to subsequent recriminations (linked to the fact that it has obtained only a small profit, compared to a much wider movement carried out by the market). Both errors arise from a lack of confidence in one's methodology, which, after being evaluated and tested, should instead be followed consistently and rigorously.

Desire

When a position does not go in the right direction, it is hoped that later, the market will end sooner or later to give us a reason. In some cases, the exposure is increased, carrying out a very dangerous "average price" operation. Often, we do not accept that we have wronged the initial analysis (or to recognize that the market has changed its technical structure). You want to prove at all costs that you are right and that you know more about the market. The reality, however, is that the market is always right, and in trading, you must put aside your ego and know how to accept it.

Defeats

Then there is a form of desire that concerns the desire for revenge. When you suffer losses, at first, there is a sense of frustration and disappointment. Then the desire to make a new return to resume what has been lost. This behavior often leads us either to increase the operation (with the danger of going into overtrading, that is, to operate with extreme frenzy, to enter and exiting the market several times without the conditions) or to increase the size of the positions that are opened. This behavior usually leads to additional negative results, generated by taking higher risks than those you can manage. If you do not accept that a good part of the positions is destined to be closed in stop-loss, it means not understanding what trading is, an activity that is based on strategies that have a statistical basis. And since there are no strategies that have 90/100% success, it means that in most cases, we will be dealing with operational techniques that will have a positive result in 60/70% of cases.

Disappointment

After a series of closed trades at a loss or after a period in which the desired results have not been achieved, it is normal that there are disappointment and despair. However, this situation must not lead us to take greater risks, just because of the desire to do it again. Many are tempted to significantly increase their exposure to the market, with the sole aim of returning to profit as soon as possible. Trading requires patience and perseverance: Positive results can only be achieved if we can calmly and disciplined deal with the various situations that the markets offer us. Trading is not a speed race: It can be compared to a 10,000-meter race, where you must first maintain a steady pace. There may be stages when you can accelerate, but you must be aware that there are also periods when you must suffer.

Uncertainty

Uncertainty often arises from some negative results, which have undermined security in its operational strategy. In these situations, some traders play defense and prefer to stay out of the market for a while. This attitude, which is prudent, could prevent some interesting situations that, in addition to generating a good profit, could return a little confidence in their operations. Other traders prefer to reduce the size of the positions to reduce the level of risk and regain confidence with the market. In these situations, however, it is preferable to re-examine the latest trades made, to understand the mistakes made, analyzing both the technical situation on the market and how the various positions were managed.

Anger

When you suffer losses of a certain size, it is normal that you get angry, first towards the market, and then with yourself. The first reaction, quite normal, is blaming others for our mistakes: We think there is a conspiracy against us, ordered by the "strong hands," which, by moving at their leisure prices, aims to make us lose. This is, of course, a completely unmotivated thought: often, in fact, the losses resulting from a misinterpretation of the technical situation on the market or the fact that it has not correctly identified the graphic levels on which the strategy should be set. The most emotional traders, in the wake of this feeling of anger, often increase the way their operations are indiscriminate, creating the conditions for further failures. Often you decide to enter with a large capital on a single operation, doing a kind of "all in" and hoping to make the trade that suddenly heals the budget in the red of our operation. It is useful to point out that this bet results in a new and burning disappointment in most cases. As a result of positions that have generated or are generating heavy losses, panic then subsets.

Panic

It is the mental situation that takes place when losses have taken on such a dimension that they can no longer be endured and managed. The position was not closed when prices fell below the stop-loss level and when the loss was small (the entity of which had been defined and accepted during the construction of the strategy). The loss has become more and more substantial, to the point of becoming so substantial that it leaves no other way for the trader/investor: To abandon the position to itself and in the medium/long term the market will return, if not all, at least some of the initial capital. Confidence in our strategy is undermined, and the danger is that we are then afraid to return to the market (both for the insecurity that comes with it and for fear of trying such negative sensations).

Euphoria

There are periods when we have become in total harmony with the market, with the latter appearing to move according to our indications. If we decide to enter long, prices immediately accelerate upwards, and if we open short positions, the market immediately drops decisively. In this situation, where there is absolute confidence in our operation, we often run the risk of exaggerating, deciding to excessively increase exposure, and taking ever higher risks. The danger, however, is around the corner: It will take a few loss-making trades to bring us back to earth and bring everything back to normal (made up of many transactions that generate low profits/losses and few transactions that manage to produce appreciable results).

Chapter 29.

Setting Up Your Own Trading Account

Once you've decided to trade Forex and you've gathered some funds together than can be used, you need to open a trading account. To do this, you will find a broker or dealer that is suitable for your needs. You'll want to find an established and trustworthy dealer that is in your home country. In the United States, many well-known and established stockbrokers such as TD Ameritrade also offer Forex trading. The comfort of being able to trade using a broker like this is that you know it's reliable and can trust them. However, there are many other options. Opening an account for Forex trading is a little more involved than opening a stock trading account, due to the possibilities (real or imagined by authorities) of money laundering. Because of this, broker-dealers are a little more careful about verifying your identity and so forth, but it's not a big deal to worry about.

Factors to Consider When Opening a Trading Account

Look at is simple ease of use and convenience. These days, many people want to be able to trade using a mobile device such as an iPhone or tablet.

Website-only access can be a bit cumbersome; therefore, many people are searching out dealers that also have mobile apps they can use to execute trades. Of course, having flexibility is important, too. So, traders are also going to be interested in a company that has a desktop, as well as a mobile platform. Most established broker-dealers have both, although, in recent years, some mobile-only stockbrokers have emerged. As a Forex trader, you always want to have unfettered access to your account, and you may need to access it on a desktop computer when mobile access is not available for one reason or another.

Another important factor is the tools that are made available. Charting is an all-important tool for Forex traders. You need to be able to see price movements in the blink of an eye and recognize trend reversals. So, while it sounds basic, you'll want to make sure that your dealer has built-in charts that can be used for at least a simple analysis. But the more tools that are available to the trader, the better. When looking at the charts, a line graph is nice, and it shows you the overall price movement and trend, but it does not convey the level of information a trader needs to have access to. So, you will want to make sure that any broker-dealer that you select also can make candlestick charts. Candlestick charts are important to determine the trends underlying the current pricing on the charts. They also play a central role in determining when there is about to be a price reversal. These price or trend reversals (that is, when a rising price is about to become a falling price or vice-versa), are important for traders when determining when to buy or sell currency pairs.

Another tool that your broker needs to make available are technical indicators. You are going to want to be able to use moving averages and tools like Bollinger bands and the relative strength indicator. Don't worry if you aren't familiar with these tools right now, the important point here is that you have a platform that makes them available. You might not even use them in your trading activities, but you are going to want to have them there just in case you need them.

The Basics First

In any business, whether it's a used car dealer or a Forex broker, the first things that come to mind are how long has the company been operating. Of course, new companies are rising all the time, and so this is not a make or break factor. In fact, in recent years, many new stockbrokers have come into existence that has become very popular over a short period, such as Robin Hood. But a company that has been in business for a long period is one that inspires more confidence. You can ensure that the company has some chance of weathering major economic downturns and other events if it's been in business for more than ten years. Some companies, like TD Ameritrade, have been in business for much longer, which gives us confidence that the company is mature and stable. Remember, you will be putting your money into an account managed by the company. Of course, if the company failed, you can just go trade Forex somewhere else. But what you want to avoid is a situation where the company fails, and you've got $10,000 in your account, and then you have trouble getting it back. While the FDIC insures up to $250,000 in a bank account, you may find that any money you put in a Forex trading account isn't protected. This leads us to the point where looking for established brokers is the preferred route when setting up a new trading account. Second, you might be interested in the size of the company. Again, this obviously cannot be a hard and fast rule. All companies start somewhere, and two or three individuals once operated many of today's largest corporations, such as Apple, in someone's garage. However, as a rule, a company that has a larger size is going to be one that is preferred to a new startup that only has five employees. If the company is publicly traded, this is another good sign that it's a brokerage that is reliable and trustworthy. Of course, we can point to many old, well-established, and large, publicly traded financial companies that have gone bust in the past. Three of the most famous examples include Lehman Brothers, Bear-Stearns, and Merrill Lynch. These companies were all household names, they were older and mature companies with large numbers of employees, and they were publicly traded. And they all went bust during the 2008 financial crisis. So, there are no guarantees in life, but you do have to play odds. And when it comes to probabilities, a company that is publicly traded is more stable.

Regulation

Although we prefer a lighter regulatory touch as Forex traders, you want some regulation; otherwise, you might be taken in by fly-by-night operators that have fancy looking websites. These days it's very easy to create a flashy and professional looking website that can entice people to sign over their money. The website might be based overseas and lack the usual protections that an American based company would offer for investors. A trader is better off going with a domain where there is some regulatory touch. The best locations for this are the United States, the United Kingdom, Australia, New Zealand, and Canada.

Creating Your Currency Trading Account

Opening a Forex trading account, for the most part, is no different than anything else you do online. You are going to have basic forms to fill out that asks you general information such as your name, address, and phone number. Other contact information like your email address will probably be required. To start, you are going to be required to apply for an account rather than just creating an account. Remember that Forex trading is considered risky by the authorities in that currency trading could be used for money laundering. So, a few hoops are in place that you must jump through to show who you say you are so that they have some reasonable confidence that you are not using Forex trading for this purpose. There are two main things that you must verify to pass the application—the first is that you are a citizen of the country that you are claiming. Second, you are going to have to offer some level of proof of residence—that is, you live at the location that you are giving to the broker as your address. This simply means that you are going to have to upload some documentation. The specifics may vary from broker to broker, but you may be required to send in copies of such items as your driver's license and a current utility bill. Once this documentation has been sent in, the broker-dealer will assess it and get back to you. If your application is legitimate, the broker will probably approve your application over 1-3 days. Most applications are approved in about 2 days.

Connecting a Bank Account

Once the application is approved, you are nearly ready to go. The final step in the process is to connect a bank account to move funds into an account

DAVE ROBERT WARREN GRAHAM

that your broker sets up for you. And of course, wishing you successful trading, we will want to be able to quickly move profits to a bank account we use to enjoy the fruits of our labors. You will have to wire funds to your broker. As we noted earlier, some brokers might require a minimum deposit. It could be $500 or $1,000. Check with specific brokers or dealers that you are interested in and find out what the specifics are for each brokerage. Once the bank account is connected, the money will move by wire transfer into your account with the brokerage. At this point, you can begin trading.

Trading Platform

Many Forex dealers will have their trading platform, but others will be using meta trader 4, which is a trading software designed for Forex markets. Meta trader was first introduced to the Forex community back in 2005. The software is immensely popular among Forex traders, and it's available through many Forex dealers and brokers. Meta trader 4 includes a server component that is run by the broker. Traders run client software on their desktop machines. More recently, you can download mobile apps to your smartphone or tablet to run the platform. The meta trader 4 platforms will allow you to pick currency pairs, view charts and indicators at a glance, and place your trades. It's a very easy platform to use that most people can pick up nearly instantly. While there are other trading platforms available, one of the benefits of meta trader is the ability of traders to write scripts and even build robots using the platform. This powerful capability enables small, retail traders to automate large parts of their trading activity and to engage in faster computer-controlled trades. This can help traders to earn larger profits by moving in and out of currency positions quickly. The important part of a trading platform can look at charts to spot pricing trends. Depending on what type of strategy you adopt for trading, you will be interested in using these charts—often in real-time—to decide when to place your trades. If your broker is not using meta trader 4, then you are going to want to make sure that whatever software they are using, including if it's in-house developed software, allows the capabilities that you must have so that you can not only make trades quickly but that they are also informed trades.

Chapter 30.

Different Types of Securities

There are numerous types of securities out there. In finance, we define security as a tradable financial asset. This means the financial asset can be traded, bought, or sold, at the financial markets. Securities are crucial for the global financial system. They are financial instruments that are created to afford their owners a variety of options. This means anyone with a financial tool can sell, purchase, hold, assume or relinquish ownership, and so much more.

There are specific securities that are traded more than others. Day traders generally prefer certain securities. These include stocks, currencies, and contracts for difference. Others are futures contrasts like commodity futures, currency futures, interest rate futures, and equity index futures.

Securities

These are financial instruments traded on exchanges around the globe. Some of these popular exchanges include the London Stock Exchange, New York Stock Exchange, and exchanges in cities such as Hong Kong, Tokyo, Paris, and Sydney. Some securities, such as bonds and other fixed-income assets are traded across the secondary markets. There are millions of individuals around the world who hold various securities, especially stocks, bonds, and others. Other entities include exchange-traded funds or ETFs and mutual funds. Before security is made available to the public, it must be vetted. The regulator must assess large firms and corporations that wish to list at the stock market to raise money for different purposes. In the US, this regulator is the SEC or securities exchange commission. The stock and bond markets are also referred to as capital markets. Companies need to seek funds from the public list at the markets so that individuals and institutions purchase their stocks and then trade them back and forth whenever they want. Large companies must liaise with investment bankers and underwriters to help in the preparation of listing their securities at the markets. These securities could be bonds, stocks, and so on. The investment bankers will generally examine the company's financial position and the amount it intends to raise. It is based on this that the firm will likely recommend the number of shares or securities to be issued and how to approach the entire listing process.

Stocks and bonds are generally the most common and best-known types of financial securities available. They are also the most commonly traded securities, together with a few others. However, they are not the only financial instruments traded at the capital markets. We also have options, derivatives, indexes, currencies, warrants, and debentures, and even US Treasury securities.

All these securities have a few things in common. They all carry a certain value that makes them admirable to both traders and investors. However, the risk profiles of these securities vary greatly. Different traders and investors have different risk appetites. Therefore, the choice of security to trade or invest in varies.

Take bonds and stocks, for instance. Stocks carry a higher risk level compared to bonds because of how they respond to market fluctuations and the general economic state. Bonds are a lot more stable even though the income they provide is considered fixed.

Stocks

By far, stocks are the most popular form of security sold and purchased by traders and investors at the markets. There are different kinds of stocks, such as ordinary shares. These are sold to the public by the parent company through the stock market. Stocks from very successful companies that are profitable over the years are referred to as blue-chip stocks. We also have internal stocks as well as niche-specific stocks. Common stocks regularly transacted at exchanges are also known as equities. The reason why stocks are by far the most popular sort of security traded is that they have the highest return. Stocks, on average, have a return of 9.2%. In comparison, bonds have seen a return of about 6.5% within the same 50-year period.

Bonds

Another popular security that is common among day traders is the bond. Bonds are ideally a form of investment where investors put their money in debt, either public or private. Therefore, bonds are largely considered to be instruments of debt.

Bonds are also known as debt securities, so a trader who deals in bonds is purchasing a debt instrument. Compare this to traders who deal in stocks, which are essentially units of ownership of a listed company.

Companies or organizations that issue bonds often do so to raise money for a certain financial obligation. For instance, governments may issue a bond to expand or improve the local infrastructure. At the same time, companies do so to expand into new markets or sometimes even to come up with a new product line and similar ventures.

Banks also issue instruments like bonds. These are known as certificates of deposit. Banks issue these to receive funds they need most to lend to their customers. Investors or buyers of certificates of deposit, often received a certain fixed rate of interest for their investment. Certificates of deposit are short-term investment tools used by banks to raise revenue for their operations.

Options and Derivatives

Another common type of security is a derivative. Derivatives are financial securities whose value is directly related to an underlying security. This means the price is derived from the price of the underlying asset and hence the term derivative.

A good example of derivatives is an options contract. Equity options contracts are contracts between a buyer and a seller regarding an underlying asset. The asset is most cases are most often stocks. Not many retail traders deal in options, but numerous professional traders trade-in options regularly.

Others include investment firms, commercial and investment banks, hedge funds, and other companies that need to balance their portfolios.

At the most basic level, equity options contract that award buyers a right to sell or purchase underlying stocks at a certain price and within a certain period. It is important to note that this is a right, but not an obligation. Beginner and novice traders should generally stay as far away from derivatives as possible because they are extremely risky.

Currencies

Trade-in currencies are sometimes referred to as Forex or foreign exchange. It involves the purchase and sale of currencies at an exchange. The main aim of currency trading is to make a profit. The gist behind currency trading is that currency prices fluctuate, and based on these fluctuations, and traders can capitalize and earn a profit.

There is a reason why some day traders prefer trading currencies. One reason is that the currency market is the largest in the entire world. This market has a turnover of $2 trillion every single day. This is massive even when compared to other large securities markets such as NYSE.

Chapter 31.

Forex vs. Stocks

A lot of individuals range into the Forex trading business to earn some easy returns. Anyway, everybody who expects to take up this trade must realize that it is fundamental to know the subtleties of the business preceding taking a plunge in it.

Forex for apprentices may not be as easy as it might appear to be; however, there is no reason why achievement can't be accomplished whenever traded with the correct trading strategies. Amateurs Forex includes gaining the essentials gadgets of the trade altogether and, after that doing the business in a progressively trained way.

Currently, one in each five-person needs to put resources into Forex and profit right away. This has made Forex trading world's most significant trade as far as exchange volume. Up to an individual can risk and have abundant to contribute Forex trading can be a profitable business.

Web-based trading has made things stunningly better whereby an individual can trade Forex from the solace of their homes, maintaining a strategic distance from the issues voyaging. This has likewise made Forex for tenderfoots too easy to even think about venturing into as they can get everything dealt with on the web. To make progress with apprentices, Forex, one should play the diversion particularly well. Legitimate preparation and practice, however, can make novices trade like veterans and reap high returns.

Forex for tenderfoots turns into an easy undertaking with a Forex broker. The Forex brokers empower novices to work with a demo account, which can be acquired for nothing. It is seen that fledgling Forex customers are tricked in by the Forex brokers by offering a free demo account, giving them a superior comprehension of the business, and would likewise provide the customers a chance to contribute virtual money instead of real and avoid any risk. This, in the end, causes the customers to pick up a lot of trust in the trade and leave them urged enough to join with the broker to contribute hard money. There are various presumed Forex instructional exercises nowadays, which can give a lot of expertise to apprentices Forex applicants needing to put resources into Forex. If not all, the rudiments of the Forex trading business are at any rate, which is, however, the learning, an apprentice Forex competitor needs to know, can be accomplished through a decent Forex instructional exercise. After an apprentice effectively finishes the instructional exercise classes, they can apply the essential trading tips that they have learned in the instructional exercises in the underlying period of their trade execution.

Followers of this tip can doubtlessly discover Forex for novices intriguing in a higher number of ways than one. Fruitful Forex trading accompanies tolerance, determination, promptness, and diligent work. A taught methodology towards benefit making can assist an individual with novice Forex in a long way.

Options and Stocks for Beginners

Options are a form of financial derivative, and all that means is that it derives its value from an underlying security. For example, a common type of Option is the Stock options—which derive their value from the underlying company stock's market performance. However, Options can and are traded using other derivatives such as commodities and exchange-traded mutual funds.

Commodities and Futures (ETF)

The provenance of financial Options is in the trading of Commodity and Futures contracts as these were agreements between two parties, typically farmers and traders looking for a future price for their next harvest crops.

The futures markets developed to help traders hedge and speculate on commodities, especially in the agricultural market. The options market, in turn, evolved from the futures market, hence, the similarities and the shared concepts. But, because commodities and futures deal with a physical asset, there are slight differences as to how they work. The seller of a commodity or futures option is still obligated to buy or sell the stock. However, exercising the contract is different as commodities and futures contracts set the price for delivery of a specific quantity of a physical item—a bushel of wheat, for example, is to be delivered to a specific location on an agreed date. There is nothing similar in stock options as there is no need for physical delivery of anything. Commodity options are options listed on such things as corn, oil, gold, or interest rates. Futures, on the other hand, are options trading on the underlying value of futures contracts, typical futures on commodities and currencies. Futures contracts are, therefore, derivative contracts—their value is derived from the underlying commodity/asset—that give holders the obligation to buy or sell an asset at a specified future date for a specified price. Where there is a similarity between stock options, commodities, and futures contracts is that they lock in the price and quantity of an asset and have predetermined expiration dates. But in both cases, they are in themselves tradable assets, which means you can trade away your rights and obligations if you wish to exit the contract early.

Equity Options

An equity option is an option based on the price of a share of stock of a company. However, options are not available on all stocks, but some do not have options attached. It is up to the exchanges to determine whether to offer an option—based upon perceived demand—It is not up to the companies that issue it. Most equity options are priced at 1 contract per 100 shares. Equity options are what most people think of when they contemplate Options.

Index Options

The concept behind trading options in indexes is that if you can buy an option on a stock of a company within a sector says the technology, why does the exchange not make available an option on that market sector as a whole? That's the idea behind index options; you can bet on the sector performance and not have to drill down to a specific company. The result has been a proliferation of Index options based on the performance of different market indices. There are options on the S&P 500, NASDAQ, and FTSE. Trading in indexes has become a very popular alternative to trading in stock options as they represent a collection of diverse assets.

This means that a trader can spread their investments across several sectors of interest. The index works by pooling together several stocks in the same sector or across diverse sectors, and the performance aggregate is used to measure the price of the group. There are many indexes, and these include stocks, commodities, and futures, as they are all used as components of an index. But an index is just a logical category, a convenient grouping of other securities so you can't buy an index directly. Instead, you buy a security that tracks the value of the index. An example of such an option would be one that tracked an ETF that owned the stocks in Standard & Poor's (S&P) 500 Index.

Exchange-Traded Funds (ETFs)

ETFs are mutual funds that have become very popular trading vehicles as they can be traded like stocks on an exchange. However, they are often referred to as quasi-derivatives. This is because, unlike other indexes, they can be traded and because they are not necessarily holding the same securities of the index they are tracking. For example, some leveraged ETFs use swaps to mimic the action of the underlying index while adding leverage. ETFs allow you to trade on their underlying indexes, directly or through options. One of the most popular and well-known ETFs is the S&P 500 SPDR (SPY).

Stocks and bonds

Buying a company's stock gives you part ownership in that company, whereas buying bonds makes you a debt holder. Each position has its risks and rewards. However, when we bring Options into the equation, we can see that the three assets, stocks, bonds, and options, have very different risk and reward profiles. For example, although stocks give you a piece of the company, and bonds offer you income, options offer you no ownership of any tangible assets, but all three can lead to a total loss of investment.

Interest Rate Options

These are sometimes better known as yield-based options, as they trade on the interest rate on a specific type of bond. With this type of Option, calls (buying) become more valuable as interest rates rise, and interest rate puts (selling) become more valuable as the rates fall. Importantly, the underlying value is the interest rate and not the value of the bond itself. Because interest rates aren't securities and can't be traded or exchanged as such, the settlement is in cash.

Miscellaneous Options

The way that the different options exchanges make money and compete with one another is when they develop new innovative types of contracts that capture the imagination of hedgers and speculators. As an option is just a contract, which is based on the price of another asset, options can be drawn up for just about anything where someone might want to guarantee a price, and someone else might want to speculate on that price. As a result, exchanges are always trying out new option types so you can find options on different measures of market sentiment, i.e., whether it's optimistic or pessimistic about different economic outcomes.

A swap

This is a type of insurance contract whose terms are privately agreed upon by the participants. It is an over-the-counter style option as they are non-exchange traded options. They are often used to bet on the direction of just about anything, including the weather, that the two parties agree upon. Swaps are by sophisticated design securities, and so they are not available to individual investors. Often complex financial and legal requirements required to be signed before you can trade them.

Trading in Options

As opposed to investing in stock or assets, trading Options is often a decision based upon a short-term analysis. An Option having a predetermined period, a time-to-live, will have by design an expiry date. As a result, Options are renewable and can be resold many times. This makes them suitable for both trading over the short term or over longer periods delivering income when the value of the underlying stock rises, falls, or even moves sideways.

Conclusion Part 1

S tart practicing your stock trading skills, stock market analysis, applying different strategies, and using various financial tools, including chart reading. All these are simple and straightforward. If you put your heart and mind to it, you will get to learn and understand how the stock markets function eventually. It is impressive to learn that buying and selling stocks is a pretty simple affair. Most traders and investors, including novices, can pull this off. The main challenge will be to learn how to choose the winners. There are quite several stocks in all the different industries and sectors of the economy. If you learn how to identify the winning stocks, then you can expect your investments to grow immensely over the years.

A lot of investors across America and elsewhere worldwide have managed to create wealth for themselves and their families through stock market investments. You, too, can achieve this success through prudent investments over time. There are different strategies and approaches to stock market investing. If you can find the right approach and be committed to the strategy you choose, you will enjoy long term success. Remember to start investing as soon as possible because the sooner you start, the better off you will be. Investing in the stock market can seem confusing when you are first starting. If you have tried to learn about investing only to find yourself more confused than before, don't feel bad. There is so much complex information about investing in the stock market that it can make investing seem unattainable. While many people want to overcomplicate investing in the stock market, I have good news for you. None of it is necessary. By investing in index funds and allowing your investment to grow over a long period, you will be able to grow your wealth while avoiding all the overcomplicated information. Swing trading allows short financial motion in unequivocally slanting stocks to ride the wave toward the example. Swing exchanging merges the best of two universes—the more moderate pace of contributing and the extended potential increments of day exchanging. Swing vendors hold stocks for an impressive period or weeks playing the general upward or plunging designs. Swing Trading isn't fast day exchanging. A couple of individuals call it waves, contributing considering the way that you simply hold puts that are making basic moves. By turning your money over rapidly through transient expands, you can quickly build up your worth. The basic procedure of Swing trading is to dip into an unequivocally inclining stock after its season of company or remedy is done. A swing trader will most likely make money by getting the quick moves that stocks make in their future and all the while controlling their risk by proper means of the managers' methodologies.

Swing trading joins the best of two universes—the more moderate pace of contributing and the extended potential augmentations of day exchanging. Swing trading capacities splendidly for low support vendors—especially those doing it while at work.

While day traders' wager on stocks popping or falling by divisions of centers, swing traders endeavor to ride "swings" in the market. Swing traders buy less shares and go for dynamically basic augmentations, they pay lower business and, theoretically, have an unrivaled probability of gaining progressively immense increments. With day exchanging, the principle individual getting rich is the mediator. "Swing vendors go for the meat of the move while a casual investor just gets scraps." Furthermore, to swing exchanging, you don't need refined PC catch ups or lightning smart execution organizations, and you don't have to play entirely erratic stocks.

Swing exchanging is a splendid methodology used by various sellers transversely over various markets. It isn't simply used in the Forex trade, yet it is a crucial mechanical assembly in prospects and financial markets. Financial experts will, when all is said in done, have a progressively broadened term time horizon and are not generally impacted by fleeting financial changes. Swing exchanging is only a solitary framework and should be utilized exactly when appropriately grasped. Like any exchanging strategies, swing exchanging can be risky, and a moderate approach can change into day exchanging systems quickly. If you mean to use a swing exchanging system, ensure that you totally appreciate the risks and develop a method that will presumably empower you to create more prominent rate returns on your positions.

Index funds are a great investment for people who don't have the time to go out and learn everything they know about the stock market. You can think of an index fund as a set it and forget it system. When you invest in an index fund, you don't let the market's inevitable fluctuations pull you from your course. Instead, you leave your investment, continue to add to it, and allow it to grow as the market begins to rise again.

By doing this, you will take all the emotions out of investing, and you will be setting yourself up with a nice little nest egg for the future. With all this insight, you should be able to successfully carry out a trade from start to finish. You must, however, note that the options business is not for every investor. By now, it is clear to you whether this is an investment you want to try out or not. If you are into it, you must decide the kind of trader you want to be. You can either be a day trader, long term trader, or a short-term trader. As a day trader, you will have the advantage of making several trades that close quickly. This option is good for you if you are interested in making small profits. Otherwise, consider long-term trading that can span over 30 days, but with incredible profits.

Nothing will replace your raw experience when it comes to running this kind of business. As I mentioned before, the best way to gain experience is through experience. The best way to learn how to ride a bike is to work on riding a bike. You must do, and you must try to make progress. The best way to learn how to drive a car is by driving a car.

It is important to note that the shorter the trading period, the higher the stress and risks involved. If you keep holding your trades through the night, you stand a high risk of losing all your capital and destroying your account. Other than this, we are glad that you have learned a new way of earning money from the financial market and understood all the traits and skills you need to make it in binary options trading. Note that theory is never effective without practice. So, in case you need to get started, it is best to identify a trading platform and put what you have learned into practice. Remember, the more you practice, the more confident you become.

Dave R. W. Graham

PART 2:
OPTIONS TRADING
CRASH COURSE

Introduction Part 2

An option is a financial contract called a derivative contract. It allows the owner of the contract to have the right to buy or sell the securities based on a specified period's agreed-upon price. As the name suggests, there is no obligation in this type of transaction. The trader pays for the right or the option to buy or sell a transaction such as security, stock, index, or ETF (exchange-traded fund). An option is a contract.

The option derives its value based on the value of the underlying asset hence the term derivative contract. This contract states that the buyer agrees to purchase a specified asset within a certain amount of time at a previously agreed-upon price. Derivative contracts are often used for commodities like gold, oil, and currencies, often in US dollars. Another type of derivative is based on the value of stocks and bonds. They can also be based on interest rates such as the yield on a specified amount of time Treasury note as a 10-year Treasury note.

In a derivative contract, the seller does not have to own the specified asset. All he must do is have enough money to cover the price of the asset to fulfill the contract. The seller also has the option of giving the buyer another derivative contract to offset the asset's value. These choices are often practiced because they are easier than providing the asset itself.

Securities come in several types. The great thing about securities is that they allow a person to own a specified asset without taking its tenure. This makes them readily tradable because they are good indicators of the underlying value of the asset.

The trader can exercise the option at the strike price up until the expiry date reaches. In Europe, a trader can only exercise the right to the option at the strike price exactly on the expiry date. We will more largely focus on the American way of trading options, which allows for exercising right on or before the expiration date.

Trading options and trading stocks are different because stocks and options have different characteristics. Stocks share ownership in individual companies or options, and this allows the stock trader to bet in any direction that he or she feels the stock price is headed.

Stocks are a great investment if you are thinking of long-term yields, such as for retirement and have the capital. They are very simplistic in the approach that the trader buys the stock and wagers on the price that he or she thinks it will rise at a certain time in the future. The hope is that the price will increase in value, thus gaining the trader a substantial yield.

The risk of investing in stocks is that stocks can plummet to zero at any moment. This means that the investor can lose his or her entire investment at the drop of a hat because stocks are very volatile from day to day. They react to world events such as wars, politics, scandal, epidemics, and natural disasters.

On the other hand, options are a great option for traders who would like flexibility with timing and risks. The trader is under no obligation and can see how the trade plays out over the time specified by the option contract. In that period, the price is locked, which is also a great appeal. Trading options also require a lower investment compared to stocks typically.

Another great appeal for options reading is that the specified period is typically shorter than investing in stocks. This allows for regular buying and selling as options have different expiration dates.

The drawback that makes some people hesitate in trading options is that it is more complex than trading stocks. The trader needs to learn new jargon and vocabulary such as strike prices, calls and puts so that he can determine how he or she can set up effective options. Not only does the trader have to learn new terms, but he also must develop new skillsets and the right mindset for options trading.

There are several advantages to trading options, and they include:
The initial investment is lower than with trading stocks: This means that the options trader can benefit from playing in the same financial market as a stocks trader without paying as much upfront. This is called hedging.

The options trader is not required to own the asset to benefit from its value: This means that the trader does not incur the cost associated with the asset. Costs can include transportation and storage fees if applicable.

There is no obligation to follow the transaction: Whether the trader exercising a call or put option, at the end of the day, the loss is limited because the trader is only obligated to pay for the contract and nothing more. Only if the trader feels it worth it does he or she take action to move forward with exercising the contract.

The options trader has many choices: Trading options gives the trader great flexibility.

The strike price freezes the price: This allows the options trader the ability to buy or sell the asset on or before the expiration date without the worry of fluctuating prices.

Options can protect an asset from depreciating market prices: This is a long-term strategy that can protect assets from drops in the market prices. Exercising a call allows the trader to buy the asset at a lower price.

The trader can earn passive income from assets that he or she already owns: You can sell call options on your assets to earn income through traders paying you premiums.

Successful options traders weigh the pros and cons carefully and implement strategies to minimize the costs and potential losses while leveraging ways to make maximum profit.

Chapter 1.

Understanding Options

W e're going to explore the fundamentals behind options pricing on the market. It's easy to predict how the market prices of options will change by knowing the expiration date, the price of the underlying stock, and a few other details. You can also find options pricing calculators online that will give you the future price of an option for various changes in stock price.

The fundamental problem in trading, whether you are a day trader, on Forex, or trading options – is estimating future price changes. You can do simple analysis like studying price trends and keeping up with company news, including earnings reports and product releases, or major announcements such as the departure of a CEO. Any news coming out about a company can cause a major price move, and random trading can cause ups and downs in price as well, although it takes big news to cause big price changes. The overall economy can have an impact too. If there is a good jobs report or GDP growth rate, it can send stocks soaring, at least for a short period. Of course, the converse is true too, so staying on top of the news helps.

The good thing about options is that since (in most cases) they involve short-term deadlines, they make it a little easier to plan. That is, over a year, anything can happen, but over the succeeding 5-10 days, odds are it will just be business as usual. Of course, you don't want to time an options trade around some earnings call unless you are prepared and have an idea of how it will turn out, or you have set up a trade to benefit either way.

One of the coolest—and dangerous—things about options is that there is a direct relationship between the price of the options and the price of the underlying stock. It does not make a significant change in the stock price to move options prices by a large amount. A $2 change in a stock that is worth $200 is not all that significant, but it can move options prices up or down by as much as $200.

Part of dealing with this is implementing good options strategies to ensure that you don't get nailed by bad trades. Unfortunately, many new traders are not going to be able to get a high designation or high-level trader designation, so they are limited as to the types of trades they can enter. For now, let's start educating ourselves to find out how various factors influence options prices.

Call Option

It gives the buyer the right to purchase the shares at a preset rate, on or before the predetermined date. Nevertheless, the buyer, at this point, expects the price to rise.

This is tricky, and you need to be cautious because if you buy the stock at an increased price and decide to go along with it, you may end up losing all your investment.

Remember, once you buy the stock, there is no limit to the amount of loss you can make. Once your loss increases, the losses keep on increases.

Once you put the call option into actions, you have the following rights to:

- Buy a specific quantity of the asset
- Buy at a specific date
- Buy at a specified price

Those who buy options are called holders.

Put Options

The slight difference between the put option and the call option is that the holder has the right to sell the stock or asset at a predetermined price in the future.

The put option is like when you have a "short on a stock." This means you expect the stock's price to fall, and once that happens before the contract expiration period, you make a profit. Take note that the price may never fall but, instead, rise before the contract expiration.

This should not discourage you because the best part of a put option is once the price falls, you are certain to earn high profit. Alternatively, if things did not go as you expect, you will not lose your money.

If you want a quick profit without investing in the asset for a longer time, then you may consider taking the put option strategy.

Most experienced investors look for opportunities when the asset price falls before they make a move. When the price falls, it places them in an advantageous position to reap the market. Those who sell options are called writers.

In the Money

The first term we need to know is called "in the money." Calls are easier for people to understand because if you are not experienced as an in-depth market trader, you are not used to thinking in terms of shorting stocks. Normal people want stock prices to rise. As you learn more about options trading, you will find out that it is not always the best thing. But calls have an intrinsic appeal to that natural belief, thought process, and desire.

When the stock's market price is higher than the strike price of the option, a call option is in the money. So, if you have an option with a strike price of $75 and the stock is trading at $80 a share, it is in the money. In short, in the money call options are worth a lot more than options that are not in the money. We can look at the options calculator to see what the differences can be.

So, I have set up a hypothetical stock that is trading at $80 a share. We will consider an option that expires in 14 days. Just for the record, the implied volatility is 16%, and the risk-free rate is 0.3% (we will explain what that means in a minute).

Setting the strike price at $75, we find that the option (in this case, a call) is priced at $5.03. Once again, remember that it is for a single share; the option would be $503.

Now let's consider another option with all the same characteristics but say that this one has a strike price of $70. The price of this option is $10.01, or $1001 to buy the option. The option with the strike price of $70 is also in the money, but it's more in the money than the option with the strike price of $75. Another way to express this concept is by saying that it is deeper in the money. If the share price is exactly equal to the strike price, the option is said to be at the money. The odds of an option being exactly at the money in the real world are slim, but they can be very close to the money. These options can be of interest because, if the stock price goes beyond the strike, the value of the option can suddenly increase by a large margin. For a call option, the probability of the share price moving above the strike price can be high. Using the example of a strike price of $75, the option would be $0.92 (you would have to pay $92 to purchase the option). If the share price rises to $76 later that afternoon, the price of that call will jump to $1.53. This kind of price change illustrates why people find trading options so appealing. If you sold right then, that would net you $61 in profit for each option contract.

Out of the Money

An option is out of the money if the strike price is higher than the share price on the market. Options don't need to be in the money to make a profit. Depending on the direction of price movement, you can earn profits from out of the money options as well. We can illustrate this with call options. If the stock price is rising, the prices of out of the money calls are going to rise as well. So, we shall set up a similar scenario where there are 14 days until option expiration, but, this time, assume that the strike price is $77. Suppose the share price is $75, which is lower than the strike, the option is out of the money.

If the share price rises over the following couple of days, you can make a decent profit. The good thing about out of the money options is they are relatively cheap.

Using our example, the $77 strike would cost $0.27 ($27 to buy).

Now let's suppose that, two days later, the share price rises to $76.50. The option is still out of the money. However, the price of the option will rise because the share price is rising. It turns out that under these conditions, the option's price would be $0.66 at that point. That means you could turn around and sell it for $66 when you had purchased it two days earlier for $27.

Many experts don't recommend trading out of the money options. But they remain a great alternative for people that don't have much money to start making profits. This can work if there is a large price move for the underlying stock, and you only hold the option for a couple of days. If there is a lot of movement within a single day, you can make substantial profits. If an option expires and it is out of the money, it is also worthless (it "expires worthless"). This holds for the money options as well. If the option is in the money at expiration, the price of the option is (share price – the strike price).

Chapter 2.

Buying and Selling Options

This gives you the capability to shop to open a function. So, you may purchase alternatives at what you desire is a low fee, and then sell them at what you wish is an excessive rate. Knowing when to shop for and sell is something you need to learn from experience. However, we can come up with some general advice. You will additionally install guidelines for reducing your losses.

Making Profits Buying Call Options

The net is full of nonsensical advice. The problem is that all people can create a blog and write something that looks authoritative, or they can make a YouTube video. Even some authoritative web sites have articles that might be no longer written through someone who trades alternatives. Many websites and YouTube motion pictures are made using humans that recognize what they're doing, and they're likely promoting a training direction or something so that you can take what they say.

Can your earnings buy call options? The solution is manifest, yes. But to do so, you must do it carefully. The first step in doing that is to keep away from letting "luck" decide your fate. You are going to want to pick while the right time is to get into options. The second component to keep in mind is the expiration date of the options. Third, to have a successful and profitable enterprise buying alternatives, you must set a pre-determined income restriction on the way to take a set quantity of earnings.

Never Let an Option Run to Expiration

Options suffer from trouble called "time decay." The price of the options is the sum of two prices, the extrinsic rate, and intrinsic price:

Option Price = Extrinsic Price + Intrinsic Price

The intrinsic charge comes from the rate of the underlying shares of stock. Depending on many exceptional factors, it can be extra or much less influential on the total charge of the options. The extrinsic fee is "time price." So, it's getting smaller as time passes. If the options are inside the cash, the intrinsic fee can crush the extrinsic cost, if the options are out of the cash, then it's going to be all extrinsic price. In that case, the option can quickly dwindle to zero price if it stays out of the money. For that purpose, you shouldn't preserve directly to an alternative hoping the matter will turn around. If you're hoping that the percentage fee will turn around at some point, but the option is some days away from expiration, it's no longer worth retaining onto. Cut your losses and purchase another option with a further-out expiration date.

If you let your alternatives run out to the expiration date, or even multiple days earlier, you will end up losing all or a massive fraction of your cash. Options might be out of the money 'expire worthless' on expiration day, so if you are still preserving them, you lose all your money.

Set a Cutoff to Exit Your Trade

Before you begin trading, make guidelines that you're going to stick to. As an example, you may want to offer an option if the fee drops with the aid of $25. That offers it enough room in case the percentage charge of the stock goes down but has enough momentum to turn around and upward push once more in rate. If that doesn't happen, $25 isn't a huge loss. So, you can take the loss and move on. A trader must be sensible, and investors aren't going to win on all trades. Selling at a $25 loss is higher than dropping your whole funding. Be sure to hold things in perspective, and a $25 loss could be something you'd practice for an option that costs one hundred dollars or more, for smaller fee options pick out smaller values.

Pay Attention

You will pay near interest to the markets. So, you may need to closely watch the charts to peer if you go out cutoff is reached. Become familiar with restrict orders and use them.

One way to protect yourself is to enter a restriction order. A limit order is an order you place to buy or sell economic protection at a hard and fast charge. When selling your options, it's a fee you're simply willing to accept for the options. If you want to get out of options due to the fact the charge is strongly declining, then you should use a restricted order so you can get out of the option quickly before you lose most of your investment. Submit a fee that fits the low end of the variety when you need to get out.

Follow Trends

If you are buying call options, the great ones to look for are for shares which can be coming into a fashion. Generally, all you want is to find out where the stock is going to locate candlestick charts with a 9-duration and 20-period moving average on the chart. You can study candlesticks and their meaning if you want to count on what takes place next. To buy a call option, you're going to need to shop for the option when the stock is at the bottom of a downward trend, with signs and symptoms of a trend reversal. You can learn to spot a possible fashion reversal by getting to know approximately candles on stock charts. Also, you may look for crossovers between the moving averages.

Following a trend can be a great manner to earn a quick income. Just be equipped to exit the fashion at the right time. That is something you will discover ways to do with any stage of precision. To advantage the sorts of abilities you need, you should buy some books on technical analysis or watch YouTube motion pictures about the topic. Make sure that you're watching videos about shares, not the Forex market, even though they both use some overlapping ideas.

Buying Multiple Contracts

When you're first beginning in the world of trading, you possibly want to enter an operation quickly, you likely need just to exchange one option settlement at a time. But as you advantage experience, you are probably going to need to shop for and promote multiples of the equal options to magnify your winnings. You need to hold in mind to enlarge your losses as well, and it does make sense to shop for 5 contracts of an alternative and make an income of $250 than it does to simply earn $50 if you recognize what you're doing and you've got the capital to enter the positions. However, you need to be conscious there may be sure troubles that arise in case you purchase multiples of one alternative at the identical time. The day trading boundaries are usually hiding inside the background. You'll be able to shop for the 10 options or 5 alternatives whichever you pick out, but you would possibly wait till the subsequent day to find a good way to promote them all. Remember that if options fluctuate in a few ways, either with a different strike price or expiration date, they're no longer considered independent financial securities even though they manage the same underlying stock.

Types of Trading Option

The current financial market has seen numerous types of options being traded. The contract agreed by option trading parties should have a clear indication of which type of option is being traded. The types of options that are known in the current world tend to be categorized and named depending on the varied features they pose. People across the globe are familiar with two types of options. Calls and puts options are popular in the financial markets.

Entering into a contract of American options allows a financial trader to trade his or her underlying assets between the date he or she has purchased them to the date they are bound to be invalid. On the other hand, trade options contracts that contain European options bound an individual to perform his or her trades on the edge of the expiry time.

Strike Price

The presence of a strike price is a common phenomenon in the trade of options. It can be described as a major component when it narrows down to penning down of an option contract. Options such as calls, and puts are heavily dependent on this factor. Its critical nature can be shown by an option trader who needs the call options. It is important because it determines the value possessed by the option. Several people have familiarized strike prices with a different name, which is known as the exercise price.

The criticality of this component of the contract makes it one of the components between the contractual parties before entering an agreement or contract. It can inform an investor or trader what in-the-value money is supposed to be achieved. The underlying price value of the traded assets is supposed to be lower than the strike price. In many cases, the strike price is always affected by the time frame of the contracts. One is supposed to remember that strike price operates on fixed amounts that can be converted to dollars. However, they vary depending on the contract an individual has.

Premium Price

The premium can be described as the price an option buyer in a contract pays the seller of the option. Terms of an option contract state that the amount is always paid upfront. It is always important for a trader to remember that this component of a contract is not refundable. The rule extends itself to the side that one cannot be refunded his or her money even if the contract has been exercised. The premium quotation in a contract is always done in a certain way for efficiency. The most common way across the globe entails the quotation of option in the foundation of shares, which is termed per share basis. The amount of premium is always affected by several variables before it is agreed on. The common determinants of premium prices are swayed by three major factors: the volatility value of the option price, timing, and intrinsic value.

Expiration Date

One can easily understand the term expiration date of a contract as the last day, and he has the right to exercise either buying or selling the underlying financial instruments. A contract is termed worthless in moments the expiration date has passed. The expiration date tends to differ depending on the type of contract an individual has entered this despite the general principle of the contract being worthless after the last days. A contract using the American style of option trading gives the trader the right to trade his or her options from the date he or she purchased them to the day they expire. However, European style trading fixes an individual to only performing his or her trades on the last days of contract expiration.

Settlement Option

The settlement of options can be described as the process by which the holder and writer of an options contract resolve and exercise the terms stated. The process entails the participation of two parties in the trade of options, and it differs depending on the options one has decided to trade.

Chapter 3.

Options Greeks

To quickly evaluate the variables in the option price, the option price will be determined by the price of the underlying security, the strike price of the option, the time to expiration, the value of the underlying security, any outstanding dividends, and the present risk-free interest rate. So why are seasoned traders worried about the "Greek Option?" It's because they are a valuable way to forecast what will happen to an option's price as market variables change.

This can seem at first difficult to understand, but the option prices do not change with the price of the underlying asset. Any trader who takes the time to learn the basics, however, will begin to understand the variables and the effect of each factor in moving the prices of an option.

Many business traders are using the Greek option to handle several multiple options effectively in a variety of strikes over many time frames. Market professionals will also use the Greeks to ensure that their risk exposure is efficiently hedged and adjusted accordingly, to build a balanced portfolio.

As far as the day trader or investor is concerned, the Greeks demonstrate how and why an option price changes when one of the variables changes.

Delta

The Delta is first and most frequently referred to in Greek. As reported, the Delta is the rate of variation in the option price relative to the underlying stock rate of change. This is crucial to understand because many of our option strategies are designed to take advantage of a strong prediction of the underlying security price shift.

For an example of Delta, we have a $50.00 stock and a $50.00 cash flow option. There are 30 days before expiry; the call option is $2.32 and the Delta 0.53. The Delta represents the predicted change, given that there are no other variables.

If the stock price rises to $51.00 by one dollar, we should assume that the call option will rise from $2.32 to about $2.85.

Likewise, if the stock price drops from $50.00 to $49.00, we expect the call option to decrease in value to approximately $1.79 from $2.32.

Note that the price has changed by the sum of the Delta in both cases. Several of the Delta's main characteristics are: When a call option becomes broader, the Delta reaches 1.

There is always a favorable delta for call options. At the point where this option delta hits 1, the call option will represent approximately the dollar's price movement of the underlying stock.

If we look at the Delta of a put-on option, the larger the option is, the Delta is less than 1. Put options should have a negative delta always.

Gamma

Since the Delta is always rising, this radical shift had to be calculated. As a result, the Gamma was created to measure the rate of delta transition. This is mostly used by practitioners to change the hedged portfolios of the Delta.

Vega

Vega is the calculation of the variance of the option price with the increase in implied volatility percentage. For this example of Vega, there is an inventory at $50.00 and an alternative at $50.00. There are 30 days before the expiry. The call rate is $2.06, with a 35% Implicated Variance and a corresponding Vega of 0.057.

If the implied stock volatility increased by 1% to 36%, the call option will increase from $2,06 to approximately $2,12 the Vega price.

In the same way, if the implied volatility drops from 35 percent to 34 percent, we would expect to decrease the value of the call option from $2.06 to about $2.00.

Theta

The Theta is a function of the price shift relative to the time change to maturity. A choice loses some value every day that passes, and the Theta calculates the decay rate.

For this example, we have a $50.00 stock with the $50.00 cash option and a $50.00 cash option. There are 30 days before the expiry. The call is priced at $2.06 for a Theta of less than 0.041. If the number of days before expiry dropped from 30 to 29 days, the Theta option would decrease from $2.06 to around $2.02.

Rho

Rho is a calculation of the increase in the option's price relative to the increase in the risk-free interest rate. This Greek is much more important in terms of long-term choices as the short-term interest rate effect is less evident.

For this example of Rho, we have a stock that costs $50.00 and an option for $50.00. There are 30 days before the expiry. The call option is $2.06, with interest rates at 3.00% and a Rho of 0.02.

If the rates rose to 4 percent, the option price would rise from $2.06 to $2.08, Rho's value, while the option price would decline from 3 to 2 percent, from $2.06 to $2.04.

An investor or trader will understand by studying the Greek option why the option is or isn't linked to the underlying security.

Through knowing certain factors influencing option prices, regular traders or investors have the confidence to incorporate options into their portfolios and use various approaches to help them achieve their goals.

Binomial Option Pricing Model

Option pricing theory uses all the variables mentioned above to calculate the value of an option theoretically. It is a tool that allows trainers to get an estimate of an option's fair value as they incorporate different strategies to maximize profitability. Luckily, there are models that traders can use to implement option pricing strategies to their advantage.

More commonly used to develop pricing for American options, this pricing system was developed in 1979. Even as popular as the Black Scholes Model is, this model is more frequently used in practice because it is intuitive. This pricing system allows for the assumption that there are two possible outcomes – one where the outcome moves up and one where the outcome moves down.

This system differs from the Black Scholes Model because it allows calculations for multiple periods, whereas the Black Scholes Model does not. This advantage gives a multi-period view, which is very advantageous to options traders.

This model makes use of binomial trees to figure out options pricing. These are diagrams with the main formula branching off into two different directions. This branching off is what gives the multi-period view that this pricing system is famous for.

For this pricing system to work, the following assumptions are made:

- There are 2 possible prices for the associated asset, hence the name of the pricing system. Bi means 2.
- The 2 possibilities involve the price of the asset moving up or down.
- No dividends are being paid on the asset.
- The rate of interest does not change through the life of the option
- There are no risks attached to the transaction.
- There are no other costs associated with the option.

Just like with the Black Scholes Model, there is some limitation with those assumptions. Still, the pricing system is highly valuable in the valuing of American options since such options can be exercised any time until the expiration date.

Chapter 4.

Volatility

W e can define volatility as a statistical measure of the levels of fluctuations of stock, shares, or the entire market. The value is calculated as the ASD or annualized standard deviation of the price swings of security in terms of daily percentage. The value is expressed as a percentage.

Historical volatility

Historical volatility is simply a measure of a security's volatility in the past. When computing this figure, you will have to define a specific period for consideration. One of the most common figures used for historical volatility is 20 days. This specific measure approximates total trading day numbers within a month.

Implied Volatility

Another useful term is implied volatility. This measures the volatility that is implied by the prevailing market price of the stock's options. Implied volatility is computed using one of the main option pricing models, like the

Black Scholes Model. Using this or similar models, you can work out volatility where a mathematical relationship has been established relating to the price of an option and the volatility of the underlying stock.

Implied volatility provides insights into the market's view of the options contracts' underlying security. It can be determined by making use of the following:

- Option's current market price
- The value of the underlying security
- Expiration dates
- The strike prices
- Any applicable interest rates
- Any applicable dividend yields

In an ideal situation, we would expect the implied volatility figure to be the same for all options that have the same expiry date. This is regardless of the strike price that was used in our computations. In practice, however, this is hardly accurate because the figures we get vary mostly due to strike prices. This variation in volatility is known as the volatility skew.

The Impact of Volatility on Options Trades

We have already established what the term volatility means in options trading. It is simply a measure of the size and rate of the price change of the underlying security. High volatility implies a high option premium. The reverse is also true.

If you can accurately assess the value of statistical volatility for the underlying security, you will be able to use this value into a pricing model for purposes of computing a fair market price for the option. It is crucial that, as an options trader, you keep in mind the fact that changes in volatility can greatly impact your trades either negatively or positively.

Historical volatility generally measures the speed at which a futures commodity or stock price has moved in the past. This enables you to predict with some degree of accuracy, its expected movement in the future.

For instance, if we have a vehicle that is traveling at 50 miles per hour, we can determine how many miles it will travel for the entire year.

Distance = speed * time

In our case, distance = 50 mph * 24 hours/day * 365 days/year = 438,000 km

If everything remains constant, then we can accurately predict the distance that the car will cover. However, in real life, this is hardly the case because the car could make stops, break down sometimes, and so on. The same is true for stocks and options. Although our calculations depend on known factors, if the variables keep changing, the outcome could be different.

How to Compute Historical Volatility

Historical volatility is quantifiable and is based largely on previous changes to a futures or stock options contract. To calculate this figure, you need to consider the past prices and all price changes, then average them out into a percentage.

For instance, you can consider the historical volatility for 10 days. If you have the price change for 10 days in percentage terms, you should subtract the daily percentage price variations to find deviations from the average daily change for the period.

One of the most common methods that can be used to compute historical volatility is the close-to-close changes in percentage for daily values. There is another method known as the high minus low prices. Another approach would be to take an average of low, high, and median prices. The purpose of all these models is to obtain some intraday information that is usually not included in a close-to-close system.

It is also advisable to spend a few moments calculating historical volatility as well as the trending vs. trading range markets. A stable trend will likely emerge, and it can go either up or down but will not affect the size of percentage price changes.

While the changes in average daily price may increase, historical volatility as calculated may become smaller. Also, it is possible to demonstrate that historical volatility figures can increase if the average daily price reduces in size regardless of the market trends. One of the most popular methods uses 10 days of daily percentage price changes. This information is then used also to compute a standard deviation. Commonly used are 20 and 30 days and specific time frames for your computations.

How to Compute Implied Volatility

It is a lot easier to look at implied volatility with common pricing models such as the Black-Scholes model. You will need to have at least five inputs or variables. These variables are:

- Historical volatility (or statistical volatility)
- Strike price
- Stock price
- Risk-free interest rate
- Number of days to expiration

With these inputs, you will receive a more accurate and reliable theoretical option price. However, most of the time, the markets do not set the fair value price for the same option. Options prices will normally deviate from these theoretical values. The fair price is a result of the input of five independent variables.

In general, if the market price exceeds the theoretical price of an option, then market participants such as traders and investors have added a premium to the price. A lot of these concepts are best viewed with real-life examples.

Commodity options usually portray excellent volatility. When the markets portray high volatility, then traders should be careful of buying options straight up. It would be a lot better to sell than to buy at this point. When the volatility is low, then options buyers should start buying.

Chapter 5.

How to Trade Calls and Puts Effectively

The first thing about options is that you will be looking to trade options on stocks that are going to move in price. While an options trader does not want to be reckless, being excessively conservative is not going to lead to profits. Remember that a small change in stock price can lead to a large change in the value of an option, putting traders in a position where they can make significant profits. But to get it right, you should be thinking in terms of percentages. Different people are going to have different trading styles, but these examples show that you will be able to make significant profits going with stocks that have higher share prices. Of course, you could make up for it by buying many options with smaller stock prices, but there are day trading rules that you need to be aware of when taking that approach – and that could cause trouble for your plans.

Day Trading Rules

An option on a stock that is the same type, same expiration date, and same strike prices is the same security. The basic day trading rule is that if you buy a stock and sell that same stock before the market closes, that is a day trade.

Consider options with the same ticker in the options chain as a "stock" for this rule. It is important to note because sometimes, you must get out of an option on the same trading day. You might either earn large profits and want to take advantage of it before momentum shifts, or you lose value from time decay, or you might need to get out of a losing trade before you get wiped out. Consider selling options for income rather than buying options hoping to profit by trading. Many traders prefer selling options. Although there are risks, selling options is a more reliable approach for earning money than trying to speculate with trading. There is still a level of speculating when you are selling options, but the speculation is one-sided, making it less risky. We will see how this works in a minute.

Covered Call

The simplest way to sell options for income is by using covered calls. To sell a covered call, you must own 100 shares for each option you want to sell. So, if you have been investing in some of your favorite stocks over the years and you have built up some shares, you can start earning money off the shares by selling call options against them.

The strategy involves selling the options with a strike price that is out of the money. If you sell in the money options, while you are going to be able to get a nice payment, your options will be "called away" if they expire in the money, and there is even a risk a buyer might exercise the option before expiration. So, beginning traders are better off selling out of the money options, even though you earn less money. The money you are paid for selling an option is called the premium. This is analogous to an insurance premium, and many people trading stocks invest in options for insurance.

This is especially true to get protection against falling stock prices, buying a put option can give you insurance by giving you the out of being able to sell the stock at the strike price of the put if prices drop significantly.

With a covered call, you find the option that you want to sell in the options chain, and then use the interface of your broker to sell to open the option. You will be credited with the amount that the option is trading at the time. If the option expires, and the share price did not put your option in the money, you will be able to take that out as cash.

Breakeven Price

The breakeven price is important to note when selling options. If the share price has not gone above the breakeven price, nobody will exercise the option. To take a simple example, if the share price is $100 and it costs $2 to buy the option (per share), then the breakeven price for a call option is $102. So, the stock price must rise above $102 to make it worth it to a buyer to exercise the option.

For a put option, subtract the price paid for the option to get the breakeven price. For our $100 stock, if a put option costs $2, then the breakeven price is $100- $2 = $98.

Buying an Option Back

One strategy used by traders who sell options is to reduce the risk of having the option exercised; they will buy the option back before it expires. This will reduce your overall profit but eliminate the risk that a sudden price movement will put the option in the money (past breakeven) and it will be exercised. Remember that if a call option is exercised, you will be required to sell 100 shares of stock at the strike price. If a put option is exercised, you will be required to buy 100 shares of stock at the strike price. The key to this strategy is time decay. So, if you sell an option for $2 a share or $200, if it is out of the money as it nears expiration, it will be worth pennies on the dollar. So, you can buy it back without losing too much income. In the event, an option goes in the money, and it looks like it is not going to move again in your favor, you can always take a slight loss and buy it back to avoid having to sell the shares.

Protected Puts

Another strategy is to sell put options, and if you are only a level 1 or level 2 trader, you can sell a protected put. However, this requires tying up a large amount of capital. To sell a protected put, you must have enough money in your account in the form of cash to buy 100 shares of the stock in the event the option is exercised. While this could be a way to earn a regular income, it requires a lot of money in proportion to small earnings, and there are better ways to earn money.

Debit Spreads

Now let's consider one of the most popular ways to earn money from selling options that don't involve having to own the shares of stock or putting up large amounts of cash. This is done using so-called bull and bear spreads or put and call spreads. A spread involves buying and selling two options at the same time. With a credit spread, it is a form of earning income. With a debit spread, you are essentially trading options but reducing the risk. So, let's look at that first. Consider a call debit spread. With a call debit spread, you will buy an option at a lower strike price, and then sell an option at a higher strike price. Traders do this because you lower your risk by selling an option at a higher strike price. A trader can buy a call option in the money, earn higher profits, and then sell a cheap call option to mitigate the risk. This strategy is used when you expect the stock price to rise. You can also invest in a put debit spread. In this case, you buy an in the money put option with a higher strike price, and then mitigate your risk by selling an out of the money put option with a lower strike price. You use this strategy when you expect the stock price to drop.

Credit Spreads

Credit spreads are an income-generating strategy. The most frequent type of credit spread used is a put credit spread. In this case, you are going to trade 2 out of the money put options simultaneously. However, you will sell a put option with a higher strike price, and then buy a put option with a lower strike price. For a put credit spread to work, all you need is for the stock price to stay above the strike price (less breakeven, technically) of the put option with the highest strike price. What the stock does beyond that is immaterial.

Selling Naked Put Options

A simpler trading method is to sell one option without buying another one to mitigate risks. Professional traders prefer this method, but you must open a margin account to do it. This will require a cash deposit of $2,500. You will also have to deposit some collateral cash, and the requirements are higher than what is required for a credit spread. However, it is far less than what is required for a protected put, a small fraction of the money. You can also sell naked call options.

The principles are the same, but when you sell naked put options, you will be doing so, expecting the stock price to stay above the strike price of your option. So, you will sell naked put options when you are neutral or bullish on the stock. For naked call options, you will sell one when you expect the stock price to be neutral or drop so that it will remain below the strike price. So, you sell naked call options when you are bearish.

Chapter 6.

ETF Options vs. Index Options

ETF

We first need to know and understand Exchange Traded Funds. You can think of ETFs like mutual funds that are traded in any regular stock exchange, just like how stocks and shares are traded. An Exchange Traded Fund usually consists of representative stocks and shares held in trust and managed by big institutions such as Vanguard, Merrill Lynch, State Street, Barclays, and others. The ETFs are also normally subject to a management fee like mutual funds though the magnitude of the fees is much smaller than that of MFs.

ETFs are tradable on any regular stock exchange, so you can buy and sell ETFs from any brokerage firm that helps you deal with stocks and shares. And just like stocks, ETFs can be traded via the options trading route too. ETF options, like stock options, normally use the American style of trading wherein the buyer can exercise his right any time till the expiration date after which the option has no value.

ETF options offer you more diversity than that offered by individual stock options. ETF options deliver a broader market to you, reducing the risk associated with the price movements of a single stock. So, to give examples, for stock-related ETF options, the choices include options contracts based on SPY (an ETF that represents S&P 500) and for commodities such as oil, gold, and silver, the choices of ETF options including those based on USO (United States Oil Fund), GLD for gold, and SLV for silver.

Large trading volumes in ETFs and ETF Options – Many ETFs trade in large volumes owing to their broad market perspective, which is highly attractive for the discerning investors. Many large institutions, high-net-worth retail traders, and individual investors like you and me are also attracted to ETF Options. Because of this trend, EFT trade volumes match that of many popular stocks. EFT options are also traded in high volumes and hence are highly liquid, which in turn results in tight ask/bid spreads. Hence, when you place an order price between the bid and ask price, you will be able to trade easily.

Risks associated with trading in ETF Options:

As any trading investments, ETF Options also carry risk, and some of them are enlisted below:

- The first most basic risk that the underlying asset may turn into losing money (as with any other market-related security)
- Another risk is that ETFs themselves are a complex investment vehicle and hence add to the complexity of the corresponding ETF Options.

To overcome these challenges is to enhance your knowledge and expertise in the field by continuously learning information, data, and new products as when they come into the market.

Index Options

An index option gives the holder the right but not the obligation to trade in the value of an index, such as Standard & Poor 500, at a fixed price within the expiration date. It is important to note that index options contracts are always cash-settled.

Investors using index options are essentially speculating on an underlying index rather than single security, stock, or share. This option allows investors to gain exposure in a specific market, giving them a choice to bet on whether the specific index is going to go up or down in value. There are two types of indexes that are widely used throughout the trade:

- Dow Jones Industrial Average – This type of index is made up entirely of large-cap companies
- Nasdaq – A sector is driven towards the technology division

Choosing an Index

Many investors trading in index options invest in broad indexes, such as the Standard & Poor 500. However, some investors may sense that a sector – perhaps in the technology area – is doing well and may choose to invest within a Nasdaq index type. Depending on their outlook, an investor will choose an appropriate index to match the sector in mind, whether it's an airline, utility, or pharmaceutical sector.

Advantages of Investing in an Index Options Contract – You can invest and gain exposure in multiple stocks, reducing the risks involved when investing in just one index option type.

Settlement

As stated before, all index options are cash-settled. The settlement price is determined by the differing value of the specific index and the strike price.

Capped Index Options

A capped index option is automatically exercised when the capped price is reached. If the capped price is not reached during the length of the contract, the capped index option can be exercised on – and only on – the expiration date.

Predetermined Risk and Leverage for the Buyer

Like stock options, index options give the buyer predetermined risk leverage. The leverage received is due to the premium being a fraction of the contract value. This means that, even for small price movements, the buyer may gain or lose a large sum of money.

Contract Multiplier

Index options obtain a contract multiplier of $100. This multiplier is used to calculate the cash value of an index options contract.

Premium

The premiums of index options contracts are received in dollars. The cost of one stock index options contract is calculated by multiplying the contract multiplier with the quoted premium.

Options on Futures

To understand futures options, let us recall what stock options are; a stock option is a contract with stocks of a specific company as the underlying asset. For example, Microsoft Call options' underlying asset would be stocks of Microsoft. As investors more commonly use stocks, it is quite easy to understand how the stock options work too.

Similarly, to understand the working of futures options, you would have to know how futures are traded. A futures contract between two parties is transacted in such a way that the parties agree to transact physical commodities or financial instruments to be delivered in the future at a fixed price. When you buy a futures contract, you are purchasing an asset that the seller does not yet have or not yet produced at a fixed price.

As expected, the futures market is complex, layered, and risky. It requires a high level of financial sophistication to play around with futures and futures options. However, now that you know how futures are traded, we can go into how futures options are traded too.

Let us use examples to see how futures options operate. Suppose there is a current upward trend in the gold market, and you wish to invest in a gold futures option. You believe that the present rising trend in gold prices will continue, so you choose to buy a call option. Suppose you are willing to invest $2000 in buying this option.

Suppose you choose to buy a 1405 gold call option with expiration in September. You keep a close watch on gold prices. And within a short while, true to your belief, the price of gold goes up to 1430. The present value of your option is $3700. As you believe the gold prices are only going to decrease or remain stagnant from here on, you choose to exercise your option and make a profit of $1200 by offsetting the option. Offsetting an option can be done simply by selling the options you bought earlier.

Things to know before trading in Futures Options:

Expiration Dates: Futures options normally expire on the third Friday of the month before the month of delivery of the underlying futures contracts. For example, the options for March futures will expire in February and usually on the third Friday.

Strike Price: The strike price is the rate at which the Futures position will be opened in the buyers' and sellers' trading accounts if the option is exercised.

Exercise and Assignment: When the Futures option is evoked, a Futures position is set up in the buyers' and sellers' trading account at the predefined strike price. Based on whether a put or call option was exercised, the option seller and buyer will assume a short or a long position, respectively.

Futures Options Pricing: It is critical to remember that the futures contract is the underlying asset in futures options and not the commodity. So, the price of the option aligns itself with that of the futures contract. Although the futures contract's price is closely related to the price of the commodity, the two are not the same. In leveraged products, these small differences can create large profits or losses.

Currency Options

Currency (or Forex) options are financial tools that allow investors to make a profit without purchasing the underlying asset in the currency options contract. Within this contract, investors can use leverage to maximize profit and make decent returns, even when price movements are small. It is important to remember that profits need to be limited to keep a manageable cap on losses.

Because selling currency options involves a high amount of risk, it is common for investors to only buy currency options. The ability to sell currency options is usually limited to individuals who can maintain large amounts of capital protection.

Two currency/Forex trading options are available to you as an investor: Single payment options trading (SPOT) options and call/put options.

SPOT options are generally more expensive than regular options, but they are easy to set up and manage. For example, say you buy a SPOT option as you determine that the EUR/USD currency rate will be over 1.3225 in twenty days. If this prediction comes true, the SPOT will be paid out to you automatically.

Chapter 7.

Trading Strategies

Whether you are a beginner, average trader, or experienced options trader, there are strategies you need to use to make options work for you. When it comes to options trading, you do not need to be a genius to make it.

Many traders invest in options without the necessary information. This is one mistake that results in self-doubt and lack of confidence in the trade. People who do this often give up as soon as they start. With the right strategies in place, you can easily make income, secure your capital, and make the volatile nature of options to work in your favor.

Trading strategies help you reduce risks and maximize profits. If you do not have any strategy to follow, the business can become difficult and costly. Options strategies vary from simple to sophisticated ones but have one thing in common – they are all based on put and call operations. The payoffs do vary greatly, and before you settle on a strategy, be sure to understand how it works, the expected gain, and the risks involved. As a beginner, do not get overwhelmed with many strategies since you only need a few basic ones to get started. You can add more of these to your trading plan as you master the game.

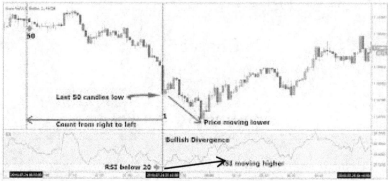

FIG10. e.g. of strategy, Bullish divergence pattern, you can buy

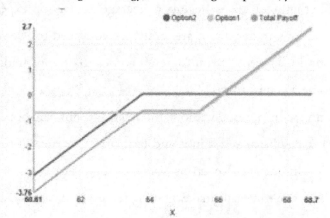

FIG11. Example of Options Trading Strategy

Options trading strategies can be divided into three categories - conservative long-term strategies, semi-conservative or short-term, also known as aggressive strategies.

- Conservative strategies are accomplished on a long-term basis. These allow you to build your capital in a slow but steady process. The benefit of such strategies is that they reduce the risk of losing your capital.

- Semi-conservative strategies consist of four to six trades per day. These are more aggressive than conservative strategies and involve more risk as well.

- Aggressive strategies allow numerous trades each day. These often result in higher risks and small profits.

You can define the type of strategies you need. If you are a day trader, then aggressive strategies will suit you better. Now, let us look at some of the strategies you need to understand to get started in options trading.

FIG12. Example of entry and exit points for day trading activities

Strategies Related to Calls

The process of buying and selling calls is one of the easiest in the options trading field. It is one of the popular and frequently used ways to get into options trading. This is because it allows you to own stock, using very little capital. Buying calls also presents you with a higher profit potential than purchasing stock.

- Covered Calls
- Bull Call Spread
- Long Call

- Long Call Butterfly Spread
- Short Call

Strategies Related to Puts

Buying of puts is one strategy you should use anytime you notice the market taking a direction against your call options. Traders buy puts whenever there is a possibility of the prices going down. Buying puts is the opposite of buying calls. Here are some strategies related to the put option that may be of benefit.

Cash Secured Puts

This is the opposite of covered calls. This strategy requires you to sell puts against a liquid cash balance in your broker account. The only people who use this strategy are investors anticipating a decline in the stock price or those traders who wish to generate some profit from excess cash that is in their possession. Through selling puts against their cash, they can make some profit. Generally, this strategy involves selling put options while saving enough cash on the side to purchase the underlying stock. It allows you to get stock options at discounted prices and sell them at a profit. The goal is to acquire the underlying stock at a price that is below the market price. When the stock goes below the strike price, the put is assigned, and the trader is allowed to buy the stock. The process involves a lot of risks since the stock may decrease way below the strike price, and this means that you may be required to purchase the shares at an amount that is above the current stock price. This comes as a loss to you, especially if the prices keep going down.

Married Put

This is where an investor buys stock and equivalent put options simultaneously. You can sell the put option at the strike price. Just like the covered call, each married put contract requires 100 shares. In this case, the trader is positive that the stock value will rise but uses a put option as insurance should the value go down. The married put strategy is common in investors who have a vision of minimizing the downside risk of their stock. When an investor buys the shares and an option, he protects his stock from loss should a negative event occur and makes some cash as the stock's value increases. However, if the stock does not go down, the investor loses the cash placed on the put option as a premium.

The married put has so many similarities with the covered call. It gets its name from combining or marrying a put option with the underlying stock. For every 100 shares, you are only allowed to buy one put option. The maximum profit for this strategy is undefined. The more the stock appreciates, the higher the profits. One downside of this strategy lies in the cost of premiums. The put option increases in value as the stock value declines, and because of this, the trader loses the costplaced on the option. Such losses, however, cannot be compared to the value of the underlying stock, which would have been saved in the process.

Protective Collar

The protective collar strategy comprises of an out-of-the-money put option and a call option that run concurrently. This strategy is not so common in beginners, but if you master it correctly, you can lock some good profits from it. The combination of call and put options allows you to have downside protection to your stock while enjoying potential profits on the upside. It is the same as running the covered call and protective put strategies at the same time.

Investors use this strategy as another option to stop orders since they have the right to choose when to exercise their options. You can use this strategy with little or no cost since the premium you get from the short call can be used to cancel out the long put. The strategy is called a collar because it helps you limit both downside and upside risk.

Chapter 8.

Bullish Options Trading Strategies

This procedure is used when there is a foreseen ascend in the estimation of the basic stock. As it were, it is utilized when there is a normal increment in the costs of the basic instrument. Securities exchanges are going up or down, contingent upon the encompassing developments. Every development has a positive or negative effect contingent upon the gathering in question. One may wind up winning gigantic benefits while the other may wind up with misfortunes.

Long Call Strategy

It is the most basic strategy in options trading and the one that is quite easy to comprehend. In the long call strategy for options trading, aggressive option traders who happen to be bullish are pretty much involved. It implies that bullish options traders end up buying stock during the trading activities with the hope of it rising shortly. The reward is unlimited in the long call strategy.

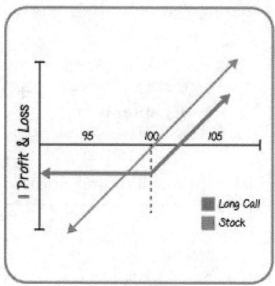

FIG13. Long Call vs Stock

Covered Call Strategy

In an exposed call, a dealer sells call alternatives without fundamentally having responsibility for the hidden instruments. The broker must claim the hidden instrument whose call choice is being sold or composed in a secured call system. The speculator can limit dangers and increment benefits. The financial specialist needs to practice its offers at a predetermined cost. A financial specialist purchases the hidden resource a similar way the person buys different resources. This technique guarantees that in any event, when there is a probability of the estimation of the basic instrument diminishing, the earning of income through premium.

Bull Call Spread Strategy

Financial specialists buy call alternatives at a predetermined strike cost and, thus, sell them at an expanded strike cost. While purchasing or selling, the call alternatives hold the expiry date and the fundamental resource. This system can be used when there is a potential increment in the costs of the basic stock. It can likewise be alluded to as a vertical spread procedure. They can limit the odds of bringing about a misfortune as they expand the potential benefit. While doing this exchange, the premium spent might be limited, and the financial specialist's upside might be decreased.

Bull Put Spread Strategy

Bull Put Spread is a vertical spread strategy where the investor sells a put option at a higher strike price, indicated in point B, and buys a put option with a lower strike price, point A, during the same month of fall.

The investor uses this strategy if they believe the market will make stable or trade higher. The lower position option is used as hedging in case the market is trading lower so that the investor can limit his maximum loss.

Bearish Options Trading Strategies

This kind of technique is used when a merchant envisions that the estimation of a hidden resource will decrease. We can say it is utilized when the costs of the basic resource are relied upon to fall. At the point when this occurs, it presents an enormous chance of getting loses.

Long Put Strategy

In this kind of plan, when you become bearish, that is the moment you may purchase a put option. Put option puts the trader in a situation where he can sell his stock at a time before the expiration date reached. This strategy exposes the trader to a mere kind of risk in the options trading market.

Covered Put Strategy

One or more contracts sold with 100 shares multiplied with the strike price amount for every particular contract involved in the options trading. Most traders use this strategy to acquire an extra amount of premium on a specific stock they would wish to purchase.

Synthetic Put Strategy

An option strategy that involves buying or owning the stock and then buying a put option at the strike price A.

This strategy is generally applied when the investor is nervous about the market and wants protection in disguise while allowing a return on investment. The protection option acts as a minimum price, limiting the amount an investor can lose if stock continues to fall. Once the stock moves below the protective position option's strike price, the investor is protected from additional losses.

Bear Call Spread Strategy

A vertical spread options strategy in which the investor sells a call option at a lower strike price, represented by point A, and buys a call option at a higher strike price, lower, point B, during the same month of fall. An investor entering this trade has a potential profit that is limited to the premium he received during the execution of the trade and a potential loss once the stock exceeds the short strike price by a greater amount than the first receipt.

Investors use this strategy if they believe the market will be stable or trade lower. The higher option is used as hedging in case the market is trading higher so that the investor can limit his maximum loss.

Bear Put Spread Strategy

A bear put spread is a sort of methodology whereby a speculator foresees that the costs of basic resources lower. When there is a decrease in the costs, the financial specialist can experience misfortune or a benefit contingent upon the side they are in during this frequency. At the point when the market is in support of themselves, they are probably going to encounter a benefit.

It guarantees that the financial specialist acquires negligible misfortunes and diminished dangers. Simultaneously, the speculator is probably going to encounter expanded benefits or capital increase.

Short Straddle Strategy

In this kind of strategy, the trader sells both the call and put options at a similar price and bearing the same expiration date. Traders practice this strategy with the hope of acquiring reasonable amounts of profits and experience various limited kinds of risks.

Short Strangle Strategy

A small strike involves selling put and put options with the same underlying value, the same strike price, and the same expiration date. Point A represents the sales pitch and point B, the call sales in the chart below. With a short acceleration, credit is received, and they reach a maximum profit when the stock remains around the two strike prices. This strategy works perfectly when the stock has little movement to expire.

The investor will receive his maximum profit if the trade ends at strike prices at maturity, which means the investor will win the call and put the sides on hold, keeping the full premium of both positions.

Neutral Options Trading Strategies

They are additionally alluded to as non-directional systems. This technique is used when a broker doesn't have a clue whether the estimation of the fundamental instrument will increase or diminish.

The costs of the advantage may move upwards or downwards; however, the speculator may not know about the bearing that the stock is probably going to take. At the point when the costs go upwards, the financial specialist could cause misfortune or a benefit. On the other hand, when the costs go downwards, the speculator could acquire a misfortune or a benefit.

Long Call Butterfly Strategy

In a long butterfly margin using call options, an investor will combine a bullish margin strategy and a bearish margin strategy that uses three different strike prices which options are for the same underlying asset and the same expiration date.

Long Put Butterfly Strategy

This strategy involves three parts where one put option is purchased and then selling the other two options at a price lower than the buying price and purchasing one put at even lower price during a specific trading period.

Long Straddle Strategy

The puts profit by a descending movement, and the calls profit by an upward development of the fundamental resource. Contingent upon the side in which a financial specialist ends up, they can either benefit from a major misfortune.

This methodology endeavors to acquire a pay from flighty moves. It includes buying a put or a call alternative. If you are a learner, it isn't fitting to use this procedure. You might not be able to foresee the conceivable market move and wind up getting tremendous misfortunes. It is consistently prudent that you do a historical verification of the procedure before giving it a shot.

Long Strangle Strategy

The financial specialist holds a situation in both a put alternative and a call choice. The call and the put alternatives have comparable basic resources and the lapse date yet with various strike costs. On the off chance that the financial specialist is cheerful that the costs of the basic resources are probably going to expand, this is a decent procedure to embrace. The drawback is that the costs of the basic instrument may rise strongly. At the point when this occurs, a financial specialist may wind up bringing about a misfortune as opposed to the normal ascent in benefit. In a long choke, the speculator will buy an out-of-the-cash put alternative and an out-of-the-cash call choice. The present market cost is lower than the basic resource strike cost of the call choice.

On the off chance that you are sure that there will be an upward development in the stocks, this is a decent technique to utilize.

Chapter 9.

Brokers

For selecting brokers, you have many options available. Understanding the differences between them and selecting the ones best suited for your purposes is crucial if you wish to succeed. Another area that many beginners ignore and then receive a rude lesson in is the regulations surrounding options trading.

Choosing a Broker

Generally, there are two major varieties of brokers: Discount and full service. A lot of full-service brokers have discount arms these days so that you will see some overlap. Full service refers to an organization where brokerage is just a part of a larger financial supermarket.

The broker might offer you other investment solutions, estate planning strategies, and so on. They'll also have an in-house research wing, which will send you reports to help you trade better. Besides this, they'll also have phone support in case you have questions or wish to place an order.

Once you develop a good relationship with them, a full-service broker will become a good organization to network. Every broker loves a profitable customer since it helps with marketing. A full-service broker will have good relationships in the industry, and if you have specific needs, they can put you in touch with the right people.

The price of all this service is you paying higher commissions than average. It is up to you to see whether this is a good price for you to pay. You need not sign up with a full-service broker to trade successfully. Order matching is done electronically, so it's not as if a person on the floor can get you a better price these days. Therefore, a full-service house will not give you better execution.

Discount brokers, on the other hand, are all about focus. They help you trade, and that is it. They will not advise, at least not intentionally, from a business perspective, and phone ordering is nonexistent. That doesn't mean they reduce customer service, far from it.

Commissions will be lower as well, far lower than what you can expect to pay at a full-service house. The downside of a discount brokerage is that you will not receive any product recommendations or solutions outside of your speculative activities. Many people prefer to trade (using a separate account) with the broker they have their retirement accounts with; they keep so everything in-house.

So, which one should you choose? Well, if you aim to keep costs as low as possible, then select a discount broker. Only where you're keen on keeping things in one place should you choose a full-service broker. These days, there's no difference between the two options otherwise.

An exception here is if you have a sizeable amount of capital, the worth of half a million dollars. In such cases, a full-service broker will be cheaper because of their volume-based commission offers. You'll pay the same rate or as close to what a discount broker would charge you, and you get all the additional services. Whatever additional amounts you need to invest can be handled by the firm through their wealth management line of business.

There are a few terms you must understand, no matter which broker you choose, so let's look at these now.

Margin

Margin refers to the number of assets you currently hold in your account. Your assets are cash and positions. As the market value of your positions fluctuates, so does the amount of margin you have. Margin is an important concept to grasp since it is at the core of your risk management discipline. When you open an account with your broker, you will have a choice to make. You can open either a cash or margin account. To trade options, open a margin account. Briefly, a cash account does not include leverage within it, so all you can trade are stocks. There are no account minimums for a cash account, and they're minuscule even if they are. A margin account, on the other hand, is subject to weird rules. First, the minimum balances for a margin account are higher. Most brokers will impose a $10,000 minimum, and some will increase this amount based on your trading style. The account minimum achieves nothing by itself, but it acts as a commitment of sorts for the broker.

The thinking is that with this much money on the line, the person trading will be more serious about it and won't blow it away. If only it worked like that. Anyway, the minimum balance is a hard and fast rule. Another rule you should know is the Pattern Day Trader (PDT) designation.

PDT is a rule that comes directly from the SEC. We classify anyone who executes four or more orders within five days as a PDT ("Pattern Day Trader," 2019). Once this tag is slapped onto you, your broker will ask you to post at least $25,000 in the margin as a minimum balance. Again, this minimum balance does nothing, but the SEC figures that if you screw up, this gives you enough of a buffer.

Each strategy plays out over a month or more, so once you enter, all you need to do is monitor it, and you can adjust it. However, if you avoid the PDT, you're only limited to entering just three positions per workweek. My advice is to study the strategies and to start slowly. Trade only one instrument at first and see how it goes and then expand once you gain more confidence. At that point, you'll have enough experience to figure out how much capital you need. Remember that even exiting a position is considered a trade, so PDT doesn't refer just to trade entry.

Margin Call

One other aspect of margin you must understand is the margin call. This is a dreaded message for most traders, including institutional ones. The purpose of all risk management is to keep you as far away from this ever happening to you. A margin call is issued when you have inadequate funds in your account to cover its requirements.

Remember that your margin is the combination of the cash you hold plus the value of your positions. If you have $1000 in cash, but your position is currently in a loss of -$900, you'll receive a margin call to post more cash to cover the potential loss you're headed for. You'll receive it well in advance. If you don't post more margin, your broker has the right to close out your positions and recover whatever cash they can to stop their risk limits from being triggered.

The threshold beyond which your broker will issue a margin call is called the maintenance margin. Usually, you need to maintain 25% of your initial position value (that is when you enter a position) as cash in your account. Most brokers have a handy indicator that tells you how close you are to the limit.

Execution

A favorite pastime of unsuccessful traders is to complain about execution. Their losses are always the broker's fault, and if it weren't for the greedy brokers, they'd be rolling in the dough, diving in and out of it like Scrooge McDuck. Complaining about your execution will get you nothing. A big reason for these complaints is that most beginner traders don't realize that the price they see on the screen is not the same as what is being traded on the exchange. We live in an era of high-frequency trading, and the markets' smallest measurement of time has gone from second to microseconds. Trades are constantly pouring in, and the matching engine is always finding suitable sellers for buyers. Given the pace of the market, it is important to understand that it is impossible to figure out the exact price of an instrument. Therefore, within your risk management plan, you must make allowance for high volatility times when the fluctuations will be bigger. I want you to understand that just because the price you received differed from what was on screen doesn't mean the broker is incompetent.

There are many different types of orders your average broker offers you. Do not get bogged down trying to figure them all out. Institutional traders use most of them for specific strategies. To trade well, you do not need to understand a single word of what those orders are about. Stick to the ones mentioned here, and you can trade successfully.

Price Quotes

Many traders are stumped when they first look at their trading screens and see that there are two prices for everything. After all, every financial channel always displays one price for security, but when trading, you'll be quoted two different prices within the price box. This is a small but crucial detail for you to understand.

The lower price you receive is called the bid, and this is the price you will pay if you sell the instrument. The higher price is the ask, and this is what you will pay to buy the instrument. The single price you see on your TV screen is the "Last Traded Price" or LTP. Do not make the mistake of thinking the LTP is the actual price since the market moves constantly. Even the spread (the difference between the ask and the bid) doesn't accurately reflect the genuine state of things thanks to constant movement. There's no need to worry, if volatility is stable, the difference isn't much. Just remember to look at the spread to understand what you'll be paying. The spread increases and contracts constantly, but if you see that it is getting too big, this is a sign that too much volatility exists, and you're better off staying out.

Chapter 10.

Financial Leverage

The process of using borrowed capital (debt) to increase the shareholder's return on their investments or equity in capital structure is called as Financial leverage or Trading on equity. The financial leverage analysed by the firm is intended to earn more return on the fixed charge funds rather than their costs. The surplus will increase the return on owner's equity whereas the deficit will decrease the return on owner's equity. Financial leverage affects the EPS (Earnings per share). When the EBIT increases, then EPS increases.

For example, If the firm borrows a debt from creditors for $1000 at 7% interest per annum i.e. $70and invests this debt to earn 12% return on this i.e. $120 per annum. Then the difference of surplus i.e. $50 which is after interest payment done to the creditors of the firm will belongs to the shareholders or owners of the firm and it is referred to as profit from financial leverage. Conversely, if the firm would earn 5% return, then the firm has loss of $20 (i.e. $70 - $50) to the shareholders.

The rate of interest on debt is fixed and it is legal binding to pay the interest by the firm to its creditors. The rate of preference dividend is also fixed to pay to shareholders of the firm by the company. Highly leveraged companies may be at risk of bankruptcy if they are unable to make payment on their debt, but it can increase shareholder's return on their investment and there are tax advantages associated with leverage.

Financial leverage ratio = EBIT / EBT

Financial leverage ratio is used to analyze the Capital structure and financial risk of the company. It explains how the fixed interest-bearing loan capital affects the operating profit of the firm. If EBIT is more than EBT, this ratio becomes more than 1. A slightly higher the ratio is favorable i.e. if this ratio is marginally more than 1, that is nearer to 1, it indicates moderate use of debt capital, low financial risk and good financial judgement.

Financial leverage Measures

The most common measures of Financial leverage are as under:-

(i) Debt ratio :-
Debt ratio is also referred to as Debt-to-Assets ratio. It is the ratio of total debt to total assets that are financed by debt. The Debt ratio is also known as Ratio of Debt to total capital.

Debt Ratio = Total Debt (TD) / CE or Total Assets

Here :-
CE (Capital Employed) = Total Debt (TD) + Net worth (equity)
TD = Short term Debt + long term Debt + Secured Loans + Un secured loans + Bonds + Debentures
Net worth = Equity Share Capital + Preference Share Capital + Reserves + Surplus

- Fictitious assets
Fictitious Assets = Unabsorbed portion of Deferred revenue expenditure i.e.
Advertisements, Preliminary expenses, Samples, Loss on issue of shares, etc...
Total assets = NFA + Current Assets (CA)
or
Total assets = Total liabilities + Shareholder's equity
Current Assets mean the assets which are converted in to cash within a short period of
one year i.e. Cash-in-hand, Cash-at-bank, Closing Stock, Sundry Debtors, Bills
Receivable, Prepaid Expenses, Advances given and Marketable Securities (Trade
investment).

The Debt ratio can help investors to determine a company's risk level. Companies with higher levels of debt compared with assets are considered as highly leveraged and more risky for lenders. A lower the ratio is more favorable because creditors are always looking about being repaid. When companies borrow more money from creditors or lenders, their debt ratio will be increase and there by the companies unable to get loans from creditors or Financial Institutions.

(ii) Debt equity ratio:

The relationship describing the lender's contribution for each rupee of owner's contribution is called Debt-Equity ratio. This ratio is used for long term solvency, capital structure & risk, financial stability and managerial efficiency of the firm.

Debt Equity ratio = Total Debt (TD) / Net worth (equity)

Here:

TD = Short term Debt + long term Debt + Secured Loans + Un secured loans +
Bonds + Debentures
Net worth = Equity Share Capital + Preference Share Capital + Reserves + Surplus
- Fictitious assets

Fictitious Assets = Unabsorbed portion of Deferred revenue expenditure i.e.
Advertisements, Preliminary expenses, Samples, Loss on issue of shares, etc...
A too higher this ratio indicates that more investment of loan capital than
equity capital which is high risk because of a higher claim of outsiders to the
firm. A lower this ratio than standard is favourable which indicates that more
use of equity capital than debt capital which is low financial risk. A very lower
the ratio indicates a sound long term solvency, low risk, conservative capital
structure, low profitability and inefficient managerial efficiency.

(iii) Interest coverage ratio:

This ratio is used to test debt servicing capacity of the firm and measures the
long-term solvency of the firm.

Interest coverage ratio = EBIT / Fixed interest charges

or

Interest coverage ratio = EBITDA / Interest

Here:

EBITDA = Earnings before Interest, Tax, Depreciation and Amortization.
Interest coverage is calculated in relation to before tax earnings.
Depreciation is non-cash item. Therefore, funds equal to depreciation are
also available to pay interest charges. Thus, calculate this ratio as EBITDA
divided by Interest. The limitation of this ratio is it does not consider
repayment of loan.

Financial leverage and Shareholder's return:

The role of a firm in using financial leverage is to maximize the shareholder's
return based on fixed- charges funds i.e. debentures or debt (loans)from
banks and financial institutions. This debt can be obtained at a cost lower

than the firm's rate of return on Net assets (RONA) or Return on Investment (ROI). Hence, EPS and ROE (Return on equity) will be increase, but if the firm obtains fixed-charges funds at a cost higher than the RONA or ROI, the EPS and ROE will decrease. Therefore, we can say that the EPS, ROI and ROE are playing a vital role in analysing the impact of financial leverage.

Chapter 11.

Tools and Rules of Options Trading

Stash

The best app for beginner level trading for their investment decisions. It is a trading and investment app. This is the best choice for your needs. Stash charges $5 to start investing, it helps in what to invest and gives you more information on your investments. The app also has essential articles and tips to help you improve your investment knowledge. Your finances go into single stocks and ETF's, which are incorporated into different investment themes. Stash also has a built-in investment coach.

Stockpile

With Stockpile, you will be able to buy and sell stocks. You can also gift single shares or buy a part of the shares with a minimum of 99-cent trade fees. Using your account, you can purchase high-valued stocks like Google and Amazon using the fractional trades. And you won't have to pay $1,000 or even more per share. Stockpile is very suitable for families because of the buying and gifting shares of a stock feature. Kids, teenagers, and the whole family can have portfolios and can be able to teach your family the importance of investing, and this can become a family activity. Teach your children about money and investment early and buy shares or gift them with some stocks. By engaging them, they will be able to grow a valued portfolio.

Charles Schwab

The app enables you to manage your investment and bank accounts all in one app. Schwab also has a feature to allow you to transfer funds, deposit your checks, and manage your finances. You are also able to buy and sell stocks, ETFs, and mutual funds. Schwab is a favorite with international travelers because it offers a checking ATM card whenever it has no extra fees. Schwab is user-friendly; you can log in to your Android, Apple, and Kindle fire devices to check your investments. You can also pay bills on the app.

TD Ameritrade

The app is very user-friendly and straightforward to navigate. It is suitable for new option traders. TD Ameritrade offers 24/7 access to customer support via the phone and through email support. The user can also visit their many local branches to get assistance, and the service can provide research to their users. TD Ameritrade has no hidden charges, and it does not charge platform fees, and there is no minimum trade fee. The app charges a flat-rate commission of $6.95 equity trade and $0.75 per contract.

Trade Station Mobile

This app is one of the high rated apps, and it is free for all Trade Station clients. The users can see different options contracts with different prices and expiration dates. Trade Station app offers up-to-date information which the traders can access, and they can run options analysis, and the traders can view charts with various technical indicators. The app has notification features, and the traders can monitor the price changes and other indicators. Trade Station is a full-service trading app that offers access to stocks, futures options, and forex trading.

The Rules Used in Option Trading

What are the guidelines to follow in options trading? What are the rules? These are essential questions new traders should be able to answer correctly. We will go through the rules that you should follow in options trading. And by the end of this topic, you will have the knowledge needed to trade efficiently. For a new emerging trader, these rules will be an eye-opener, while for an experienced options trader, it will be as a reminder. These rules won't be a get-rich tip, and the rules will help you stay out of trouble, increase your capital, and improve your money with options. Here are some of the rules used on options trading:

Trade Small Positions

When you get into the market, it's obvious to assume the worse. It only makes sense to make smaller trades and avoid big trades to reduce the risk of losing a significant amount of the money you had invested. The best tip is to make lots of small positions because if you make just one large, you risk being knocked out when you hit a loss. About 90% of options traders fail because they trade large position sizes. Trading over 5% is considered a large position, and the trader risk affecting their accounts from a bad loss.

Don't Be Emotional

The market doesn't care what you think; one of the ways to be successful in trading is not to be emotional. Don't allow your emotions, opinions, or thoughts on the market to lead you.

Have a High Trade Count

By knowing your estimated percentage chance of success, you will make a lot of trades. The higher the trade count, the higher the chances of leveling out at that expected percentage. Options trading is a number game and math, and you can pinpoint your probabilities of success in each position. You can see your percentage chance of success; however, this can be the reason for your failure as you will have the same expectation in all your trades. So, the higher the trade count you make, the more consistent your percentage success rate will be.

Balance Your Portfolio

You can bet the price direction if it goes up or down when you invest in options trading. Traders tend to focus on the investment value going up; however, you must learn how to balance your portfolio with positions going down.

Trade According to Your Comfort Level

If you are not comfortable trading naked options or if hedged positions give you sleepless nights, then you should trade options as a speculator forming opinions and act on them accordingly. Once you are in tune with your strategies, you will realize it will be much easier to make money. Each strategy is unique and individual, and it might not work for all traders. By doing this, you will lower the individual's risk level.

Always Use a Model

Failure to check the fair value of the option before it's sold or bought is one of the biggest mistakes option traders make. It can be hard, especially if you don't have an exact real-time evaluation capability. These are the basis of the strategic investment and be aware of the bargains and the amount you are paying for the option.

Have Enough Cash Reserve

It's essential to have a lot of your investment money in cash. It might be useful for brokers as they need a margin requirement when trading. They partition some amount to cover potential losses on your position. Try to keep about 50-60% of your investment portfolio in cash.

Reduce Commissions and Fees

Paying commissions and fees to transact and rebalance your portfolio might be crippling you. One of the ways to lower the percentage of the charges is by using low-cost ETF's. But for a beginner, you shouldn't pay any fees to invest in stocks.

Chapter 12.

Benefits of Options Trading

With the mention of an investment, you want to make sure that you are working with a choice that will make you money. No one wants to get into an investment that will have them lose all their money. But part of the point of an investment is that it does carry some risk. Hopefully, you can pick out an investment that has a much higher reward than the risk to it so that you can earn money.

There are a variety of options that you can choose when it comes to your choice of investments. You can choose to do real estate, put the money in retirement, trade on the stock market, and even start your own business. With all these other options to choose from, why would you want to choose options as your investment vehicle? Here are some of the benefits of choosing options trading over some of the other investment options when you are ready to put your money to work for you.

Why You Should Use Options

Some people scared of ever getting into the derivatives trading market, lamenting that it is a very risky pursuit, but that's not the case. Of course, there are instances when options can be risky, yet there are also situations wherein options can help you minimize risk. It all comes down to how you utilize them. Options take less financial commitment than equities, and they are also resistant to the negative effects of gap openings.

A good reason to go with buying options is that you will be able to limit your risk to just the amount of money you pay for the premium. With other investment options, you could end up losing a lot of money, even money that you did not invest, to begin with, but this does not happen when you are working with options.

Let's say that you saw that the prices of cows were about to go up. You could pay some money upfront and enter into a contract with someone else to sell your five cows for $2,000. Since you are working with an options contract, you do not have to buy the cows upfront.

On the other hand, if you had gone up to the other person and purchased those cows straight up for $10,000, you could end up in trouble. For this example, the price of the cows may end up falling by $500, rather than going up by $500, and you would end up losing $2,500 in the process. Since you went into the options contract, you would stand to lose no more than $250 if the prices were to fall afterward. You still stand to lose some money, but it is a lot less than you would have lost otherwise.

Cost Efficiency

The leveraging power of options is great. Thus, a trader may acquire an option position like a stock position at a significantly lower price. With options trading, it is possible to make great profits without necessarily having large amounts of money. Individuals that operate on a tight budget have found options trading very accommodating. An intelligent trader can employ leverage to increase their trading power without necessarily injecting more capital.

Let's suppose that you had $1000 and wanted to invest in a company whose stock was trading at $20 per share. On the one hand, you could elect to buy the company's stocks and thus acquire 50 shares. If the stock price increases to $25, you would make $5 profit for every share you own, and your total profit would be $250. This is a 25% return on investment! On the other hand, you could purchase call options on the same stock and gain the right to purchase it. If the call options with a $20 strike price were trading at $2, you could purchase 500 options, which would enable you to purchase 500 shares. If the stock price increased to $25, you could exercise your option to purchase 500 shares and, upon selling your shares, you'd make a total of $2500. This is a staggering 150% return on investment! The greatest appeal of options trading is that it enables traders to execute cost-efficient trades even as it widens their earning capacity.

Better Leverage for the Money

When working with options, it can provide you with some good leveraging power. A trader will be able to buy an option position that will imitate their stock position quite a bit, but it will save them a lot of money.

Let's say that you saw that there was an opportunity to make a profitable trade, you were only able to spare about $1000 to purchase the stock, but you didn't know what options were available. If we were still talking about the cows from before, you would not be able to purchase even one cow for the money (remember that they are about $2,000 each without the options contract), and so you would completely miss out on the possibility to make a profit.

But, if you decided to purchase with an options contract, rather than purchasing the underlying asset outright, the dynamics have completely changed. This could result in an investment of just $250 to get started. The premium on the options contract is a fraction of the total cost, allowing you to get in on the trade for a lot less money. If you check options contracts, you will be able to make more purchases, and potentially more money, compared to some of the other stock choices you can make.

Higher Percentage of Returns

As mentioned, an options trader is only going to pay a fraction of the value of the asset to have some control over that asset. This will allow the trader to earn more money than what they would be able to earn when purchasing the asset upfront and then try to sell it.

Going back to the idea of the cows, the market price at the beginning of this trade is $2,000. For a regular cattle trader, one who doesn't know anything about options had the $2,000 in hand and believed that the cattle's price would go up, he would have the opportunity to purchase a cow. If the cows' price goes up to $2,500, this trader will only be able to make a profit of $500. This isn't bad, but since there is a big risk with this option, it is not always the best.

On the other hand, a trader who knows a bit about options will be able to do things differently. If you had $2,000, you could choose to purchase eight options contracts, with a premium of $50. This means that you now have the purchasing rights for a total of 40 cows rather than the one cow the other trader had.

With the same profit of $500 per cow, your profit would be $18,000 (this includes the $500 per cow minus the $2,000 you spent in the beginning to purchase the contracts). You earned thousands of dollars more than the original trader, but you used the same amount of money to get started.

Flexibility and versatility

Another benefit of options is the flexibility that they offer. For instance, if your investment approach is to buy and hold, you will buy stocks either for the long term or short term. The long-term stocks should appreciate over time, and the short-term stocks should perform faster for regular dividends. The investment strategy of buying stocks doesn't confer to investors avenues of risk limitation or strategies of increasing their earning potential. As a stock trader, the method of earning a profit is linear, i.e., you either buy stocks that you think will appreciate or short sell stocks that you think will depreciate. But when it comes to options trading, the flexibility and versatility afford many investor opportunities of earning huge profits as dictated by the prevailing markets. Options can be purchased or sold based on a wide selection of underlying assets. You can speculate on the movement of a stock price, commodities, foreign currencies, indices, etc. The challenge is to identify opportunities for profitable trades. Spreads can make your trades more flexible, and they can be applied in hedging positions as well, which is a critical step during uncertain market conditions. A trader can also profit from stagnant markets by utilizing options spreads, an action that is hard to replicate in stock trading.

Helps to Hedge Intraday or Futures Trades

It is common for traders to purchase or short-sell Futures contracts because they expect them to move in one direction or another. Intraday traders may do the same thing because they will purchase many shares in the hopes that they will move down or up during that day. If the trader ends up picking the wrong direction on the Futures or the intraday trades, they may lose a lot of weight. Unless you put in a stop-loss, you can lose an unlimited amount of money in the process.

You may not be complaining when this goes the right way, and you earn unlimited profits, but if you go with one of these trades and don't hedge your position, you will complain when you start losing a lot of money. If you understand how trading options work, you could buy a call or put options to help ensure that you are not going to end up with an unlimited loss. The right options choice is going to help control your loss when the intraday or futures positions start going against what you wanted.

Though there exist several great investment choices that you can make, none of them are going to limit your risk as much as options while still providing you with a great potential to make money in the process. This is a great investment for anyone, whether they are just getting started with investing or they have been in the market for a long time.

Can Options Work for You?

Even after you understand the benefits that the options offer, you may be wondering if you have what it takes to trade them profitably. That depends more on commitment than any innate ability. Almost anyone can learn to trade options successfully. You don't have to be a financial whiz or a stock market expert. The only math that's required is eighth-grade arithmetic.

Once you get a handle on the fundamentals, you have many choices about how to use options. Some strategies require a fair amount of skill and close attention to price movements. Others have a high probability of success and don't require a lot of time or attention.

When you're ready to start trading, it's important to get your feet wet by making simulated trades in a paper trading account where you aren't risking real money. Then you can take the subsequent step by trading in a live account and taking very small positions to limit your risk. From that point on, you can develop your options trading skills at your own pace and choose the strategies and levels of risk that best suit you. The possibilities are almost endless.

Chapter 13.

Hazard and Money Management

Great administration of your introduction to chance and your exchanging capital is crucial in any exchanging on the off chance that you can bring in cash over the long haul. There are various techniques you can use for overseeing hazards and controlling your spending plan. For example, utilizing choices spreads and position estimating; our article on hazard and cash the board covers a few of the best ones. We additionally offer guidance on the most proficient method to utilize them.

Effectively dealing with your capital and hazard introduction is basic when exchanging choices. While the chance is unavoidable with any venture, your introduction to it doesn't need to be an issue. The key is to deal with the hazard reserves viably; consistently making sure that you are okay with the degree of hazard being taken and that you aren't presenting yourself to unreasonable misfortunes. Similar ideas can be applied while dealing with your cash as well. You ought to exchange utilizing capital that you can stand to lose; abstain from overstretching yourself. As a powerful hazard and cash, the board is essential to fruitful choices exchanging. It's a subject that you truly need to comprehend. One of the reasonable employments of such an arrangement is to assist you in dealing with your cash and your hazard introduction. Your arrangement ought to incorporate subtleties of what level of hazard you are alright with and the measure of capital you need to utilize. By following your arrangement and just utilizing cash that you have explicitly designated for choices exchanging, you can maintain a strategic distance from probably the greatest error that financial specialists and merchants make utilizing "terrified" cash.

You are far more reluctant to settle on discerning choices in your exchanges when you are exchanging with cash that you either can't bear to lose or ought to have saved for different purposes. While it's hard to evacuate the feeling of being involved in alternatives exchanging, you truly need to be as centered as conceivable around what you are doing and why.

When feelings start to take control, you conceivably begin to lose your concentration and are at risk of acting unreasonably. It might make misfortunes from past exchanges turn sour, for instance, or making exchanges that you wouldn't normally make. If you follow your arrangement and stick to utilizing your speculation capital, then you should have a greatly improved potential for the success of monitoring your feelings.

Similarly, it would help if you held fast to the degrees of hazard in your arrangement. It's regularly enticing to do this, maybe because you have made a couple of misfortunes, and you need to attempt to fix them. Or perhaps you have done well with some okay exchanges and need to begin expanding your benefits at a quicker rate.

On the off chance that you wanted to make generally safe exchanges, at that point, you did so for a cause, and there is no reason for removing yourself from your customary range of familiarity given the equivalent enthusiastic reasons.

1. Overseeing Risk with Options Spreads

Alternatives spreads are significant and integral assets in choices exchanging. A choice spread is when you consolidate more than one situation on choices contracts dependent on the equivalent basic security to make one, in general, exchanging position adequately.

If, by any chance, you purchased a stock in cash approaches and, at that point, a similar stock worked less expensive out of the cash approaches, you would have made a spread known as a bull call spread. Purchasing the calls implies you remain to pick up if the fundamental stock goes up in esteem, yet you would lose a few or all the cash spent to get them if the cost of the stock neglected to go up. By composing approaches a similar stock, you would have the option to control a portion of the underlying expenses and, in this manner, lessen the most extreme measure of cash you could lose. All choices exchanging techniques include the utilization of spreads, and these spreads speak to a valuable method to oversee chance. You can utilize them to diminish the forthright expenses of entering a position and to limit how much cash you remain to lose, likewise with the bull call spread model. This implies you possibly diminish the benefits you would make. However, it decreases the general hazard.

Spreads can likewise be utilized to diminish the dangers included when entering a short position. For instance, if you wrote in cash puts on a stock, you would get a forthright installment for composing those choices. However, you would be presented to potential misfortunes if the stock declined in esteem. If you likewise purchased less expensive out of cash puts, you would need to invest a portion of your forthright installment; however, you would top any potential misfortunes that a decrease in the stock would cause. This specific kind of spread is known as a bull put spread.

As should be obvious from both these models, it's conceivable to enter positions where you, despite everything, stand to pick up if the value moves the correct route for you, and can carefully constrain any misfortunes you may bring about if the value moves against you. This is the reason spreads are so generally utilized by alternatives merchants; they are incredible gadgets for hazard the executives. There is a huge scope of spreads that can be utilized to exploit essentially any economic situation.

2. Overseeing Risk through Diversification

Expansion is a hazard the procedure that is normally utilized by financial specialists that are building an arrangement of stocks by utilizing a purchase and hold methodology. The fundamental standard of expansion for such financial specialists is that spreading speculations over various organizations and segments makes a fair portfolio, not a lot of cash tied up in one specific organization or part. A differentiated portfolio is commonly viewed as less presented to chance than a portfolio made up to a great extent of one explicit kind of venture.

With regards to choices, the broadening isn't significant in the same incredible way it does at present, have its uses, and you can expand in various manners. Although the standard to a great extent continues as before, you don't need a lot of your capital focused on one specific type of venture. You can enhance by utilizing a choice of various procedures, by exchanging alternatives that depend on a scope of basic protections, and by exchanging various kinds of choices. Utilizing broadening is that you remain to make benefits in various manners, and you aren't dependent on one specific result for every one of your exchanges to be fruitful.

3. Overseeing Risk Using Options Orders

A moderately straightforward approach to oversee hazard is to use the scope of various requests that you can put. Notwithstanding the four primary request types that you use to open and close situations, there are some extra requests that you can place, and a considerable lot of these can assist you with hazard the executives. For instance, an ordinary market request will be filled at the best accessible cost at the hour of execution. This is a flawlessly ordinary approach to purchase and sell choices, yet in an unpredictable market, your request may wind up getting filled at a higher or lower value than you need it to be. By utilizing limit orders, where you can set least and greatest costs at which your request can be filled, you can abstain from purchasing or selling at less good costs.

There are additionally arranges that you can use to robotize leaving a position: regardless of whether that is to secure benefit or to cut misfortunes on an exchange that has not turned out to be well, by utilizing requests, such as the cutoff stop request, the market stop request, or the trailing stop request, without much of a stretch control when you leave a position.

It will help you to maintain a strategic distance from situations where you pass up benefits by clutching a situation for a long time or causing large misfortunes by not finishing off on an awful position rapidly enough. By utilizing choices arranges suitably, you can confine the hazard you are presented to on every single exchange you make.

4. Cash Management and Position Sizing

Dealing with your cash is inseparably connected to overseeing hazards, and both are similarly significant. You, at last, have a limited measure of cash to utilize. As a result of this current, it's essential to keep tight control of your capital spending plan and ensure that you don't lose everything and get yourself unfit to make further exchanges.

The absolute most ideal approach to deal with your cash is to utilize a genuinely straightforward idea known as position estimating. The position estimating is fundamentally choosing the amount of your capital; you need to use it to enter a specific position. To successfully utilize position measuring, you must consider the amount to put resources into every individual exchange in terms of your general venture capital level. In numerous regards, position estimating is a type of expansion. By utilizing only, a little level of your capital in any exchange, you will never be excessively dependent on one explicit result. Indeed, even the best merchants will make exchanges that divert out severely every now and then, the key is to guarantee that the terrible ones don't influence you too seriously. For instance, if you have half of your venture capital tied up in one exchange, and it winds up losing you cash, you will have most likely lost a lot of your accessible assets. If you watch out for utilize 5% to 10% of your capital per exchange, at that point, even a couple of back to back losing exchanges shouldn't clear you out. Once you are sure that your exchanging plan will be fruitful over the long haul, at that point, you should have the option to get past the terrible periods and still have enough money to make something happen. Position measuring will assist you in doing precisely that.

Chapter 14.

Binary Options Trading

Binary Option is a method for investing in an asset price that has just two closing positions. A wise investment can be made if the closing area is estimated precisely. The most widely recognized option is the "High" or "Low" option. To begin, an understanding of the time length is fixed before making the expectation. The trader can anticipate a fixed return if, toward the end, the price lies on the right side of the started price.

The trader will lose the entirety he invested when the trade was opened If predicted incorrectly.

With an itemized investigation into buying and selling stocks, the straightforwardness at which one can place trades using Binary Options ends up visible.

An investor starts trading by selecting and purchasing a measure of a stock or an asset. By calculating the offer price individually, we can ascertain what the price of the asset is.

A trader can produce a decent return by selling his asset when the price has risen from the asset's price at the outset. In that manner, the investor will encounter a loss if the asset's selling price is not the exact price it was acquired. Complete learning and experience of numerous outcomes are fundamental to invest in these lines — an intensive understanding of how the financial market capacity is critical. The investor would need to be examined what the asset's price movements have been previously, how price-changing occasions influence the asset in the market, and how the asset's price will change in the future.

Up to now, there is no financial framework set up that can avert a Stock Market crash from occurring, and we are always updated in the media about how occasions can affect the market. To effectively bring these components together, the investor who routinely creates profitable returns knows and understands asset price switches and is sponsored by trading strategies and methods that can be actualized when the circumstance requests it.

Having no technique or understanding of assets and the market may leave you in your very own private sorrow what you have saved for investing will before long vanish. You won't have adequate assets to buy presents for the children at Christmas, and your accomplice may keep running off with somebody more proficient at investing their money than yourself!

What is appealing in the examination is that there is no compelling reason to buy into anything when investing with Binary Options. Binary investments highlight the prices of assets, and if the price of an asset will rise or fall. For this situation, you are trading exclusively on an up or down movement in the price of an asset. Consequently, it is an impressively, less unsafe investment opportunity.

Likewise, it is deserving of note that Binary Options Trading enables potential investors to get up and running without putting down enormous entireties to begin because the required investment sum can be a lot smaller. If an investor were looking to start trading on gold, which depended on the present estimation of gold, it would make it exceptionally difficult for many people to make it an advantageous asset to invest in. In Binary Options Trading, nobody is genuinely buying any gold; instead, traders are investing in price changes of gold over a set time frame.

Assets Available to Trade with Binary Options

Before we talk somewhat about gold, now would be a good time to dig into the sorts of assets regularly utilized for Binary Options Trading.

- Indices - An index is simply the market. It is conceivable to invest in the markets themselves.

- Forex - Or Foreign Exchange is worried about trade rates between significant currency sets, for example, the USD, the GBP, or the JP. You can trade on combinations of all these real monetary forms.

- Commodities - A crude material or essential rural item that can be purchased or sold, for example, Gold, Copper, or Coffee.

Selecting which asset to trade is the starting point for a trader. the magnificence of Binary Options Trading is that it is so natural to get up and to run.

Getting Started

Most trading stages give two necessary decisions regarding binary trading: The put option is chosen if the trader accepts that the cost will decline, while the call option is accessible, for if they receive that, the price will rise. All traders need to choose their position dependent on any number of market factors, and there are various trading methods and calculations that can be utilized, which will be secured later.

Before choosing your position, you will be required to pick a trading stage through which you will direct most of your trades. Selecting the correct broker to deal with your finances is essential to the accomplishment of your trades, particularly for new traders who need to benefit as much as possible from every single financial option. Not all brokers will most likely give you similar trading methods, much the same as not all brokers will have similar restrictions and profits accessible for their sites. New traders are prescribed not to stress over a portion of the more confounded binary trading methods. To start, pick a decent brokerage that offers a high rate on their profits, and check whether there are any incentive projects offered that you can exploit.

Tips to Keep in Mind

There is a wide range of tips and deceives that beginner traders can remember in request to increase their odds of profiting. A considerable amount of these tips is additionally intended to enable individuals to be more open to the trading background, particularly if they need a couple of dependable guidelines to remember as they trade. As the trader turns out to be increasingly experienced, they will most likely build up their own trading methods and frames of mind, which are explicitly structured to supplement their very own remarkable way of dealing with trading. Until further notice, in any case, merely remembering a couple of these essential tips can be enough to enable most traders to get a head start.

Let Emotions well enough alone for Your Trades

Maybe the most crucial suggestion to recollect is to never depend on hunches or natural desires. Trading binary options don't care for gambling or some other essential money-making process. While chance still assumes a job in determining your profits, most by far of them will be identified via deliberately examined indicators and adequately actualized strategies. Traders who depend on their instincts or any passionate associations with their finances will find that they will begin losing money in the long term, regardless of what inadvertent profits they may verify from the start.

Making genuinely determined trades is an extremely massive slip-up that, shockingly, numerous section level traders make. If your head isn't clear and you are not thinking objectively, you will wind up making trading botches. It is as straightforward as that. If you begin to feel baffled or irate with your trades or become too energized after successful ones, it is essential to take a step back, take a full breath, and think about taking a break.

Think About Yourself as a Trader

The best traders are simply the ones who know and realize what they need to escape their trades. These are individuals who have investigated different types of options and have chosen to work with ones that match their characters as traders. Short term trades are identified by brisk exchanges that occur in unstable situations, for example, sixty second and two-minute trades. Medium-term trades allude to any exchanges that can be made somewhere in the range of five and fifteen minutes. Long term trades, as the name infers, depict more extended expiry periods, which can go anyplace from an hour to multi-day, depending on the broker.

As should be evident from the range, there is a way to deal with each type, which defines the trader. If you flourish in quick paced situations and enjoy the dangers of dealing with instability, you will be more qualified to work with short term trades. Then again, if you enjoy a lower level of risk and plan on trading consistently if possible, you may generate profit by more extended expiry options. Understanding your degree of comfort and moving with it is essential for all traders.

Chapter 15.

How to Start Options Trading

lthough it seems complex and can include a wide range of strategic approaches, it's relatively easy to start trading options. You need a broker, and you will need to compare fees and account minimums so that you can choose one that is affordable and meets your investment style. From there, it's time to develop your strategy for trading options. Like most investment options, trading strategies is dependent on your personal goals and tolerance for risk and can range from simple to complex.

Step by Step Guide to Trading Options

Create a Brokerage Account

If you're interested in trading options, you'll need to open a brokerage to access your transactions — this can be done online or through a standard broker account. Be sure you fully grasp what's involved in creating a brokerage account before you do that.

Compare the options trading commissions between different brokerages. Some firms do not even offer commissions on trading options.

Carry out some research online and read the assessments of brokerage firms that are on your shortlist. Gain knowledge from the mistakes of other people so you won't have to repeat them.

Observe for scam trading platforms and sites. Always thoroughly research the platform before you deposit any money. Avoid any platform with negative assessments or possible fraud reported.

A cash account will only permit the purchase of options to create a position. If you desire to sell an option to set up an account without the underlying asset, you will need a margin account.

If you want to trade online, make sure that your online brokerage accepts secure forms of payment, like a secure credit card payment gateway or a third-party payment service such as PayPal, Payoneer, bitcoin, etc.

Get Approval to Trade Options

You will need approval from your brokerage before you start buying and selling options. Brokerage firms handling an account set limits based on experience and money in the account, and every firm has its criteria to ensure that the customer knows what they are doing. You can't write a covered call without an options account. Brokerage firms want to make sure that customers have a full understanding of the risks before trading.

Covered call writing means selling the right to purchase your stock at a strike price during the duration of the option. The buyer has the right to do so, not the seller. The stock must be in the brokerage account and cannot be sold or exchanged while the call is pending.

Understanding Technical Analysis

Options are typically short-term investments, so shortly, you will be searching for price movements of the optioned security to make a healthy return. To accurately forecast these price fluctuations, you would need to grasp the fundamentals of the technical analysis.

Learn about the level of support and resistance. These are points where the stock hardly ever decreases below (support) or increases above (resistance). Support is the level at which significant security purchases have historically occurred. Resistance is the price level, where significant security sales have occurred in the past.

Understand the significance of the volume. If a stock changes towards a specific direction with a lot of volume behind it, it typically means a strong trend and can be a money-making opportunity.

Understand the patterns of the chart. History usually repeats itself, even in the case of stock prices. There are common trends that you can look for in stock price fluctuations that show where the price is going.

Learn more about moving averages. It is the same case when the stock price is above or below the common moving average of the previous prices. A 30-day moving average is perceived to be more accurate than a 10-day moving average.

Start with "Paper Trading"

Resist every temptation to risk hard-earned money with a technique you've just learned.

Instead, go for paper trading or practice. Make use of a spreadsheet or a practice trading software to enter "pretend" trades. Then check your returns for at least a few months. If you make a decent return, work your way to real trading slowly.

Paper trading is different from real trading, as there is no mental pressure or commissions involved. It's a good idea to learn mechanics, but it's not a predictor of actual results. Real options trading is a very high risk, which can result in substantial losses for the investor. You can only trade with money that you can afford to lose.

Use the Limit Orders

Avoid having to pay market prices for options, as the execution price can be higher than expected. Instead, state your price with limit orders and maximize your return.

Reassess Your Strategy Regularly

Determine if there is anything that can be done to enhance your return. Learn from your mistakes, but repeat your effective strategies as well. And maintain a focused strategy; traders concentrate on a few positions, not on diversification. You should have not more than 10% of your investment portfolio in options.

Join a Forum of Traders of Like Minds Online

If you're experimenting with advanced trading options strategies, you'll discover that vital information (and help, after a few tough losses) is an online trading platform. Locate a forum to enable you to learn from the successes and, also, the failures of others.

Think of Other Strategies for Trading Options

After you have made some successful trades, you can get cleared for more advanced options trading strategies. However, start trading on paper as well. This will make it much simpler for you to carry them out in real trading.

One such strategy is the 'straddle,' which includes trading on both sides of the market, purchasing a put and a call option with the same strike price and date of maturation, so that you restrict your exposure. This strategy is most successful when the market moves up and down rather than in a single direction. There is also a risk that only one side will be exercisable.

A related strategy is the "strip." The strip is like a straddle but is a "bearish" strategy with twice the earning power of a downward price movement. It is comparable to the straddle in its implementation, but with twice as many options purchased on the downside (put options).

Know more about the Greeks

Once you've perfected simple options trading and choose to move on to more advanced options trading, you will have to learn about the "Greeks." These are measuring that traders use to maximize their returns.

Chapter 16.

Risk Management

Many experienced options traders find it relatively easy to make money but holding it can prove harder. As anyone can do, there must be another dimension to the trading option that has been ignored so far; otherwise, any trader would be through. This is the risk management dimension. Most of what professional traders can do is manage risk, play defense, and try to keep profits. If a market maker manages to keep a third of the bid-ask range, it will be very successful in the long run. Danger management tension is a key differentiator between amateurs and experts. There are two things to remember when putting risk management in perspective.

At times, it's fun to "take a shot" when you make a trade. This could have been for some reason. You might want to start trading with a new strategy. You might have a hunch that you simply can't get the hard evidence to validate. And you might need to swap to help the trader. It is never necessary, however, to "take a shot" when handling the risk. Risk management is far too important to take the chance. You just don't need to have any patience for errors. Professional option trading is not about making significant, unforgettable trades. It is about making low, predictable gains and keeping risks under control.

We should take care of the risks in the order of their Risk. We will split the risks into three groups.

Primary Risks
- Inventory
- Delta

Secondary Risks
- Gamma
- Jump risk

Vega (including skew and calendar risk)
Tertiary Risks
Correlation risk
- Rho
- Dividend risk
- Buy-in risk
- Early exercise
- Strike risk
- Pin risk

Stock Risk: Dividends and Buy-In Risk

Let's have a look at the case when a corporation declares a special dividend. Assume the stock is at $100, so we're long 1,000 out of a one-year 80 strike order. Assume the interest rate is negative, and the conditional uncertainty is 30%. The sum of this option is 23.53. When the corporation pays a dollar dividend, the interest of the call will decrease to 22.73. We're suddenly wasting $80,000. Remember that this is not going to support being hedged in the underlying. The dividend is gain to those who hold the shares, not to those who own the options.

It doesn't happen very often. So, when it does, it can be a huge concern. In

2004, Microsoft paid a special dividend of $3.08 as the shares traded $29.97. Beware of businesses sitting on a lot of funds. It is, of course, entirely probable to be harmed if we have a long stock, and the planned dividend is that. Nonetheless, the business option tends to be better at forecasting this. Generally, the rumors of payout cuts are beginning to surface well in advance of the real reduction, and the option sales are continuing to be sold at a lower cost. Finally, regular dividend yields appear to be much smaller than special dividends, so the cut in the normal dividend will not be as expensive as the declaration of a special dividend.

Pin Risk

Pin risk arises as the underlying interest reduces the effective interest of the option at expiration. Anyone short of these options is exposed to pin risk. The main risk is that it is difficult to determine whether the decision will be exercised.

Note that since the Risk of a pin is triggered by the probability of a given investor having an unplanned role in the underlying stock that he eventually must liquidate, it is not a matter of cash-setting options. There we earn cash for any expiring shares. Cash does not need to be unwound or liquidated until the economy is reopened. Nevertheless, cash-setting options have their expiration wrinkle.

Forward Risk

For most options, as the in-the-money option expires, we will obtain the corresponding position at the bottom (a long position for long calls, a short position for medium calls, a short position for short calls, and a medium position for short calls). As we keep the offset position as a buffer at the start, we're not going to have a net advantage until expiry.

That is not the case for cash-setting options. Here we usually have a future or another traded commodity, but at the end of the day, we obtain cash. As a result, our expiry status does not balance our shield. If we don't want to be directional, we need to flatten our options for deltas in the month to come.

Irrelevance of the Greeks

As the expiration approaches, the utility of most Greeks as risk control declines. Vega and rho are now obsolete, as the trend towards zero, as the time to expiration tends towards zero. More specifically, gamma and theta become confusing.

At the time of expiration, gamma is infinite if our preference is at-the-money and zero otherwise. That's because we're precisely at a point where the option switches from being equal to the underlying situation to being useless. The delta will transform from one to zero when the underlying price passes the hit. To avoid incurring huge hedging costs, the investor will postpone worrying about persistent delta hedging and then wait until he is confident that the delta option has exceeded its expiring value and then hedged. This isn't as troubling as it seems, because it is expected to entail a change of less than a buck.

Theta is also becoming unreliable. Less significance of theta starts earlier than gamma, sometimes yielding very odd numbers many days before the expiry date. The main issue here is that theta has been configured to display the deterioration of option interest over one day. Normally, this is a good thing as it transforms theta into a directly relevant number, however close to its expiry, it becomes irrational when theta shifts too rapidly for one day.

Chapter 17.

Options Trading as a Business

I f you are only planning to do options trading as a hobby, you can buy small numbers of options and try to profit on them and see what happens. Most people hope to build up their options trading activities, eventually turning it into a business so that they can earn a living from it.

Start Small

The first thing to do is to learn the way of the industry. Having smaller ambitions that can be realized is going to be a part of laying a successful foundation for an options trading business. Many new traders want to get going fast and so purchase lots of options simultaneously, and if they can get higher approval levels, enter multiple strategies all at once. The reality is that options trading is complicated and a lot more complicated than buying and selling stocks, and so you should keep things under control rather than jumping in and getting in a situation where your mind cannot possibly fully comprehend, analyze, and keep track of a dozen complicated options trades. Begin by limiting yourself to five companies and/or index funds to use in your trading. In fact, during the first three months, you might limit yourself to 2-3 companies. You should study the stock of those companies and learn its fundamentals, studying the stock charts to see how the stock has moved in the past. Learn important facts about the companies, such as when they are going to have their next earnings call. You should also learn some basics about spotting and tracking trends in the markets. This can include learning how to read candles, using moving averages, and spotting levels of support and resistance, which can tell you when to enter a trade and when to get out of a trade. Starting small also means setting small goals and meeting them, rather than hoping to make $10,000 a month in profits right away. So, plan on entering trades to make a hundred or a few hundred dollars a week and realize that you are not going to win at every trade.

As you gain experience, you can increase the sizes of your trades. But rather than entering 10 different trades, you should always aim to do multiples of the same options contracts instead, so you don't run into the problem of having too much to manage at once. Remember that options have an expiration date and change fast, so keeping close track of them is important.

Adequate Capital

You can trade options for as little as less than $100, but it is unlikely that you are going to be able to build a full-time income that way. You should plan on setting up an account with $5,000 or more in capital to get started. If you don't have access to that much money now, you can start trading 1-2 options per week using small amounts of money to start learning and trying out different strategies. But plan on having a minimum of $5,000 when you transition to doing options trading as a business and plan on growing the size of your account with time.

Use a Broker with Complete Resources

We've mentioned Robinhood, and it's a great platform for beginners. If you've never traded options before, we recommend that you open a Robinhood account and spend 2-3 months trading on Robinhood to gain some experience.

However, when you are ready to transition trading as a business, a more comprehensive platform is going to be necessary. One thing you'll want to make sure of is that you can sell options naked. That isn't possible on Robinhood.

You should also seek out a broker that has comprehensive resources that can be used to do all your research, analyze your trades, and execute the trades all in one platform. A good example is tasty works.

Make Sure You Have Proper Computer Equipment

As you are trading and keeping track of your trades on a real-time constant basis, you are probably going to want to have multiple computers or computer screens so that you can easily check things. As an options trader, you're going to be wanting to track your options, but also keeping a close eye on the stock itself and even on the news about the company. At the very least, you should be able to comfortably view the stock and your options simultaneously. Depending on your brokerage, you may be able to set things up so that you can see everything associated with one stock ticker with a click.

Make a Business Plan

You wouldn't open a restaurant without making a business plan, and if you are going to have a trading business, you should treat it the same way. Write out a business plan that outlines goals, expenses, and other items so that you have everything laid out, including capital that will be available for funding. Simply starting to buy and sell options and seeing what happens is not a business, although it can be a start.

Also, keep track of all your trades, so you can carefully monitor profit and loss. Part of your business plan will be setting goals for annual returns. Possible returns on options are quite high compared to stocks, but you should set realistic goals in order to ensure you're staying grounded and meeting them. Also, remember that you must take losses into account and not just looking at wins to determine your total return on investment.

Decide on a Business Structure

Are you going to set up a business to run your trades? It's worth doing so. Otherwise, you're going to have a hard time deducting a loss from your taxes. The IRS views trading as ordinary passive income, and there are limits to what you can deduct. You can try to get the "trader" status, but this is difficult. The easiest way to set things up so that you can fully deduct losses and expenses, and possibly offer yourself bankruptcy protection if it came to that, is to set up an official business entity that you can use to trade through. You will not be doing this as a sole proprietor but will instead need to set up an LLC or S-Corporation. An LLC is simpler to set up and acts as a pass-through, but you will be able to manage your expenses deduct everything as a professional trader and then pass on the profits as income to your personal life. Stay focused!

It is better to stay focused on one type of trading, learn it thoroughly, and commit to it 100%. Don't be all over the map, such as trying to trade Forex or Crypto and options at the same time. If you are going to try options trading, then stick to options trading. Be serious about it if you want success to the level of having it provide a full-time income.

Are You Going to Utilize Debt?

This is a personal decision, but it's not recommended that you utilize debt unless there is some compelling reason that you start with an account with a big size. The ease of doing small options trades and earning profits means that most people are better off starting small and then reinvesting profits to increase the size of their trades going forward. If you take out loans to get started, keep the loan size reasonable, and don't get more loans if you have a string of losses, you don't want to dig a hole you can't get out of. Set a reasonable maximum for borrowed capital, such as $5,000-$10,000.

Set a Time Limit

If a year goes by and you are constantly losing money, you will have to evaluate whether options trading is for you. The reality is it's not for everyone. That doesn't mean that stocks or trading full-time aren't in your future, but if it is not working out after putting in significant effort, you should re-evaluate your position and consider alternatives. For example, maybe you would be better suited to work as a swing or day trader or get into Forex, rather than trading options.

Constantly Educate Yourself

You should be continually improving your knowledge of the field. That means educating yourself by reading books on options trading, watching YouTube videos, taking Udemy courses, and possibly taking more expensive courses. You wouldn't try becoming an engineer, doctor, or lawyer without getting the education first, so treat trading the same way if you are expecting to earn a full-time income from it.

Chapter 18.

Right Mentality to Grow Trading Business

O ptions trading is a great way to earn a profit, but many people find it difficult and complicated. It is suitable for beginners as well as experts. It contains detailed information regarding options trading and how you can perform it efficiently. It would be best if you got rid of the limiting belief that what you are currently is all you can be. It would help if you had a mindset that promotes growth. Your mindset is your frame of mind. Thus, your mindset determines how you perceived the outside world, yourself, and what you can achieve. Your attitude is a manifestation of your mindset, and it shows whether your mindset limits you or helps you grow. A growth mindset is one that encourages making in extra time and effort to improve intelligence and experience to make a better standard of living. On the other hand, a fixed mindset is one where all our qualities are fixed, and born talent is the only factor determining success. This mindset limits a person's capacity for learning, while a growth mindset is one where there is no limit to potential or achievement.

Mental Balance Is the Key

What do we fathom by mental prudence? It is the ability to think indisputably despite when markets are unusual, and the financial expert is under tremendous weight. Usually, this is when the most financial expert will as a rule sway and accept utter contributing failures. Believe it or not, mental attitude is about the calm that you can keep up despite when the market appears to go against you. There are two extreme perspectives on mental balance. Stock exchanges drive by fear and insatiability. Financial experts will ask ordinarily when all is said and done, get energetic at the most elevated purpose of the market, and terrible at the base of the market—smart contribution connected to doing the cautious reverse. For example, if you had kept up your balance at the market lows of 2003 and 2009, you would have ended up with surprising assumptions at remarkable costs.

Find After the Right Framework

If you are more focused on the results than the technique, if you are more worried about the closures than about the strategies, you have an attitude problem to contributing. Remember, providing is substantially more of getting the framework right.

- How you recognize stocks
- How you screen stocks
- What are the non-cash related parameters you consider?
- How might you impact the channel
- The boundaries of security
- How might you incorporate a motivation by aligning your passage and leave levels

Your consideration should be on fulfilling this methodology, and the results will like this come after.

Be a Self-Motivated Student

The stock exchange is a remarkable teacher yet to take in the fundamental activities from the market, and you should be an excited observer and a self-motivated student. The best way to deal with gain from the exchange is to listen energetically to what the market is trying to tell you. Endeavor to record the leanings from the market consistently, and it can transform into your Bible for exchanging. The embodiment of the issue is that your viewpoint should be that of a self-student. The market isn't the place you will demonstrate the nuances. It is a large gathering of data from which you can liberally draw.

Be Humble to Recognize Challenges and Your Mistakes

If you don't practice calmness in your practices, then contributing isn't for you. The best financial experts get their assumptions wrong. Attempt to be humble enough to concede that you weren't right and make appropriate necessary changes. If pride drives you to either average the position or outflank the market, you will have a certifiable attitude problem when you are contributing. Recognize that the market has a lot to demonstrate to you and recognize your mistakes. That is the route into the right contributing attitude.

An Ounce of Movement Justifies a Pound of Orchestrating

You can make the best of plans within the planning stage before trading. There are a couple of things about the stock exchanges that you can adjust

just once you start exchanging with real money. Amusement can take you so far! Grasp a frame of mind that is an action planned rather than delighting a great deal in craftiness. You need to develop a growth mindset for you to move from your current financial position to one where you are financially free. The characteristics of someone who has a growth mindset include:

- Believing that talent and intelligence can develop through effort and learning.

- Believing that mistakes are a part of education and that failure is an opportunity for learning and growth.

- Believing that failure is a temporary setback and not permanent feedback to ability and talent.

- Embracing challenges and change as opportunities.

- Openly receiving constructive feedback from other people to further learning and development.

- Viewing constructive feedback as a valuable resource of information.

- Viewing the success of other people as a source of information and inspiration.

By opening your mind and imagining the possibilities, you can find fulfillment in not just your financial life but in your life as an entirety. Developing a growth mindset is not innately ingrained in every human being. It is something that you must work on, and the best way to do so is to develop habits that will encourage you to think differently and adaptively. Such habits include:

- Developing your mission statement. Success is a personal and individualized process. Therefore, if you would like to be financially free, you must know how this is meaningful to you and what financial success means to you on an individual basis.

- Being goal-oriented. You need to be clear on what you want out of your future and then work diligently to earn it.

- Continually learning and seeking new experiences. It lets you broaden your horizons and gain you more skills to shape your mind into forward-thinking.

- Taking action. You will not get any results by sitting on the couch and dreaming about it. Successful people know this and get up and do something about earning the results that they would like.

- Being health-conscious. The body and mind that you have now what you will have for as long as you remain on Earth. Eat right, exercise daily, keep hydrated, and keep looking to keep both your body and mind fit enough to enable you to accomplish your goals of financial freedom. Financial freedom will elude you if either of these things starts to fail you.

- Being self-disciplined. Successful people have mastered themselves so that they can control their actions and thoughts. You cannot drag by your wants and desires and expect to be successful in your pursuit of financial security and independence.

Trading Options to Gain Financial Freedom

Trading options have the great potential to be a form of passive income. It is the opposite of active income, which is what most people engage in. Active income is one where a person invests time in exchange for money. Passive income allows you to enjoy your time still, as you dictate while earning money. It comes to you automatically even while you sleep. While it usually takes time, effort, and maybe monetary input at the beginning, over the long-term, if done right, you can sustain the lifestyle you want if you put forth that investment now.

Chapter 19.

How to Be a Successful Trader

Monitoring the Trend

Trends are a graphical measure of the actual activities that are taking place in the day trading market. Any trader closely following up the trend makes him informed and accurate in his or her levels of predictions, and the chances are that winning may be their middle name. They can purchase when the prices are high and short sell when they drop. Analyzing trends has several assumptions in that, if there are continuous cases of rising prices, possibilities are that they will constantly happen and vice versa.

News on Trading

News always comes in two ways; good news and bad news. Good news on day trading always gives the traders and brokers a huge motivation to purchase prices at good rates. On the other hand, when bad news comes in, the traders can short sell prices. This kind of strategy can be a great move in making huge profits at a season and inducing high volatility rates.

Scalping

Scalping takes advantage of the small kind of prices that happen drastically during the day trading sessions. This kind of mechanism involves getting engaged so quickly and so fast and then leaving right away.

Contrarian Investing

This kind of strategy describes the assumption that prices will go up and most probably reverse and drop. The contrarian buys during fall or short sell during the rise periods. The attitude in this kind of strategy defines that the whole expectation idea is to subdue to change and that things are to head in a reverse kind of direction.

Financial Management

Capital is so lucrative in any kind of income-generating activity. There are always going to be several wins and losses. Not to sound so risky, most of the traders will not input 2% of their capital in any line of trade. Be careful in whatever you consider as an investment; money loss is ever an option too.

Also, there may be cases where brokers demand high commissions. Do not fall into that trap. That is going to cause you problems big time. Consider the rates of commissions demanded by brokers in the first place, because too many commissions expenses can incur low rates of profits, meaning that losses will be incurred.

Proper Time Management

Day trading is a journey. A certain market trading journey means that for it to be called a journey, a process is established. A certain planned period is encouraged. Monitor everyday trading move that occurs and will occur, for it makes you learn and experience all about day trading. Good things take time, mastering the day trading occurrences is quite an investment. Remember those good investments imply good rates of profits.

Consistency/Stability

Another point to add, day trading is quite logical. Day trading cannot be analyzed by fear or even greed. Mathematical approaches must be considered. Set strategies must be put in place too! Examine every logical operation bound to happen during day trading to possess certain clear stability. Once stability has been established, expect some big-time profit rates and an excellent reputation.

Timing

The trading market becomes volatile every single trading day. Experienced traders have mastered the moves and are quite sure about what steps to take once they get to read the structures. As a beginner, do not be quite in a rush to predict. Take one or more time to examine every single trend and get your desired prediction. Do not be too slow, though, and you may end missing so much.

Momentum

This kind of strategy defines revolving around new sources and identifying the substantial trending moves at a high stake. You basically should maintain your current position, be alert with the reversing signs, and face a different direction.

Strong Focus on One Particular Market

Many traders become overexcited and want to trade with all markets. This should not be the case because you will end up being confused, not knowing which trade to focus on. It is normally healthy for the business when you decide and focus on one trade, be good at it. Focusing on many trades at a go will make you lose.

Trading pivots

Trading pivots come in when you buy low at the end of the day and sell at the high end of the trading day. Once you get to master these tactics, the chances are that you will be an expert in comprehending the volatility of the market and therefore declare yourself successful using this kind of tactic.

Risk Control

For beginners, it is highly recommended that they engage in trading infrequently as a way of avoiding too many risks. The essence of this is to help them master their moves and learn a lot. Day trading is not just about profits only, and it is about taking each day as a learning trading progress. Predict the trends at least after some minutes and not just seconds. I am familiar with the adage that declares that you commit many mistakes to learn highly, but honey, some real cash is being retrieved from your pocket; you can become poor at any minute. Slow but sure steps are highly recommended. Take each trading day as a lesson. With this knowledge and tricks, you will be so equipped, and you will be okay in no time.

Passive Position Management

A novice day trader is prone to adjust their target and stop abruptly because certain emotions are taking control. These kinds of emotions are caused by the sudden updates of the figures and trends on the screen that keep changing with time. This is so confusing for the beginners and, after all causing them to alter their predictions hence leading to a great downfall. Only highly experienced and confident day traders can analyze the updates because they may know what they are doing.

For the novice day traders, leave the targets and the stops on their own, and learn how you would passively control all these. Reach for some paper material and sketch and assume how the aftermath would be without interfering with your active trends. Do some in-depth examination and comprehend why every move is happening. In the end, compare how you would have affected your trading account if at all, you altered the last trends. This is a learning process. Do this for quite a while, and within no time, day trading becomes your all-time income-generating hobby. Yes!

Protect Your Capital

Losses are normally involved in almost all businesses despite that try your best and protect the capital of your business. This can be achieved by shunning from all unnecessary risks that come along in businesses. This will bring success to your business.

Risk reward ratio of 3:1

Comprehending the proper 3:1 risk-reward ratio is so important. This kind of ratio reward encourages a trader to lose small and win big despite the frequent times you lost on the trading platform. The moment you gain some wide experience, the risk-reward ratio gets higher and higher, meaning that you are slowly advancing and enjoying some good profits. This is the kind of measure we need to strategize to grow as traders.

Patience and Persistence

Plan your trades and then trade your plans. This kind of strategy defines the behavior where most traders do not trade daily. They have this kind of paradoxical behavior where they just check up on the trends without necessarily acting up because of the fear of outlining the wrong prediction. Well, this is not a way of learning. Day trading calls for patience and persistence where several wrongs did are part of the journey, and learning happens a lot through that. Plan your trades carefully and then predict, see how this goes. Be patient and persistent in every move you make. After all, good things always take time.

Hard work

Day trading requires you to be hardworking to be successful. It is not like the entertainment business which you can joke around with. It needs maximum practices into trading and discipline. You must be trading frequently and stay updated on the stock price fluctuations.

The above strategies help to improve time factors, skills, financial management operations, to grow as a person, risk management, and, most importantly, you get to learn.

Chapter 20.

Market Trends

A market is a chaotic place, with several traders vying for dominance over one another. There are countless strategies and time frames in play, and at any point, it is almost impossible to determine who will emerge with the upper hand. In such an environment, how is it then possible to make any money? After all, if everything is unpredictable, how can you get your picks, right?

Well, this is where thinking in terms of probabilities comes into play. While you cannot get every single bet right, if you get enough right and make enough money on those to offset your losses, you will make money in the long run.

It's not about getting one or two right. It's about executing the strategy with the best odds of winning repeatedly and ensuring that your math works out with regards to the relationship between your win rate and average win.

So, it comes down to finding patterns which repeat themselves over time in the markets. What causes these patterns? Well, the other traders, of course!

To put it more accurately, the orders that the other traders place in the market are what create patterns that repeat themselves over time.

The first step to understanding these patterns is to understand what trends and ranges are. Identifying and learning to spot when they transition into one another will give you a massive leg up not only with your options trading but also with directional trading.

Trends

In theory, spotting a trend is simple enough. Look left to right, and if the price is headed up or down, it's a trend. Well, sometimes it is that simple. However, most of the time, you have both with and counter-trend forces operating in the market. It is possible to have long counter-trend reactions within a larger trend, and sometimes, depending on the time frame you're in, these counter-trend reactions take up most of your screen space.

Trend vs. Range

This is a chart of the UK100 CFD, which mimics the FTSE 100, on the four-hour time frame. Three-quarters of the chart is a downtrend and the last quarter is a wild uptrend. Using the looking left to the right guideline, we'd conclude that this instrument is in a range. Is that true, though?

Just looking at that chart, you can see that short-term momentum is bullish. If you were considering taking a trade on this, would you implement a range strategy or a trending one? This is exactly the sort of thing that catches traders up.

The key to deciphering trends is to watch for two things: counter-trend participation quality and turning points. Let's tackle counter-trend participation first.

Counter-trend Participation

When a new trend begins, the market experiences an extremely imbalanced order flow, tilted towards one side. There's not much counter-trend participation against this seeming tidal wave of trend orders. Price marches on without any opposition and experiences only a few hiccups.

As time goes on, though, the with trend forces run out of steam and must take breaks to gather. This is where counter-trend traders start testing the trend and trying to see how far back they can go. While it is unrealistic to expect a full reversal at this point, the correction or pushback quality tells us a lot about the strength distribution between the with and counter-trend forces.

Eventually, the counter-trend players manage to push so far back against the trend that a stalemate results in the market. The with and counter-trend forces are equally balanced, and thus, the trend comes to an end. After all, you need an imbalance for the market to tip one way or another, and balanced order flow is only going to result in a sideways market.

While all this is going on behind the scenes, the price chart is what records the push and pull between these two forces. Using the price chart, we can not only anticipate when a trend is coming to an end but also how long it could potentially take before it does. This second factor, which helps us estimate the time it could take, is invaluable from an options perspective, especially if you use a horizontal spread strategy.

In all cases, the greater the number of them, the greater the counter-trend participation in the market. The closer a trend is to end, the greater the counter-trend participation. Thus, the minute you begin to see price move into a large, sideways move with an equal number of buyers and sellers, you can be sure that some form of redistribution is going on.

Mind you, and the trend might continue or reverse. Either way, it doesn't matter. What matters is that you know the trend is weak and that now is probably not the time to be banking on-trend strategies.

Starting from the left, we can see that there is close to no counter-trend bars, bearish in this case, and the bulls make easy progress. Note the angle with which the bulls proceed upwards.

Then comes the first major correction, and the counter-trend players push back against the last third of the bull move. Notice how strong the bearish bars are and note their character compared to the bullish bars.

The bulls recover and push the price higher at the original angle and without any bearish presence, which seems odd. This is soon explained as the bears' slam price back down, and for a while, it looks as if they've managed to form a V top reversal in the trend, which is an extremely rare occurrence.

The price action that follows is a more accurate reflection of the power in the market, with both bulls and bears sharing chunks of the order flow, with overall order flow in the bull's favor but only just. Price here is certainly in an uptrend, but looking at the extent of the bearish pushbacks, perhaps we should be on our guard for a bearish reversal. After all, the order flow is looking sideways at this point.

So how would we approach an options strategy with the chart in the state it is in at the extreme, right? Well, for one, any strategy that requires an option beyond the near month is out of the question, given the probability of it turning. Secondly, looking at the order flow seems to be following a channel, doesn't it?

While the channel isn't very clean if you were aggressive enough, you could consider deploying a collar with the strike prices above and below this channel to take advantage of the price movement. You could also employ some moderately bullish strategies as price approaches the bottom of this channel and figuring out the extent of the bull move is easier thanks to you being able to reference the top of the channel.

As price moves in this channel, it's all well and good. Eventually, though, we know that the trend must flip. How do we know when this happens?

Turning Points

As bulls and bears struggle over who gets to control the order flow, price swings up and down. You will notice that every time price comes back into the 6427-6349 zone, the bulls seem to step in masse and repulse the bears. This tells us that the bulls are willing to defend this level in large numbers and strength. Given the number of times the bears have tested this level, we can safely assume that above this level, bullish strength is a bit week. However, at this level, it is as if the bulls have retreated and are treating this as a sort of last resort, for the trend to be maintained. You can see where I'm going with this.

If this level were to be breached by the bears, it is a good bet that many bulls will be taken out. In martial terms, the largest army of bulls has been marshaled at this level. If this force is defeated, it is unlikely that there's going to be too much resistance to the bears below this level. This zone, in short, is a turning point. If price breaches this zone decisively, we can safely assume that the bears have moved in and controlled most of the order flow.

Turning Point Breached

The decisive turning point zone is marked by the two horizontal lines, and the price touches this level twice more and is repulsed by the bulls. Notice how the last bounce before the level breaks produces an extremely weak bullish bounce, and price simply caves through this. Notice the strength with which the bears breakthrough.

The FTSE was in a longer uptrend on the weekly chart, so the bulls aren't completely done yet. However, as far as the daily timeframe is concerned, notice how price retests that same level, but this time around, it acts as resistance instead of support. We can conclude that if the price remains below the turning point, we are bearishly biased. You can see this by looking at the angle with which bulls push back as well as the lack of strong bearish participation on the push upwards.

This doesn't mean we go ahead and pencil in a bull move and start implementing strategies that take advantage of the upcoming bullish move. Remember, nothing is for certain in the markets. Don't change your bias or strategy until the turning point decisively breaks.

Some key things to note here are that a turning point is always a major S/R level. It is usually a swing point where many trend forces gather to support the trend.

The current order flow and price action are what matters the most, so pay attention to that above all else. Also, note how the candles that test this level all have wicks on top of them.

This indicates that the bears are quite strong and that any subsequent attack will be handled the same way until the level breaks. Do we know when the level will break? Well, we can't say with any accuracy. However, we can estimate the probability of it breaking.

The latest upswing has seen very little bearish pushback, comparatively speaking, and strong push into the level. Instinct would say that there's one more rejection left here. However, who knows? Until the level breaks, we stay bearish. When the level breaks, we switch to the bullish side.

Putting it all Together

So now we're ready to put all of this together into one coherent package. Your analysis should always begin with determining the current state of the market. Ranges are straightforward to spot, and they occur either within big pullbacks or at the end of trends.

Trends vary in strength, depending on the amount of counter-trend participation they have. The way to determine counter-trend participation levels is to simply look at the price bars and compare the counter-trend ones to the trendy ones. The angle with which the trend progresses is a great gauge for its strength, with a steeper angle being stronger.

Chapter 21.

Exit Strategies to Capture Profits Reliably

How many times have you turned unrealized gains into losses? If this happens to you, you may need to learn how to implement your exit strategy reliably. There is an old saying: "Never make a profit at a loss." This simple rule is always so crucial for successful trading. Unless you always implement a reliable exit strategy, your trading success is far from what it could or should be. Your profitability is unreliable. You increase your chances of success against yourself. This can lead to a more significant loss, dissatisfaction with the trading performance, and even distrust.

Why You Need an Exit Strategy

By reliably applying your exit strategy to each trade, several of your trades will be profitable. Your winnings are usually more substantial. Over time, you become more successful. And for losing trades, your losses are generally smaller. Emotions will no longer pollute your decision. And you will never allow unrealized gains to become losses. You need to have complete confidence in your exit strategy. Because if you trust my exit strategy, it is psychologically easy to implement it into every transaction automatically. You should never experience doubt, confusion, or hesitation.

Three Phases of the Transaction

Each transaction has three phases: input, knowledge, and go out. Each step has an exit strategy. Your trade will be more successful if you let the profit run, and the losses will be reduced. It means that you should always determine where your prognosis is bad before opening a position. As soon as your prediction turns out to be incorrect, close your position immediately. Leave what's left.

Stop-loss determines when a trade needs to be closed. I use three-loss methods, one for each phase of my trades:

- Loss of input loss, set before opening the position
- Loss of rear brake, set if the trade moves in my favor
- Profit stop-loss gain profit after reaching my waypoint

Before opening my position, I always set a loss. I put it one percent below the recent strong swing on the daily stock price chart for bull trades. If the stock creates an everyday closing price during this loss of income, I will leave in the morning. My prediction was wrong: stocks are falling, not raising. If the stock rises as expected and does not stop when entering at the entry-level, I will increase the rear stop losses by one percent in the event of subsequent damages due to fluctuations. I was rattling them. The ratchet effect reduces potential losses and blocks profits. My stops are also due to the daily closing price. The following day, each regular closing price is activated in the event of another loss of a stop.

Your Business Waypoint

You should also estimate where you reasonably expect the stock price to go. You need to decide how to close your trade to maximize your profit when you reach your waypoint. Once the transaction reaches your waypoint, implement your exit strategy with strict discipline. It is not good to end a trade when you reach your point on the route. It is better to stay in the trade if it continues in your favor.

However, you should leave your trading at the first sign that the market poses an unrealized risk of your unrealized profits. When I reach my waypoints, I use much stricter termination criteria that make it easier to activate the output. After start-up, stocks are reduced rather than continued. I'll stay in the box while stocks keep growing. Every day I move my surplus to the intraday layer. As soon as the shares are trading below yesterday 's minimum, I will immediately leave as at. Stocks fell. At this point, the population is more likely to continue to shrink than to keep.

Adjust Your Excessive Losses

The market provides a lot of advice that your unrealized profit is at increased risk. Profit losses cease to threaten unrealized gains. You can use one or more of the following criteria to make a profit. You can stop:

- As soon as the share price turns towards you
- As more quickly as the trend line breaks
- As more quickly as price support is interrupted
- As more quickly as a simple moving average break

Each of these terms warns you that your trade is likely to start. And that your unrealized gains are more likely to be at risk. If all these criteria are met, you must close the course permanently. In addition to this standard procedure, I will be able to override other stop-loss strategies based on the pricing model, indices, options, and time. In the bear, I'm just about the process. This way, you manage your Exits Strategy. You can make profits and reduce losses. And that should keep you from turning unrealized gains into losses. Options trading, like any other type of trading, requires careful planning and execution. I could say that every day you have some participation in the market. We are all in the business. As a trader, it is easy to enter and leave the market at the touch of a button. But once you're inside, do you mean a clear exit strategy?

Trading is like a business that requires planning with strategies that show that you want to grow your business. In trading, a solid business plan is necessary for successful trading. Blinding in the market is just a sign that you are speculating or "rushing" to see which direction you are heading. Like all plans, you need the right approach and an even better exit strategy.

What do you do when your trade goes bad? Can you find a way to save what's left, or will you just let go when you think the market can recover? Most of us can choose the first opportunity to try to keep what we can and therefore propose a strategy to save the current situation.

Depending on the trade, you should have a good exit strategy that complements your trading strategy and timing. In short time frames, such as 5-15 minutes, an exit strategy must be planned before executing a trade, because you do not have time to think about your termination. If you have 1 hour - 4 hours, you have much more time, and you can still afford to come up with your exit strategy. In professional trading, these "professionals" always have in mind an entry and exit strategy after analyzing market conditions and only need to follow their plan. They emphasized the balanced conduct of trade and already favored entry or exit. Both are equally important to them.

Chapter 22.

Kinds of Trader and Trading Styles

M ost options merchants utilize a trading style when purchasing and selling contracts. It's helpful to understand the distinctive trading styles and what is included, as eventually, you will need to choose which trading style is best for you. A ton will rely upon your venture goals, how much time you need to focus on trading, and what sort of abilities you have.

For instance, if you are anticipating full trading time and are especially skilled at settling on quick options under strain, then day trading might be a decent style. On the other hand, you might need to begin utilizing a style that doesn't need to be so tedious – swing trading.

Any person would agree that, even though the nuts and bolts trading options are not unbelievably hard to get a hold of, there is a great deal of data that should be acclimatized before you are probably going to feel good with the beginning. The basics are generally clear; you must see precisely what is included, what the advantages are, what the dangers are, and how options truly work.

We spread these specific angles, and that's just the beginning of our "Introduction to Options Trading." Yet, there are likewise a few different things that you truly need to know as well if you need the most obvious opportunity with regards to profiting. One such model is the distinctive trading styles that can be utilized alongside the various kinds of options dealers.

As a rule, brokers can be isolated into two classifications. To begin with, you have the experts, those that ordinarily work for huge monetary foundations, trading straightforwardly for those organizations or customers. These experts can likewise fill the job of market creators.

Besides, you have private people that trade carefully, who individually benefit utilizing their very own capital, and by and large, they trade from home. A few people trade full time, depending on their profits as their essential wellspring of pay, while others trade on a low maintenance premise while likewise having a fundamental activity.

Day Trading

This is a full-time style that can be utilized to trade options, or other money-related instruments, such as stocks. It's a style frequently supported by experts yet has additionally gotten even more broadly utilized by private people as of late as well. This is a serious and tedious style that requires consistent checking of the business sectors during the day. It was named properly because it includes making trades that last no longer than a day –

for example, you would ordinarily close all situations before the day to understand any profits and afterward adequately start the following day again.

Swing Trading

This is another style that can be utilized for a trading scope of money related instruments expansion to options. It's one of the most generally perceived styles and can be utilized by an investor or merchant. It's especially reasonable for low maintenance merchants who can't devote a few hours every day to their exercises, and for beginners who are not set up for the force of day trading. This style is referred to as swing trading as the thought is fundamentally to distinguish value swings and purchase and sell fittingly to benefit from them.

Position Trading

This is the style that is, for the most part, utilized for trading options and prospects. It's a moderately okay style, and it requires an exceptionally exhaustive comprehension of the mechanics of options and options trading. It is anything but a style that should be considered by beginners, and it is principally utilized by experts that have the important experience and information to be effective.

Market Makers

Market creators/makers are experts that are fundamental to the options trades. They guarantee that there is, in every case, enough profundity and liquidity inside the market for the brokers to have the option to execute their ideal trades. Market creators purchase and sell in high volumes and assist dealers with encouraging trades if there is no related purchaser or merchant. This ensures the market moves effectively. Market creators are, for the most part, workers of money related establishments.

Open Interest

This is the total number of outstanding contracts, in this case, options that haven't been settled for the asset. This doesn't count every buy and sell contract. It is the trading activity on the option, whether the money is flowing, if the underlying stock increases, or decreases under it all.

So, what does that mean? Well, open interest is one of the data fields that you see when you look at the option, and that also includes the bid price, ask price, implied volatility, and the volume. Many traders ignore this, and this is a really bad thing to ignore.

Why is that? Well, essentially, it doesn't update during the trading day, and you may not realize it, but sometimes this causes contracts to be exercised without you knowing it.

Let us use an example. You have 1000 shares of ABC, and you want to do a covered call, selling 10 of these calls, and you essentially would enter this into the open. It is an open transaction and adds 10 of these shares to the open interest. You're essentially entering the transaction to buy from closed one, which would decrease the open interest of this by 10. Let's say you are buying 10 of the ABC calls to open, and the other will buy ten calls to close, the same number, so it won't change.

But why does this matter? Well, if you're looking at the total open interest, you won't know immediately whether the options are sold or bought, and therefore many ignore this. But the truth is, this also has important information, and you shouldn't assume there is nothing there. One way to use this is to look at the volume of the contracts that you trade. When this starts to exceed the existing open interest, it does suggest that trading in that option is super high, which means lots are acting on it. You should potentially act on this if you feel that you're going to profit from acquiring that underlying stock.

Let us take another example. You see, the open interest on a stock, such as maybe IBM, is 12,000. This suggests that the market is active, and there might be investors that want to trade at this point. You see, the bid price is just $1, and the option is $1.06, which means you can buy one call option contract at the mid-market price.

But, let's say that the open interest is like 3. This is practically no activity on those call options, and there isn't a secondary market. People aren't interested, so you will struggle to enter and exit this at a reasonable price. Let us take a look at GameStop, for example. After their recent reports, their stock is probably at an incredibly low open interest. That means you shouldn't try to act on that. But Apple is currently putting out more products and is getting ready to shell out more flagship products. Hence, their stock has a huge open interest on it, which means you should consider entering and exiting it and possibly buying covered calls on that stock for a good price. Open interest doesn't get updated as much, but it is still an important case to understand, and it can affect you to rush in and approach a trade. It will give you the overall trading volume on the stock, which makes it very significant.

Chapter 23.

Technical Analysis

It is essential that you understand technical and fundamental analysis, as they will help you tremendously with the growth of your option trading endeavors. Both techniques work very well when it comes to helping you make more profits out of your trading.

Technical analysis is a way options traders find a framework to study the price movement. The simple theory behind this method is that a person will look at the previous prices and the changes, hence determine the current trading conditions and the potential price movement. The only problem with this method is that it is philosophical, meaning that all technical analysis is reflected in the price. The price reflects the information, which is out there, and the price action is all you need to make a trade.

The technical analysis banks on history and the trends and the traders will keep an eye on the past, and they will keep an eye on the future as well, and based on that, they will decide if they want to trade or not. More importantly, the people who are going to be trading using the technical analysis will use history to determine whether they will make the trade. Essentially the way to check out technical analysis would be to look up the trading price of a stock in five years. Many options traders used to determine the history and the future of the capital, and whether they should trade using technical analysis. There are many charts you can look up online to figure out how technical analysis takes place. However, we have given you a brief explanation of what technical analysis is.

When using technical analysis, they also look at the trends that took place in the past. Most of the time, the stock fluctuates simply because of the trends that took place at that time, keeping that in mind, the traders will look at the future and see if the trends will retake the position. If so, they will most definitely trade or not trade, depending on whether it will benefit them. Many people say that technical analysis as more of a short-term thing; however, some still believe the technical report can be used in the long-term. In our opinion, we think that technical analysis is short. The reason why we believe technical analysis is short-term is that we are mainly basing our assumptions based on the past and the trends that took place.

Keeping that in mind, the capital gains you might see from technical analysis might be short-term. This means that the tray you will make will not keep going in the long-term and will be a quick gain for you. Keeping that in mind, technical analysis is a great tool to use for people who are looking to make more money from options trading rather quickly. However, make sure that you do research properly on the stock before you make a trade on it. Many people make a trade on it by looking at the 5-year chart. However, it's much deeper than that you need to make sure that the trends that took place during those five years are going to retake the position. If not, then it will be entirely subjective for you to make a trade or not. The great thing about technical analysis would be that if you do it correctly, you will have a better chance of seeing success from it, and it can build a ton of confidence in new traders. This will be a significant thing for newbies or be a bad thing for them since you will become extremely confident and make a blunder. Technical analysis believes that the current price of the underlying asset in question is the only metric that matters when it comes to looking into the current state of things outside of the market. Specifically, because everything else is already automatically factored in when the current price is set as it is. As such, to accurately use this type of analysis, all you need to know is the current price of the potential trade-in question as well as the greater economic climate.

Those who practice technical analysis are then able to interpret what the price is suggesting about market sentiment to make predictions about where the price of a given cryptocurrency is going to go in the future. This is possible since pricing movements aren't random. Instead, they follow trends that appear in both the short and the long-term. Determining these trends in advance is key to using technical analysis successfully. All trends are likely to repeat themselves over time, thus using historical charts to determine likely trends in the future.

When it comes to technical analysis, what is always going to be more important than why. That is, the fact that the price moved in a specific way is far more important to a technical analyst then why it made that movement. Supply and demand should always be consulted, but beyond that, there are likely too many variables to make it worthwhile to consider all of them as opposed to their results.

Technical indicators are used in options trading to determine trends and potential turning points in the price of underlying stocks. When used correctly, they can accurately predict movement cycles as well as determine when the most profitable time to buy or sell is going to be.

Technical indicators are typically calculated based on the price pattern of a derivative or stock. Relevant data includes closing price, opening price, lows, highs, and volume. Indicators typically take the data regarding a stock's price from the past few periods depending on the charts the analyst favors and use it to generate a trend that will show what has been happening with a specific stock as well as what is likely to happen next.

Two primary types of technical indicators:

Lagging indicators are used to determine if a new trend is forming or if the underlying stock is currently moving within an expected range using existing data. If the lagging indicator points to a strong trend, there is a better than 50 percent chance that the trend will continue moving forward. Unfortunately, they are not especially useful for determining pullbacks or rally points that may appear in the future.

Leading indicators tend to come into play when traders need to predict a likely future price point when it is currently unclear if the current price is going to crash or rally. They tend to manifest as momentum indicators that help determine the strength of the current trend's movement, which will help determine if the trend is going to continue or reverse. As no trend will continue forever, the momentum indicator will allow you to determine how long of a timeframe your options should be in to ensure that you get out before the disruption begins.

Leading indicators are also useful if you find yourself needing to determine if the price of a specific stock has reached a point where it is unsustainable.

This means a slowdown in the price is forthcoming. As overbought or oversold stocks experience a pullback when a slowdown occurs, knowing when this type of movement is coming can be supremely useful for several different trading strategies.

Chapter 24.

Fundamental Analysis

Fundamental analysis aims to figure out what a company is worth. It takes the approach that a stock is a piece of a business and that to understand what the stock is going to do; you need to understand the business itself and its work. The degree to which you do this depends on what you're comfortable with. There's no single 'right' way of analyzing the market. If you're someone who finds a solely technical approach comfortable, then so be it. This means that it is right for you and not that it is the only right way to do things. As you can imagine, a lot of it is subjective because there are no set criteria for a 'great' business. You could say that all great businesses make money, but things like profit margins and management quality have a large impact on the bottom line. For example, Apple makes more money than Walmart, but does this mean the latter is a bad business?

Either way, our aim for trading options is not to get under the skin of the business entirely. Remember, we're trying to screen for opportunities that we can take advantage of. This means that when we do spot an opportunity, we need to look at the company's financial reports in question and determine whether it is a suitable candidate for any of our chosen strategies.

Reading

It doesn't sound revolutionary to say this, but to make fundamental analysis work well, you must read. A lot. A lot of fundamental traders make their task easier by focusing on the sole industry and narrowing their scope. This is a very good approach since there are always opportunities present everywhere. Also, keep in mind that options strategies are varied. Hence, it isn't as if you're not able to take advantage of any potential opportunities in each sector. A crucial step before crunching any numbers is to get a feel for the sector or industry. Pick something easy for you to understand. For example, Facebook might be a tempting stock to speculate on. Still, if you barely use the platform and don't know anything about what drives the tech industry, there's not much in trying to dive into Facebook's fundamentals.

Getting to Know Them

Research all the news you can find about the companies in the sector of your choice. If you feel as if you would rather focus on just one or two companies in that sector, then so be it. Either way, get to know them better. If there are too many companies in the sector or industry you've picked, seek to narrow your list down to a more manageable size.

Getting to know your companies in question is all about figuring out what their character is like. This might seem odd, but every company has a certain personality that comes through in the way they conduct business. Coca Cola's approach to advertising its brand is different from what Pepsi does, for example. If you look at the car industry, the way Mercedes-Benz advertises its cars is different from what its main competitors, Audi and BMW, do. One of the best ways of figuring this out is to look at the management and their philosophy with regards to the industry they're in. Another possible thing to search for is restructuring announcements or earnings announcements of a large company after a series of bad quarters. Given the relative size of the company in question, the market will be poised to push prices up massively on positive news or depress prices tremendously on receiving negative news.

Financials

There is no end of financial ratios you can use to evaluate a company. When trading a company's options, all you want to figure out from a financial perspective is whether something is alarming going on that might derail your plans. For example, is there something that looks off, or is there another issue that might cause its stock to behave in ways that are detrimental to your strategy. Your objective is not to figure out whether it is a great business or not. This is beside the point. There are things you need to keep in mind when looking at the financial side of things:

Debt to Total Capital Ratio

This is sometimes expressed as a percentage as well. It is simply the total amount of debt divided by the sum of debt and equity. You can get these two numbers from the balance sheet, which will give you the total debt and total equity (which you'll find at the bottom.)

Price to Earnings Ratio

Also called the P/E ratio, this is the price divided by the earnings per share. This number is not relevant by itself as much as it is compared to the ratios of the other companies in its industry. For example, if company A is selling at a P/E of 60, but the rest of the companies in the industry are selling at a ratio of 20, then obviously, something is up.

This is where fundamental analysis becomes more of an art than a science. If you feel that the market will push prices down, you could look for some corroboration from the technical side of things. If both types of analysis say the same thing (that a decline is due), then employing a short strategy might be the best move forward.

Free Cash Flow

Free cash flow is an important metric to track if you're looking at investing in a company for the long term. Given that we're seeking to speculate on its options, this doesn't quite have the same significance. The easiest way to get a sense of how strong a company's financials are is to compare it to the P/E ratio. Almost always, you will see that the former number will be higher than the latter. This isn't a bad thing by itself.

Insider Trading Disclosures

The SEC heavily regulates the stock market, and the likelihood of a senior manager of a publicly listed company trying to dump company stock while talking it up is slim these days. However, insider trading disclosures will give you a good idea of who owns how much in the company. The form you want to look for is the 13-F disclosure. Anytime significant changes in ownership take place, or whenever the existing bunch of significant owners of the stock changes their holdings, they will need to file a 13-F disclosure. These are delayed by a month, so they aren't real-time. These days you will find that a lot of the publicly listed companies are owned by institutions such as mutual funds or index funds. As such, you will see a lot of 13-Fs coming from these institutions, and you might think that they're running away from the stock by selling their holdings or buying it up in anticipation of huge bullishness. While this might be the case in a few instances, you must understand that mutual funds and index funds have different rules to follow. A mutual fund manager has one of the hardest jobs in the market.

Chapter 25.

Cryptocurrencies

Since the technology is still new, the community around the cryptocurrency market is small and can be very beneficial if used correctly. We will talk about useful trading tools, describe the best of exchanges, and talk about how not to let cryptocurrencies take over your personal life.

Cryptocurrencies have also known to threaten the price of credit for traditional financial institutions. More trades are occurring with cryptocurrencies, and it is quickly becoming apparent that the customers of conventional banks are losing confidence in fiduciary currencies. There will be a lot of difficulties to occur for the financial institution when it comes to gathering data to look and figure out what is taking place in the economy. This data is given to the government for them to steer the economy in the direction that they want it to go.

You may have heard of cryptocurrency or crypto assets; the remarkable thing is that they are all the same. It will be a trade of money that will utilize the controlling of units that are going through negotiations. These are digital currencies that will cover topics such as Ethereum and Bitcoin. The first digital currency that worked with a decentralized system was Bitcoin, which happened back in 2009. Ever since Bitcoin came out, other cryptocurrencies have come out, such as altcoins and Ethereum. Altcoins are going to be an alternative to Bitcoins.

Like it was just mentioned, the cryptocurrency program is going to be decentralized, and it is going to work on a blockchain where each negotiation will locate on a block. It is also going to make it different from typical banks because a conventional bank runs on a centralized system.

Some people call cryptocurrencies the best distribution of wealth there has ever been, and it is hard not to agree when we see all those 20-year old changing their lives thanks to this market. Since social media has become the primary means of communication between young people, Cryptocurrencies are no different as new generations dominate them—leading social media platforms to include Facebook, Reddit, and, most importantly, Twitter. That is, apart from private groups being active on Telegram and Discord, where access is usually requested.

Having an account on those channels is essential to do proper research – it provides you with a community to share ideas with, a lot of rumors and news that you would not find anywhere else, and a vast base of knowledge from the best traders out there. Since Twitter possesses the most significant number of experienced traders, we would highly suggest having an account on one of these platforms to soak everything the crypto-sphere has to offer.

It is not only an excellent research base but also a fun place where you will be able to network with the most creative and exciting personalities this market can offer.

The growing popularity of cryptocurrencies on social channels has also led to the appearance of influencers that, in such a small community, can have enormous powers. We can confirm from our experience that one of us owns an account of significant size as well. Most of the big accounts are 100% anonymous, hiding behind cartoon avatars without revealing real data about themselves. As a result, popularity leads to them being able to influence the market in various ways.

It is a natural occurrence that a lot of people try to build a brand of their own that gives a lot of benefits to the person. Having followers not only helps in research (as people interact with you and often share their results with you) but also provides a lot of opportunities to earn money, which is probably the most significant threat we would like to warn you.

Being a big personality on Twitter not only allows you to cause movements on the market but also attracts companies offering money to promote their products (usually Initial Coin Offerings but other coins do this as well). Unfortunately, this happens often; therefore, you should always do your research and keep this in mind.

Let's not put everybody into one basket and let's see how you can benefit from being a part of the community:

Learn from the Charts

There is no right or wrong way to create charts as everybody has their style that either works for them or not. Being exposed to dozens of traders, everyone has a different approach to Technical Analysis helps enormously to grow as a chartist. The study which indicators bring the most success and compare those scenarios with your trading ideas – this way, you will always have many different perspectives on how trade can play out.

Look for Unknown Tickers

Go through random threads and look for people shilling their coins. You would be surprised how often the biggest gainers appear in threads like this before a high profile picks them up, and the run starts. Never fall for the suggestion of investing, always do your research on it occasionally that might be a potential big move.

Reach out to other people to share ideas and help each other with so many good traders in the crypto sphere. It takes a lot of weight – in this case, work- from your shoulders and opens you up to the parts of trading you might not be good at (finding shallow caps and margin trading – you name).

Be Up to Date with All Important Events

You will be able to understand what is currently going on in the market and maybe find some excellent investment opportunities along the way if you can filter through some obvious shills.

One last thing that we would like to address in this topic is paid groups. It is a common phenomenon that during the bull market, there are a lot of traders that open paid signal groups. Places, where you pay a monthly fee, where your "guru" gives you, buy/sell signals that theoretically should outperform the market.

We understand that there is a massive demand for that kind of service because not everybody has enough time to learn about trading themselves or spend so much time in front of the computer. However, as we have experienced two of the most massive alt seasons ever, we can confidently say that most of these groups are not worth the money. During a serious bull run, losing money is almost impossible, as even blind guesses tend to give 50-100% gains (this is not an exaggeration, the crypto market is very irrational in its growth during alt season).

Successful traders often outperform the market with their calls, and we will not take that away from them. Things, however, get interesting when the bull market takes a break, and people must guide through retracements. We have seen groups holding through 70% losses as the group owners were not able to give profitable calls during the bear market.

If you need a service like this, because you lack time, make sure you talk to the current members. Get an honest confirmation on group makes profits in both bull and bear markets and that it provides lessons on how to trade as well. Otherwise, we highly recommend learning how to trade with you. Not only because it will save you money from the fees, but because there is much free content to learn from by yourself.

Knowing how to trade will not only bring you a quick profit now but also remain a valuable skill for the future as you can use your knowledge for stocks. Trading requires enormous amounts of self-control and patience that cannot achieve by following calls from others, as it comes strictly from experience and being on your own with a trade.

Chapter 26.

ABCD strategy

The ABCD strategy is an essential strategy that looks for a pattern in stock to get an idea of what the trend is in the market. What you are looking for is a stock that starts low and rises to a high point A, and then drops back down to a low point B. Point A represents the breakout level, that is if the stock passes point A, a second time during the trading day, you're expecting it to rise significantly, representing an opportunity where you can sell for profit. So why would point A drop down? It is a point when many investors have decided to sell because they are happy with their earnings, and they are suspicious of the stock continues to increase.

As the stock begins to be sold off, at some point, it will reach a low point, which will be point B in the chart. The low point occurs when new buyers overtake sellers that began selling as a result of the stock reaching the high point A. Then, when more buyers come in the stock will settle on a new low point, C, which will be higher than point B. If this pattern established, you take your risk level as point B. After it hits point C, it may begin moving upward again. It is a signal of an excellent buying opportunity, so we may jump in at this point. If the ABCD pattern realized, it would move up to a new high point D, where we can sell and take our profits. In the chart below, if the stock goes above point A, this is considered a breakout it is time to consider selling. It is a bearish ABCD, which means you see a time to market and take profits before the stock drops again. Point B, could you're your stop-loss point. It is a bearish ABCD, meaning we expect it to fall.

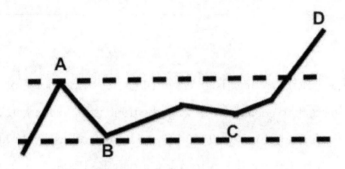

FIG14. ABCD Strategy

Example: suppose that XYZ Stock opens strongly, going from $50 a share up to $60 a share. Then over the succeeding hour, it drops to $40 a share. It then raises to $55 a share and drops a little bit to $53 a share. At this point, we will consider buying. Our risk level is the lowest point which was $40 a share. If the stock starts turning upward, we buy. So, we can take any point between that and our purchase point as a stop-loss, so, for example, we could set a stop-loss at $45. It then continues upward to point D, say it raises to $63 a share, where we sell to take our profits before the stock drops again. We can also have a bullish ABCD pattern. It is where the stock looks to rise. In this case, we buy at point D. it can do buying calls or go long on the stock. When we see ABCD patterns, the lines AB and CD are known as the legs. The line BC is either called the correction or the retracement. A retracement is a temporary reversal of the stock price. In that case, the stock has an overall upward trend for the day. So, the retracement is seen as a temporary downturn that is going to reverse. A correction is a downturn of 10% or more in the price of the stock. A correction is an ideal time to buy a stock because odds are it's going to go back up and possibly strongly so. In the second chart, at point D, there has been a correction. In the first ABCD graph, we see a retracement, on the way to an overall upward trend. Ideally, the lines AB and CD should be of equal length.

Bollinger Bands

Bollinger bands are a trendy indicator for day traders, looking for price actions and signs for strengthening or weakening. These developed by none other than John Bollinger. Bollinger bands are adaptive trading bands. A trading band is simply a range of prices for security (aka stock). Bollinger bands represent:

- Volatility
- The extent of price movement
- They indicate trend lines defining support and resistance

Bollinger bands calculated using standard deviation. It is calculated relative to some average of prices, for example, the moving average over a given number of periods. What the Bollinger band represents then, is the spread of prices about that average. Bollinger bands only measure closing prices and how to spread out they are. Typically, they measure the 20 periods moving average, but they used for 50 or 100 periods.

Bollinger bands are dynamic. You will see them around the candlesticks in a stock chart. When they narrow, that is known as a volatility squeeze. If they spread out, that is a volatility spread.

- If the bands are narrow, which indicates that the prices over that period are falling within a smaller range (i.e. the closing prices for each period are relatively like each other).

- If the bands are more extensive, that indicates a greater spread in prices, that is individual prices differ from each other a lot more – put another way, there is more volatility.

Bollinger bands signal that a day trader looks.

- If wick of a candlestick at the bottom hits the Bollinger band, that can take as a buy signal. The stock oversold, so it's a good time to buy.

- When the candlestick touches or crosses the upper Bollinger band, then the stock is overbought and time to sell.

Of course, the vice versa applies, if a candle hits the top band, it may not be a sell signal, you may want to short or buy puts. When the candlesticks are hitting the Bollinger bands, this may indicate a reversal. A hammer at the bottom of a reversal touching the bottom Bollinger band is an excellent buy signal in many cases. Reversal candlesticks that touch a Bollinger band are a reliable indicator that there is a reversal coming.

When using Bollinger bands, you will want to look at the shape of the candlestick itself. It can strengthen or weaken your indicators. If you see a hammer at the bottom of the Bollinger bands, this can indicate a coming upturn in the stock, so it's a good time to go long.

Moving Average

Another trading strategy that can exploit is the moving average. It may help when a trader is looking for entry and exit points while trading. First, we will look at the simple moving average crossover strategy. Look at candlestick charts when considering moving averages with a two-minute interval.

You can include multiple moving averages in a chart with different periods. A faster-moving average on a chart is colored red, and a slower moving average is shaded green. A buy signal is a red line moving above the green line. That is, it breaks above the green line. A sell signal is when the green line is above the red line. If the lines are overlapping, then that means to wait. So, to profit, when the faster moving average tops, the slower moving average, you go long, which means buy the stock or buy a call option. When the red line or faster-moving percentage goes below the slower moving average it is a sell signal. If you went long, you sell your stock. It could also be an indication to buy puts.

A stop loss should be five or ten percent below the moving average line. Stable profits can realize when the stock breaks out high above the moving average. You can choose to take a half-position at this point, in order to lower your risk.

Chapter 27.

When to Exercise Options

I f you offer to close after you buy to open and buy to close after you offer to open, when do you practice your options?

Practicing options are used when you need to change over your options spot into stock. Most brokers never really need to change over their options to stock; in this manner, practicing options are seldom used.

There are times you might need to claim stock by changing over your options. To practice your options, you must make a long put or long a call.

Short options never can practice their options; these must be allotted.

To return to our options, a long put gives you the privilege to sell the stock, and a long call gives you the privilege to buy a stock.

You now are long 1 contract of a TOP 40 call, and TOP is trading for $45. You concluded that you need to claim the TOP stock, so you practice the agreement. When you practice the agreement, you will buy 100 portions of TOP at $40 (the strike cost).

Presently, when you buy the stock, fight the temptation to go back and sell it for $45. If you plan to just buy the stock and pivot and trade them for a benefit, you would prefer not to work out. You can accomplish similar outcomes with less expense if you offer to close your position.

When we look at practicing a long put, you will sell the offers as opposed to buying the offers.

You are long 1 contract of a TOP 30 put, and TOP is trading at $25. You choose to short the stock, so you practice your agreement. When you practice the contract, you will short 100 portions of TOP at $30 (the strike cost).

Much the same as with our long call, you would prefer not to practice the agreement so you can quickly close the position and gather the profit. If that were the situation, you would offer to close your long put. This will enable you to get the profit at a lower expense.

If you need to practice your option, you should contact the option company and let them know about your expectations. A few financiers will have catches to assign that you need to practice your option. However, most businesses will have you bring in to affirm your arrangements. Most financiers are going to charge you an additional expense to practice your options. You can rapidly observe and think about your financier expenses at StockBrokers.com.

If your options are one-penny in-the-money at lapse, it will consequently be practiced by your business. If you want to practice your options, you must finish it off with a buy to close or offer to close requests before termination. Holding up too long could be hindering to your portfolio. You could rest on Friday with 5 entries that are marginally in-the-money and wake up Monday with 500 portions of stock in your portfolio.

Don't Exercise/Practice Out of the Money Options

Never practice an out-of-the-money option. Practicing options are intended for in-the-money options as they were. This is effectively clarified with a model.

You now are long a call at 50 strike. Your fundamental is at present trading at $40, and you choose to practice. Presently you have changed over your options into offers at $50.00 even though the basic is just trading at $40; you have a loss. If you needed to get the portions of the stock, you ought to have offered to close, finished off your options, and bought the offers in the market for $40 rather than $50. Try not to set yourself up by beginning with a loss, just options that are exercise in-the-money.

Don't Exercise an Option Before Expiration

When practicing your options before termination, you are giving up the properties of the options for which you've officially paid.

In the first place, you will relinquish the time price of the options. If your basic is trading at $50, and you're on a long call option at the $45 strike, you will have at any rate a $5 benefit (50 - 45). If you practice your options before the expiry, that is your lone benefit in that position.

If you have time staying before the lapse, your call will have a greater benefit without anyone else's input. The benefit of your call would be $5 + time value. When you practice, you lose the time value.

You could offer to close the options in the market for more than $5 if it is before lapse. The closer you get to lapse, the more your time worth abatements until it comes to $0. Your call would be worth $5 at termination, and that is the point at which you practice.

The second reason you don't practice before lapse is because you will relinquish the protection options give.

You are long an approach the $30 strike that cost $3.00 and terminates in about fourteen days, and your fundamental is trading for $40. You concluded you're close enough to lapse and need to practice your call. You never again have those options and now hold 100 offers at $30. The following day an unexpected declaration is discharged that the organization is under scrutiny for misrepresentation. The stock starts to sink, and toward the day's end is worth $20. You are presently sitting on a $1,000 loss. If you had held those options, it would be useless now. However, your all-out loss would have just been $300.

Even though you will begin your options instruction finding out about practicing options at the strike value, you will find that you occasionally will practice genuine positions. Most options brokers never need to claim the stock. They trade options to deal with the agreements forward and backward.

When you buy to open, go long, or pay a net charge for a position, go long or open; you will use an offer to near close the position.

If you offer to open, go short, or get a net acknowledgment for a position, you will use a buy to near close the position.

When you manage a place that is progressively confused and has both long and short options, you will recollect how the first exchange was set up. Did you go long on the position and pay a charge, or did you go short the position and get credit?

If you would like to practice your options, ensure your spot is in-the-money and at termination.

Never practice a situation to finish off the exchange and gather the benefit. You will get a similar outcome for less expense if you use a buy to close or offer to close requests.

Chapter 28.

Options Trader Common Mistakes

As a new options trader, it is very common to easily feel overwhelmed or obsessive in your pursuit of this business. Even though the risks of such a business are relatively low, making mistakes can be very costly.

Mistake #1 - Not Having a Trading Plan to Fall Back On

Unfortunately, many people enter the arena of options trading out of desperation or greed with no plan as to how they will make this a successful venture. They are looking to make a quick buck and do not think things through because they are not thinking rationally. This leads to them trading with their emotions rather than with logic. There is no place for emotions and feelings in options trading. While gut instinct has a time and a place in options trading, being led by anger, sadness, and other emotions can lead to heavy financial losses.

Many factors need to be considered if an options trader wants to make maximum profit. Therefore, going in half-cocked, desperate, or greedy will only lead to failure and unnecessary losses. To make the best out of this business venture you need to have a sound trading plan before you do a single thing. Your trading plan will serve as your comprehensive decision-making guide for all your trading activities.

Mistake #2 - Choosing the Wrong Expiration Date for Options

Having expiration dates that are too short or too long can be costly. While you develop your trading plan, you will come across the factor of how you will select expiration dates for your options. Each option is unique, and this requires setting up a system whereby you can select proper expiration dates so that profits are maximized every time.

Mistake #3 - Not Factoring in the Volatility of the Financial Market

Even the most stable financial markets can have days where they take off in an unexpected direction. This affects the value of the associated asset and so the options trader needs to be aware of this. Some traders only look at the reactivity of the financial markets during one-time period and not others and doing so, they do not rely on historical data or focus on forecasting the future. These are costly mistakes.

Ensure that the factoring of the market and stock volatility are always considered even after the option has been finalized. Volatility in the market is inevitable. Look at the stock market and you will see how quickly it moves up and down over the short term. You must not get carried away with short-term fluctuations. Know your strategy before you invest so that you are not distracted by short-term fluctuations.

Mistake #4 - Not Having a Sound Exit Plan

This is a trading strategy that many novice options skip in their eagerness to get started. While they may have a strategy in place for entering options trading, they forget or are ignorant of the fact that an exit strategy is just as important.

One of the biggest reasons for developing an exit strategy is to prevent emotions from clouding your judgment during that time when tough decisions need to be made. As a result, make the plan before things hit the fan to take out that emotional aspect.

There are two factors that need to be considered when creating an exit plan for an option. They are:

- What is the absolute point you will get out of the trade if things are not working out in your favor?

- How will you take profits if things are working in your favor?

Many experienced options traders place a percentage cap on the trade to know at which point they will back out of the trade if things are not working out profitably for them. While it is normal for the value of the transaction to fluctuate between 10% and 20%, most experienced traders will cut their losses if their fluctuation goes between 30% and 50%. This fluctuation needs to be also considered if things are working out in your favor. If the transaction has increased in value between 30% and 50%, you need to be thinking about how you can protect your profits or how to ensure that you do not lose any money through that option. Your exit strategy can also be time-based. You may decide that pursuing a certain option is only worthwhile for you for a certain period and not beyond. Having a target profit can also be the foundation of your exit strategy.

Mistake #5 - Not Being Flexible

Never say never with options trading. Many traders get stuck in their ways when it comes to options trading and refuse to try out new strategies. Remember that having a growth mindset is necessary for success in any part of life and this philosophy also applies to trade options. You must be willing to keep in the know when it comes to options and be willing to learn and try new strategies. That does not mean try any strategy you come across. It simply means that when you do come across new strategies; assess them carefully to see if they have the potential to fit into your trading plan to help you accomplish your goals.

Mistake #6 - Trading Illiquid Options

Liquidity describes how quickly an asset can be converted to cash without a significant price shift. The more readily the asset can be traded, the more liquid it is. Having a liquid market means there are ready and willing active buyers and sellers. Highly liquid options have certain characteristics. Being high in volume is one such characteristic. The higher the volume of options, the easier they are to enter and exit. Having the ability to move in and out of a contract is a huge advantage to an options trader. Being easily adjustable is another characteristic. Seeking out option with these characteristics makes the job of an options trader that much easier

Examples of highly liquid assets attached to options include stock and ETFs. On the other hand, there are illiquid options, and establishing such a contract is a mistake that many novice options traders make. These are not easily moved or converted into cash. They drive up the cost of doing business because of this characteristic. This makes the trading cost of that option higher and thus cuts on the trader's profits. To avoid this, trade options that are higher in liquidity. For example, stocks that trade less than 1 million shares per day are liquid. Pursue such options at the beginning of your career as an options trader. Also, seek options with a greater volume and that are easily adjustable.

Mistake #7 - Not Factoring in Upcoming Events

The financial market is volatile and unpredictable. Some things cannot be foreseen. However, others can be foreseen, and it is the job of the options trader to keep these things in his or her foresight. There are two major common events that an options trader needs to know in advance and these things are the earnings (the measure of how much a company's profits is allocated to each share of stock) on the associated assets as well as the dividend payout dates in these assets if they apply. Not knowing these future events can mean losing out on extra payout like these because no action was made to ensure that the trader had a right to them. In the case of dividends, payment on the associated assets could have been collected by the trader if only he or she had the foresight to purchase that asset before those payments were processed. To ensure you get such extra earning, you need to be on the ball of the date of such events. Do not sell options that have pending dividends and avoid trading in the earning season to avoid the common high volatility associated with that time.

Mistake #8 - Waiting Too Long to Buy Back Short Strategies

You need to always be ready to buy back short strategies early in the game. Never assume that profits will continue to come in just because you are having a good period. The market can change any time and so your profits can be lost easily if you fail to react properly.

There are many reasons why some options traders wait to do this, and they include not wanting to pay commissions, trying to gain more profits out of the contract, and thinking that the contract will be worthless upon expiration. Thinking in such a manner is a mental trap that can lead to financial losses.

To avoid this, consider buying back your short strategies if you can keep at least 80% of your initial gain from the sale of that option. If you enter an out of money positions, reduce the risk by buying back.

Mistake #9 – Getting Legged Out of Position

Legging out means that one leg of the option closes out and essentially becomes worthless to the trader. The leg gains an unfavorable price that does not benefit the trader. This does not automatically spell the death of the option made up of several legs, but it can expose the trader to loss. Legging can be performed in several types of options, including straddles, strangles, and spreads. These types of options can be enhanced by multiple legs and gain the options trader a leg up. However, the complexity of using the legging technique can elude even experienced options traders. The timing and order of executing legs make this a delicate process that needs a fine eye for the market. Therefore, this is a technique that must be attempt only after a trader is confident in his or her experience, knowledge, and success rate.

Mistake #10 - Trading Options on Complicated Assets without First Doing Proper Research

In their overexcitement, many new traders like to go for complex assets because they believe that this where the big bucks are. Even if this is true in some cases, if the trader does not have a good grasp of how the asset works in its market, then he or she will fail to implement the right strategies to gain profits. Never just jump into an option. Do your research first. Also, as a newbie options trader, it might be best to get your feet wet with more common options rather than jumping into the deep end of the pool.

Chapter 29.

Principles to Ensure a Strong Entry into Trading Options

You need to take it a step further by applying principles that will reinforce that plan. Think of that trading plan as the foundation of your house of success. The policies below are the bricks to develop your home into what you want it to be.

Principle #1 – Ensure Good Money Management

Money is the tool that keeps the engine of the financial industry performing in good working order. You must learn to manage your money in a way that works for you instead of against you as an options day trader. It is an intricate part of maintaining your risk and increasing your profit.

Money management is the process whereby monies allocated for spending, budgeting, saving, investing, and other procedures. Money management is a term that any person with a career in the financial industry, and particularly in the options trading industry, is intimately familiar with because this allocation of funds is the difference between a winning options trader and a struggling options trader.

Below you will find tips for managing your money so that you have maximum control of your options day trading career.

Money Management Tips for Options Traders

- Define money goals for the short term and the long term so that you can envision what you would like to save, invest, etc. Ensure that these are recorded and easily accessed. Your trading plan will help you define your money goals.

- Develop an accounting system. There is a wide range of software that can help with this, but it does not matter which one you use if you can establish records and efficiently track the flow of your money.

- Use the position sizing to manage your money. Position sizing is the process of determining how much money will allocate to entering an options position. To do this effectively, allocate a smart percentage of your investment fund toward individual options. For example, it would be unwise to use 50% of your investment fund on one option. That is 50% of your capital that can potentially go down the drain if you make a loss in that position. A good percentage is using no more than 10% of your investment fund toward individual option positions. This percentage allocation will help you get through tough periods, which eventually happen, without having all your funds lost.

- Never, ever invest money that you cannot afford to lose. Do not let emotion override this principle and cloud your judgment.

- Spread your risks by diversifying your portfolio. You expand your portfolio by spreading your wealth by investing in different areas; add to your investments regularly, being aware of commissions always, and knowing when to close a position.

- Develop the day trading styles and strategies that earn you a steady rate of return. Even if you use scalping where the returns are comparatively small, that constant flow of profit can add up big over time.

Principle #2 – Ensure that Risks and Rewards Are Balanced

To ensure that losses kept to a minimum and that returns are as high as they can be, options day traders should use the risk/reward ratio to determine each and to make adjustments as necessary. The risk/reward ratio is an assessment used to show profit potential concerning potential losses. It requires knowing the potential risks and profits associated with an options trade. Potential risks manage by using a stop-loss order. A stop-loss order is a command that allows you to exit a position in an options trade once a certain price threshold has reached.

Profit targeted using an established plan. Potential profit calculates by finding the difference between the entry price and the target profit. It calculated by dividing the expected return on the options investment by the standard deviation.

Another way to manage risks and rewards is by diversifying your portfolio. Always spread your money across different assets, financial sectors, and geographies. Ensure that these different facets of your portfolio are not closely related to each other so that if one goes down, they don't all fall. Be smart about protecting and building your wealth.

Principle #3 – Develop a Consistent Monthly Options Trading System

The aim of doing options trading is to have an overall winning options trading month. That will not happen if you trade options here and there. You cannot expect to see a huge profit at the end of the month if you only performed 2 or 3 transactions.

You need to have a high options trading frequency to up the chances of coming out winning every month. The only way to do that is to develop a system where you perform options trades at least five days a week.

Principle #4 – Consider a Brokerage Firm That is Right for Your Level of Options Expertise

There are four essential factors that you need to consider when choosing a broker, and they are:

- The requirements for opening a cash and margin account.
- The unique services and features that the broker offers.
- The commission fees and other fees charged by the broker.
- The reputation and level of options expertise of the broker.

Look at these individual components to see how you can use them to power up your options day trading experience.

Broker Cash and Margin Accounts

Every options trader needs to open a cash account and margin account to be able to perform transactions. They are simply tools of the trade. A cash account is one that allows an options day trader to perform operations via being loaded with cash. Margin account facilitates transactions by allowing that to borrow money against the value of security in his or her account. Both types of accounts require that a minimum amount deposited. It can be as few as a few thousand dollars to tens of thousands of dollars, depending on the broker of choice. You need to be aware of the requirements when deliberating, which brokerage firm is right for you.

Broker Services and Features

There are different types of services and features available from various brokerage firms. For example, if an options trader would like to have an individual broker assigned to him or her to handle his or her account personally, then he or she will have to look for a full-service broker. In this instance, there minimum account requirements that need to meet. Also, commission fees and other fees are generally higher with these types of brokerage firms. While the prices are higher, this might be better for a beginner trader to have that full service dedicated to their needs and the learning curve.

On the other hand, if an options trader does not have the capital needed to meet the minimum requirements of a full-service broker or would prefer to be more in charge of his or her option trades, then there is the choice of going with a discount brokerage firm. The advantage to discount brokerage firms is that they tend to have lower commissions and fees. Most internet brokerage firms are discount brokers.

Other features that you need to consider when choosing a brokerage firm include:

- Whether or not the broker streams real-time quotes.
- The speed of execution for claims.
- The availability of bank wire services.

- The availability of monthly statements.

- How confirmations achieve, whether written or electronic.

Commissions and Other Fees

Commission fees paid when an options trader enters and exits positions. Every brokerage firm has its commission fees set up. These typically developed around the level of account activity and account size of the options trader.

These are not the only fees that an option trader needs to consider when considering brokerage firms. Many brokerage firms charge penalty fees for withdrawing funds and not maintaining minimum account balances—the existence of costs such as these cuts on options trader's profit margin. Payment of fees needs to be kept to a minimum to gain maximum income, and as such, an options trader needs to be aware of all charges that exist and how they are applied when operating with a brokerage firm. It needs to be done before signing up.

Broker Reputation and Options Expertise

You do not want to be scammed out of your money because you chose the wrong brokerage firm. Therefore, you must choose a broker that has an established and long-standing reputation for trading options. You also want to deal with a brokerage firm that has excellent customer service, that can aid in laying the groundwork for negotiating reduced commissions and allows for flexibility.

Principle #5 – Ensure That Exits are automated

Even though I have stated that emotions should set aside when trading options, we are all human, and emotions are bound to come into the equation at some point. Knowing this is imperative that systems develop to minimize the impact of emotions. Having your exits automated is one such step that you can take to ensure that emotions are left out when dealing with options day trading. Using bracket orders facilitates this.

A bracket order is an instruction given when an options trader enters a new position that specifies a target or exit and stop-loss order that aligns with that. This order ensures that a system set up to record two points – the goal for-profit and the maximum loss point that will tolerate before the stop-loss comes into effect. The execution of either order cancels the other.

Chapter 30.

Tips and Tricks

Growth at Reasonable Price (GARP) Investing:

The GARP method of investing is a combination of both growth and value investing. It looks for companies that are currently slightly undervalued and have sustainable growth potential. It typically looks for stocks that are currently somewhat less undervalued than those that value investing looks for while expecting slightly less from the stocks it chooses than growth investing. Much like growth investing, GARP investing is concerned with the growth of a prospective company. When using this method, see positive earnings from the past few years as well as positive earnings projections for the coming years. Unlike with growth investing, however, the ideal range of growth in the next five years is going to be between 25 and 50 percent instead of 100 percent. The theory here is that higher growth rates lead to high rates of risk.

GARP investing is also going to share metrics for potential companies with growth investing, though the ideal levels are going to be lower. A good company to invest in with the GARP method sees positive cash flow and positive earnings momentum. Outside of that, however, you are going to have some more freedom when it comes to choosing the best companies when using this strategy, as subjectivity is an inherent part of GARP investing. Regardless of the specifics, it is important to always analyze companies in relation to their unique contexts, as there is no ideal formula for what makes a good GARP investment.

Growth Investing

Whereas value investors are the most concerned with where a company is currently, growth investors are more focused on the potential future growth of a company to the point of barely considering the current price at all. This investment strategy focuses on buying into companies that are currently trading above their intrinsic value with the belief that this intrinsic value will continue to grow to the point that it exceeds current valuations. To utilize this strategy effectively, primarily keep an eye on young companies, as they are traditionally going to grow more rapidly than more established companies. The theory behind this strategy success is that this growth in revenue or earnings will then directly translate to an increase in the underlying stock price. Other common investments include companies in rapidly expanding industries, frequently those that are related to new technologies. Profits are then realized not through dividends but through capital gains, as it is uncommon for growth companies to pay dividends as they typically reinvest the money that would be going to dividends directly back into the company instead.

Unlike most of the other strategies, there are no hard and fast guidelines when it comes to investing in growth companies. However, there are certain criteria which can be used as a framework for your analysis; these must be applied to each company with an eye towards a company's unique situation. Some of the things you will want to keep in mind include the company's current state as compared to past performance and its performance compared to its industry as a whole.

Value Investing

This investment strategy is exceedingly simple to understand, though it can be difficult to execute in practice. To successfully value invest, all you need to do is seek out companies that are currently trading below their current worth. In order to do so, you will want to start by looking for stocks that feature quality fundamentals including cash flow, book value, dividends, and earnings. When you find a company that is currently undervalued based on these fundamentals, pounce to take full advantage before the market corrects itself. You need to understand that the key here is to look for value, not junk. This is a crucial difference, otherwise, you will simply find yourself holding on to a stock whose company continues to decline in value.

One of the biggest proponents of this type of investing is Warren Buffet. He held the stock for his holding company Berkshire Hathaway starting in 1967 when it was worth $12 per share and by 2002 it was worth $70,900 per share. While these results are far from average, it goes to show how potentially profitable this type of strategy can be if pursued correctly. If you intend to venture into value investing, you need to ensure that the share price is not greater than two-thirds of stock's value. Additionally, you are going to want to look for companies that have a P/E ratio in the bottom 10 percent of all equity securities. The price/earnings to growth ratio, which is the P/E ratio divided by the growth rate of the company's earnings, should be less than one.

Furthermore, the stock price should never be more than the tangible book value, and the company should have less debt than it does equity. The company's current assets should be at least twice that of its current liabilities, and its dividend yield should be a minimum of two-thirds of its long-term bond yield. Its earnings growth should be a minimum of 7 percent per annum when compounded for the last 10 years.

Finally, it is important to always factor in a margin of safety as well. A margin of safety is simply a little wiggle room when it comes to potential errors that may have occurred when you were calculating the intrinsic value of the company. To add in a margin of error, all you need to do is subtract 10 percent from the intrinsic value number.

Buy and Hold

The buy and hold strategy is a type of passive investment in which, as the name implies, shareholders buy into a stock that has strong long-term potential and then hold onto it even when the markets see a downturn. This strategy looks to the efficient market to be a hypothesis for success, which states that it is impossible to see above-average returns when adjusting for risk. This means that it is never a good idea to resort to active trading. It also says that seeing decreases in value in the short term is fine as long as the long-term trend remains positive.

The strategy is effective in minimizing the commissions and fees that you have to pay a brokerage because you will only have to do so once before generating an eventual profit. In this strategy, you also don't have to worry about timing the market which is useful for new investors as determining when to buy low and sell high can be much more difficult than it first appears. For the effectiveness of the strategy, you need to start at an early age. If an investor first bought stocks in 1960 and held onto them for 50 years, then they would have seen nearly a 40 percent return on their investment, while someone who bought in starting in 2000 would have since seen a loss of little more than 2 percent if they sold today.

It is easy to get started with this strategy. All you need to do is research where a number of companies are currently and consider their future projections to ensure they seem to be moving in the right direction. Once the stock is purchased, all you need to do is to check in on your investments from time to time and ensure that nothing catastrophic has happened. Additionally, adopting this strategy means that you will have to pay less in income taxes; specifically, capital gains are taxed at a much lower rate in the long-term than they are in the short-term.

The disadvantages of this type of strategy include the possibility for nearly unlimited losses because you are not checking on the stock that frequently, nor are you watching the markets on a regular basis; you could easily stumble into a situation where the stock in question dropped far enough that it is unlikely that you would ever be able to see enough positive gains again to properly right the ship. Additionally, get to understand the difference between irretrievable losses and expected decreases. So, if you panic and make a move when it is not required, then you will be stuck with a loss that could have eventually been mitigated when the market righted itself.

Price Action Trading

At its most fundamental, price action trading can be thought of as a way for a trader to determine the current state of the market based on what it currently looks like, what any number of indicators says about it after the fact. This is a great strategy for those who are interested in getting started as quickly as possible, as you are only required to study the market in its current form. Additionally, focusing on just the price will make it easier to avoid much of the largely superfluous information that is circling the market causing static, which makes it more difficult to determine what is really going on. In order to determine when to trade using price action, you are going to need to use the trading platform that came with the brokerage you chose and utilize what is known as price bars. Price bars are a representation of price information over a specific period of time, broken down into weekly, daily, 1 hour, 30-minute or 5-minute intervals. In order to create an accurate price bar, you need the open price for the given stock in the chosen time period, the high for the time period, the low for the time period, and the closing price. With this data, you should end up with a box with a line through it. The line represents the high and the low for the day while the edges of the box show the opening and closing prices. In addition to summarizing the information for the timeframe in question, it also provides relevant information for your purposes. This includes the range of the stock, which is a representation of how volatile the market currently is. The bigger the box in relation to the line, the more active and volatile the market currently is. The more volatile the market currently is, the more risk you undertake when making a move.

In addition to the range, consider the physical orientation of the box; if the close price is above the open price, then the market improved over the timeframe; if the close is below the open, then the market lost value. Take into account the size of the box as a whole. The bigger the box, the stronger the market is overall. What this type of strategy provides you with is a clear idea of what the levels of resistance and support are like for the time period in question. This, in turn, allows you to pick trades with a higher degree of certainty. All you need to do is keep in mind that if demand is stronger than supply, the price is going to increase and vice versa. If the movement indicates that this is likely to continue in the same direction, then you will want to pick the point where it is likely to happen again and use that as your entry point. If the opposite is true, then you are going to want to sell ASAP to prevent yourself from losing out on gains you have already seen.

Chapter 31.

Portfolio Diversification

D ay traders generally execute trades in the course of a single trading day while investors buy and hold stocks for days, weeks, months, and sometimes even a couple of years. In between these two extremes are other forms of trading. These include swing trading and position trading, among others.

Swing trading is where a trader buys an interest in a commodity or stock and holds the position for a couple of days before disposing of it. Position trading, on the other hand, is where a trader buys a stake in a commodity or stock for a number of weeks or even several months. While all these trades carry a certain element of risk, day trading carries the biggest risk. A trader with the necessary skills and access to all the important resources is bound to succeed and will encounter a steep learning curve. Professional day traders work full time, whether working for themselves or for large institutions. They often set a schedule which they always adhere to. It is never wise to be a part-time day trader, a hobby trader, or a gambler. To succeed, you have to trade on a full-time basis and be as disciplined as possible.

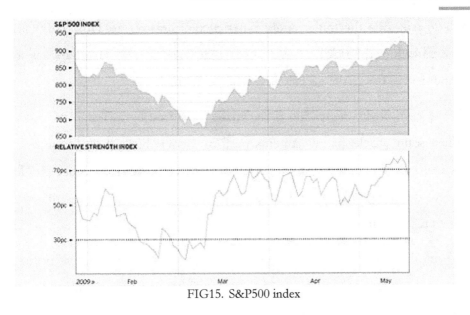

FIG15. S&P500 index

Introduction to Diversification

Diversification is considered an effective risk management technique. It is widely used by both traders and investors. The gist behind this approach is that investing funds in just single security is extremely risky as the entire trade could potentially go up in smoke or incur significant losses.

An ideal portfolio of securities is expected to fetch a much higher return compared to a no-diversified portfolio. This is true even when compared to the returns of lower risk investments like bonds. Generally, diversification is advisable not only because it yields better returns but also because it offers protection against losses.

Diversification Basics

Traders and investors put their funds in securities at the securities markets. One of the dangers of investing in the markets is that traders are likely to hold onto only one or two stocks at a time. This is risky because if a trade was to fail, then the trader could experience a catastrophe. However, with diversification, the risk is spread out so that regardless of what happens to some stocks, the trader still stands to be profitable.

At the core of diversification is the challenge posed by unsystematic risks. When some stocks or investments perform better than others, these risks are neutralized. Therefore, for a perfectly balanced portfolio, a trader should ensure that they only deal with non-correlated assets. This means that the assets respond in opposite ways or differently to market forces.

The ideal portfolio should contain between 25 and 30 different securities. This is the perfect way of ensuring that the risk levels are drastically reduced and the only expected outcomes are profitability.

In summary, diversification is a popular strategy that is used by both traders and investors. It makes use of a wide variety of securities to improve yield and mitigate against inherent and potential risks.

It is advisable to invest or trade in a variety of assets and not all from one class. For instance, a properly diversified portfolio should include assets such as currencies, options, stocks, bonds, and so on. This approach will increase the chances of profitability and minimize risks and exposure. Diversification is even better if assets are acquired across geographical regions as well.

Best Diversification Approach

Diversification focuses on asset allocation. It consists of a plan that endeavors to allocate funds or assets appropriately across a variety of investments. When an investor diversifies his or her portfolio, then there is some level of risk that has to be accepted. However, it is also advisable to devise an exit strategy so that the investor is able to let go of the asset and recoup their funds. This becomes necessary when a specific asset class is not yielding any worthwhile returns compared to others.

If an investor is able to create an aptly diversified portfolio, their investment will be adequately covered. An adequately diversified portfolio also allows room for growth. Appropriate asset allocation is highly recommended as it allows investors a chance to leverage risk and manage any possible portfolio volatility because different assets have varying reactions to adverse market conditions.

Investor Opinions on Diversifications

Different investors have varying opinions regarding the type of investment scenarios they consider being ideal. Numerous investors believe that a properly diversified portfolio will likely bring in a double-digit return despite prevailing market conditions. They also agree that in the worst case situation will be simply a general decrease in the value of the different assets. Yet with all this information out there, very few investors are actually able to achieve portfolio diversification.

So why are investors unable to simply diversify their portfolios appropriately? The answers are varied and diverse. The challenges encountered by investors in diversification include weighting imbalance, hidden correlation, underlying devaluation, and false returns, among others. While these challenges sound rather technical, they can easily be solved. The solution is also rather simple. By hacking these challenges, an investor will then be able to benefit from an aptly diversified platform.

The Process of Asset Class Allocation

There are different ways of allocating investments to assets. According to studies, most investors, including professional investors, portfolio managers, and seasoned traders actually rarely beat the indexes within their preferred asset class. It is also important to note that there is a visible correlation between the performance of an underlying asset class and the returns that an investor receives. In general, professional investors tend to perform more or less the same as an index within the same class asset.

Investment returns from a diversified portfolio can generally be expected to closely imitate the related asset class. Therefore, asset class choice is considered an extremely crucial aspect of an investment. In fact, it is the single more crucial aspect for the success of a particular asset class. Other factors, such as individual asset selection and market timing, only contribute about 6% of the variance in investment outcomes.

Wide Diversifications between Various Asset Classes

Diversification to numerous investors simply implies spreading their funds through a wide variety of stocks in different sectors such as health care, financial, energy, as well as medium caps, small, and large-cap companies. This is the opinion of your average investor. However, a closer look at this approach reveals that investors are simply putting their money in different sectors of stocks class. These asset classes can very easily fall and rise when the markets do.

A reliably diversified portfolio is one where the investor or even the manager is watchful and alert because of the hidden correlation that exists between different asset classes. This correlation can easily change with time, and there are several reasons for this. One reason is international markets. Many investors often choose to diversify their portfolios with international stocks.

However, there is also a noticeable correlation across the different global financial markets. This correlation is clearly visible not just across European markets but also emerging markets from around the world. There is also a clear correlation between equities and fixed income markets, which are generally the hallmarks of diversification.

This correlation is actually a challenge and is probably a result of the relationship between structured financing and investment banking. Another factor that contributes to this correlation is the rapid growth and popularity of hedge funds. Take the case where a large international organization such as a hedge fund suffers losses in a particular asset class.

Should this happen, then the firm may have to dispose of some assets across the different asset classes. This will have a multiplier effect as numerous other investments, and other investors will, therefore, be affected even though they had diversified their portfolios appropriately. This is a challenge that affects numerous investors who are probably unaware of its existence. They are also probably unaware of how it should be rectified or avoided.

Realignment of Asset Classes

One of the best approaches to solving the correlation challenge is to focus on class realignment. Basically, asset allocation should not be considered as a static process. Asset class imbalance is a phenomenon that occurs when the securities markets develop, and different asset classes exhibit varied performance.

After a while, investors should assess their investments then diversify out of underperforming assets and instead shift this investment to other asset classes that are performing well and are profitable in the long term. Even then, it is advisable to be vigilant so that no one single asset class is over-weighted as other standard risks are still inherent. Also, a prolonged bullish market can result in overweighting one of the different asset classes which could be ready for a correction. There are a couple of approaches that an investor can focus on, and these are discussed below.

Diversification and the Relative Value

Investors sometimes find asset returns to be misleading, including veteran investors. As such, it is advisable to interpret asset returns in relation to the specific asset class performance. The interpretation should also take into consideration the risks that this asset class is exposed to and even the underlying currency.

When diversifying investments, it is important to think about diversifying into asset classes that come with different risk profiles. These should also be held in a variety of currencies. You should not expect to enjoy the same outcomes when investing in government bonds and technology stocks. However, it is recommended to endeavor to understand how each suits the larger investment objective.

Using such an approach, it will be possible to benefit more from a small gain from an asset within a market where the currency is increasing in value. This is as compared to a large gain from an asset within a market where the currency is in decline. As such, huge gains can translate into losses when the gains are reverted back to the stronger currency. This is the reason why it is advisable to ensure that proper research and evaluation of different asset classes are conducted.

Currencies Should Be Considered

Currency considerations are crucial when selecting asset classes to diversify in. take the Swiss franc for instance. It is one of the world's most stable currencies and has been that way since the 1940s. Because of this reason, this particular currency can be safely and reliably used to measure the performance of other currencies.

However, private investors sometimes take too long choosing and trading stocks. Such activities are both overwhelming and time-consuming. This is why, in such instances, it is advisable to approach this differently and focus more on the asset class. With this kind of approach, it is possible to be even more profitable. Proper asset allocation is crucial to successful investing. It enables investors to mitigate any investment risks as well as portfolio volatility. The reason is that different asset classes have different reactions to all the different market conditions.

Constructing a well-thought out and aptly diversified portfolio, it is possible to have a stable and profitable portfolio that even outperforms the index of assets. Investors also have the opportunity to leverage against any potential risks because of different reactions by the different market

Chapter 32.

Day Trading

When trading straight calls and puts, one of the best ways to earn profits is through day trading. Although options are not stocks, the same day trading rules apply to trade options as they do with stocks. This means that you must know what the definitions are of a day trade and the legal requirements and risks.

Day trading options can be both desirable and lucrative because small price movements in stock, which happen all the time, are magnified in options. You can use day trading to get into options when prices are relatively low. You can get out when they reach a pricing level that represents an acceptable profit level for you on the same day before prices begin moving in the other direction again.

Remember that each option has its ticker. This is important because day trading involves day traders of the same financial security. If you buy and sell Apple stock on the same trading day, that is a day trade. When it comes to options, however, buying and selling two different options on Apple stock does not constitute a day trade. To understand why, note that an option is defined on the underlying stock, in addition to the predetermined factors (strike and expiration). It also depends on the type of option. A day trade involves buying a stock or option and then selling it before the close of the trading day. Anyone can do a limited number of day trades, but what is known as a pattern day trader is what brokers and regulators are looking for. A pattern day trader, by definition, is someone that makes 4 or more day trades in any five days. A five-day period means five consecutive trading days, so a weekend does not reset the counter. These days, most brokers will track the number of day trades you have in your account for you. Some brokers like to auction their stocks before the end of the market day to maintain a strategic distance from the dangers emerging out of the value holes between the end cost on the day, they purchased a stock and its opening cost on the following day. They think about this training as a brilliant guideline and follow it strictly. Different dealers have faith in enabling the profits to run, so they remain with the position considerably after the market closes. Day exchanging is purchasing and selling portions of stock within a day in attempting to deliver momentary profits.

Profits and Dangers in Day Exchanging

Informal investors make snappy bucks and brisk losses in only minutes or toward the finish of the exchanging day. Day exchanging may inspire the dreams of card sharks gaming in clubs. There is, in any case, a stamped distinction between day exchanging and betting.

While you can't make any determined moves or devise any shrewd methodologies in betting, except for when you are out to swindle others, day exchanging includes intense comprehension of the way toward exchanging.

You study the general market patterns and the development of the stocks. You make central and specialized examination and keep yourself side by the side with the most recent news reports about the many organizations that you exchange and considerably more.

Day exchanging isn't playing a visually impaired man's buff or simply discarding bones. You must be alert and mindful before each move. It would, along these lines, be uncalled for to call informal investors card sharks or outlaws as some baffling failures in day exchanging can do. Experienced and instinctive merchants produce a colossal level of profits from day exchanging. Some stockbrokers figure out how to mint millions every year exclusively on day exchanging. An enormous number of people have effectively made day exchanging the sole road of making their career. This, however, isn't to prevent the dangers from securing enormous losses in day exchanging. The individuals who exchange without a determined and astute methodology and order are bound to acquire enormous losses. This happens more with the individuals who use obtained reserves, and training is known as purchasing on edges. They need to pay back the acquired sums with gigantic interests and different punishments if they neglect to make profits. This is the thing that makes day exchanging extremely risky.

Swing Trading

Swing trading is an approach based on the observation that stock prices never evolve linearly. An increase never takes shape in some time, and corrective phases often punctuate it. As per the experts, the basic trading philosophy can be summarized as follows:

- The best opportunities lie in detecting low-risk entry points in the direction of the prevailing trend. Thus, in an uptrend, the trader will have to wait for a correction or consolidation before positioning himself for the purchase.

- Conversely, in a downward trend, the trader will have to position himself only after a rebound around a significant resistance.

In the 1980s, a hedge fund manager went in the same direction by making famous the concept of contraction/expansion. It highlights the NR7 (or smaller range of the last seven days) and specifies that a consolidating market should accelerate after the appearance of NR7.

ilder and Appel are the two most cited authors for technical indicators. They introduced mathematics in technical analysis through technical indicators development, which is very popular in trading rooms.

These indicators are based on different mathematical formulas inspired by physics. The main thesis of these authors is that the speed of an object thrown in the air is reduced during its progression, to become zero on the tops. They argue that market movements can be anticipated through these indicators, whose main function is to take the pulse of the market and answer the question: "The current trend - Is it intact or exhausting?"

These first steps have been relayed in the financial world and cause the emergence of technical analysis and many technical indicators of development. People have always been fascinated by the world of trading; however, with the risks involved, it can get to be a daunting task. Understanding the stock market and paying attention to the different kinds of trading options can be very stressful.

The swing trading system means "in the direction of the dominant movement." This system, often used by traders, allows testing the market before increasing its exposure. Indeed, if the market confirms the trader's initial scenario, it is because his reasoning is good, and he can, by crossing some pivotal points, strengthen his position.

Swing trading capacities are splendid for low support vendors - especially those doing it while at work. While casual financial specialists commonly need to stay adhered to their PCs for an extensive period without a moment's delay, fervently watching minute-to-minute changes in expressions, swing exchanging doesn't require that kind of focus and commitment. While day traders' wager on stocks popping or falling by divisions of centers, swing traders' endeavor to ride "swings" in the market. Swing traders buy fewer shares and go for dynamically basic augmentations, they pay lower business and, theoretically, have an unrivaled probability of gaining progressively immense increments.

When used precisely, swing exchanging is a splendid methodology used by various sellers transversely over various markets. It isn't simply used in the Forex trade, yet it is a crucial mechanical assembly in prospects and financial markets. Swing vendors take the capacities that they learn through assessment and can even parlay these aptitudes into various decision strategies. The transient thought of swing exchanging isolates it from that of the standard financial expert.

Financial experts will, when all is said and done, have a progressively broadened term time horizon and are not generally impacted by fleeting financial changes. Not surprisingly, one must check that swing exchanging is only a solitary framework and should be utilized exactly when appropriately grasped. Like any exchanging strategies, swing exchanging can be risky, and a moderate approach can change into day exchanging systems quickly. If you mean to use a swing exchanging system, ensure that you totally appreciate the risks and develop a method that will presumably empower you to create the most prominent rate returns on your positions.

Conclusion Part 2

T rading options have significant risks. If you are inexperienced with trading, we would recommend talking with a financial advisor before making any decision.

Always keep in mind that every investment has its own risk and reward rating, which means that if the risk is high, the reward will be high as well.

Expiration dates of American style options and European style options (the commonly used style options) are always the third Saturday in the month for American and the last Friday before the third Saturday for European style options.

The phrase "in the money" describes that the option has a value higher than the strike price for call options and lower than the strike price for put options at the time of their expiration.

The most common minimal bid for option sharing is one nickel or 5 dollars per contract. However, some more liquid contracts allow minimal bid to be one dollar per contract. 100 shares of the certain stock are 1 option contract. If you pay 1 dollar for an option, your premium for that option, whether you buy or sell it is 1 dollar per share, which means that the option premium is 100 dollars per contract.

All the examples in this guide assume that every option order ever mentioned was filled successfully. Whenever you want to open a new position, you will have to sell or buy on the market to "open". The same principle applies if you wish to close your position. You sell or buy to "close".

The phrase "Open Interest" represents the number of option contracts that are opened now. Logically, more open contracts mean a bigger number, and closed contracts indicate a smaller number. The volume of the options is the number of contracts that are traded in one single day. Be careful when signing the contracts; make sure you read all the trading options.

Trading options can be extremely profitable, but learning to trade them well takes time. You can choose to use indicators to determine your entry points, and I'm all for this approach at first, but remember that over the long term, you're better served learning the basics of order flow and using that.

There is no shortage of options strategies you can use to limit your risk and depending on the volatility levels dramatically, you can deploy separate strategies to achieve the same ends. Compare this with a directional trading strategy where you have just one method of entry, which is to either go short or go long, and only one way of managing risk, which is to use a stop-loss.

Spread or market neutral trading puts you in the position of not having to care about what the market does. Also, it brings another dimension of the market into focus, which is volatility. Volatility is the greatest thing for your gains, and options allow you to take full advantage of this, no matter what the volatility situation currently is.

Options can be a bit hard to get your head around at first since so many of us are used to looking at the market as a thing that goes up or down. Options bring a sideways and a different vertical element to it via spreads and volatility estimates. More advanced options strategies take full advantage of volatility and are more math-focused, so if this interests you, you should go for them.

Risk management is what will make or break your results, and at the center of quantitative risk management is your risk per trade. Keep this consistent and line up your success rate and reward to risk ratios, and you'll make money as a mathematical certainty.

The learning curve might get steep at times, but given the rewards on offer, this is a small price to pay. Keep hammering away at your skills, and soon you'll find yourself trading options profitably, and everything will be worth it.

Always make sure you're well-capitalized since this is the downfall of many traders. You need to be patient with the process. A lot of people rush headfirst into the market without adequate capitalization or learning and soon finding out that the markets are far tougher than they thought. So always ensure the mental stress you place yourself in is low and that you're never in a position where you 'have' to make money trading.

Dave R. W. Graham

Index of Figures

Author's Note

Thanks for reading my book. If you want to learn more about personal finance, investments, trading, and business, I suggest you follow my author page on Amazon. Through my books, I have decided to share with you the know-how that has allowed me to achieve my financial freedom, to accumulate wealth, and to live the life I want with my family.

My goal is to show you the path with useful and applicable information for reaching your targets. Only you will be able to tread that path as I did... and now, I'm sharing what I know.

To your wealth!

Dave R. W. Graham